THE ODD COUPLE: THE ABERRANT RELATIONS BETWEEN TURKEY AND ISRAEL

BY RAPHAEL ISRAELI

Strategic Book Publishing and Rights Co.

Strategic Book Publishing and Rights Co., LLC
USA | Singapore
www.sbpra.com

For information about special discounts for bulk purchases, please contact Strategic Book Publishing and Rights Co., LLC Special Sales, at bookorder@sbpra.net.

ISBN: 978-1-949483-67-3

Contents

ACKNOWLEDGMENTS

The relations between the large and populous Muslim country of Turkey and the tiny Jewish state of Israel have known many extreme ups and downs since the second half of the 20th Century and deep into the 21st. While Israel, as a newborn nation in 1948, has from its inception striven to establish good relations with all countries with a view to being accepted and legitimized around the world, it had put its special emphasis since the 1950s on the peripheral states of Turkey, Ethiopia and Iran as a way to leapfrog the tight siege around it by its Arab neighbors. For a while, that strategy seemed to work, but since the 1970s and the changes of regimes in all those countries: Iran by an Islamic Revolution, Ethiopia by a Communist coup and Turkey by the rise of Islamic parties since the Necmettin Erbakan government of 1996-7, those periods of openness and mutual rapprochement between the parties have slowly slipped back into hostility and even enmity, especially in view of the Islamic reversal that took place in Iran (1979) and in Turkey (2002). In Ethiopia, on the contrary, relations with Israel regained normalcy since the 1990s, in spite of the sizeable Muslim population of that country, but in Turkey they sank again into their lowest ebb when Recep Erdogan consolidated his authoritarian rule on the country, especially after he was elected as an executive President in 2018.

The metaphor that comes to mind when one reflects about the

ups and downs in the fortunes of this odd couple- Turkey and Israel, is that of a marriage of convenience, where the interests of both sides have attracted them to each other to conclude some sort of partnership, following a long courtship. Throughout the 1970s and 1980s, tentative contacts and low-level and discreet dates allowed the parties to get to make the acquaintance of each other, which culminated in the 1990s in an explosion of "rage of happiness" which was translated into a hot, avid and intimate honeymoon that was exhibited in public, under the civil governments in Ankara which had preceded the rise of the Islamic parties. Thereupon, alienation started between the partners, who lived separately and each took to love affairs on the side – Turkey with the Muslim Brothers, Qatar and Iran, Israel with Greece and Cyprus; while at the same time both taunting each other with their continued close relationships with the West and the US, but also with their "concubines" and with developing a close intimacy with Russia. When Erdogan came to power in 2003, his anti-Semitic and anti-Zionist zeal came to the fore as he downgraded many aspects of the previous close relationship and supported the tragic *mavi marmara* (May, 2010) flotilla to Gaza event, which tragically ended up in the death of nine of its members. The Israelis have foolishly agreed to "apologize", under the Obama Administration pressure, for a sin they did not commit, and even to pay "indemnities" for the victims who were the aggressors in that event, which turned out to be the payment of alimony in an impending divorce process.

Engrossed by their success, the Turks heightened the bar of their demands from Israel to which Israel foolishly submitted, falsely hoping thereby to calm the anti-Israel tempers of Erdogan, who unabashedly launched a campaign of lies and calumniations against Jews, Israel and Zionism. The odd couple was then on the brink of divorce, but with American mediation they tried again to make believe that they had gone back to normal, while the resentment and bitterness continued to brew under and over the surface. Using the problems of the Hamas in the Gaza Strip (2008-2018) as his anchor to champion the Islamic cause in the world, he abandoned all the diplomatic niceties that had previously somewhat restricted his outrageous accusations of Israel. For a while, in view of some Turkish practical interests to encourage the Israeli tourism to Antalya, or to secure gas supplies from the Israeli Mediterranean fields, or even more importantly, to ensure the continued Israeli procurement of military and technological hardware and the exchange of vital intelligence information, the diplomatic relations between Ankara and Jerusalem were again upgraded, but their previous warmth and intimacy had irretrievably vanished, at least as long as Erdogan's rule prevails. In the meantime, the partners have reverted to a period of alienation on the brink of divorce, amidst threats and condemnations as in the time of the *mavi marmara*, with little prospect for reconciliation.

I am indebted, as always, to the Truman Institute, my home base at the Hebrew University of Jerusalem for the facilitation of the publication of this volume. All the inadvertent mistakes remain, however, solely mine.

Jerusalem, Summer, 2018

INTRODUCTION

A Vast Muslim Land
vs a Tiny Jewish State

Turkey and Israel, by all accounts the predominant powers in the modern Middle East, have in the 1990s forged an unlikely alliance that baffled many a keen observer of the region. On the face of it, there would seem to be little historical or contemporary logic to a close relationship between the two. One is larger in size (actually 30 times the surface area) than the other, and larger in population (9 times) than the other. One is the well-established successor to the glorious and multi-centennial Ottoman Empire, the other an embattled state whose boundaries and very existence have been challenged by its neighbors, and itself a mere part of the Syrian District of the now bygone Ottoman administrative make-up. One is Muslim, and often purports to act as a champion of Islam and its 1,5 billion international *umma* that encompasses 57 Muslim-majority countries, and Muslim minorities in practically all parts of the globe, the other a Jewish-majority state barely counting 9 million people, 20% of them Muslim, and encompassing merely half the Jewish population (14 million in total) of the world. One is just emerging from the Third World and aspiring to join the EU (in addition to its membership in NATO), the other thoroughly modernized and well entrenched in Western culture. One is notoriously deficient with regard to international norms of human rights and freedom of expression, the other a respected liberal democracy with a strong independent judiciary, free press and high standards of law enforcement. One was subjected to the whims of its military until Erdogan repealed its prerogative as the curators and guardians of the Ataturk heritage, the other supremely civilian in its demeanor in spite of its false image as "militaristic" in view of the immense influence of its General Staff in its burning and perennial security problems which warrant this influence. All in all, Turkey has known in our lifetime 3 or 4 military *coups*, while Israel has not even approached that threshold and kept strictly to its democratic conduct and state of mind.[1]

No one would suggest that some sudden love affair suffices to explain the extraordinary *rapprochement* between Turkey and Israel which marked most of the 1990s. Nor could one point to new common interests attracting the two to each other, because their common borders with Arab states, common stand against fanatic Muslim terrorism, cooperation in Central Asia and rivalry in the Balkans, and envisaging certain economic interests, had all predated the stunning *entente* which evolved in those years between them, but had occasionally also caused as much hostility as amiability, depending on the mood of the time. Rather, the momentous shift, which began to impact the contours of Middle Eastern politics, exactly as it has now reversed course since Erdogan came to power, may be found in a triad of new concatenations.

1. The end of the Cold War;
2. The Gulf War of 1991; and
3. The technological evolution in Israel.

The new configuration of regional and global forces unleashed by these three contingencies had enabled Turkey and Israel to

---

[1] This and the following passage are based on this author's "The Turkish-Israeli Odd Couple", *Orbis,* January 2001, pp 165-179.

pursue a partnership in military and civil, strategic and economic, institutional and human affairs, amounting to a close relationship based on shared interests that had the potential to develop into an intimate and lasting rapport. However, all those basic factors of rapprochement, were present and evolving only as long as the pragmatic civil governments of Demirel, Ozal, Ecevit and Ciller commanded the ruling majority in Ankara. But the moment doctrinal- Islamic Necmettin Erbakan, Erdogan's teacher and mentor, won the plurality (though not yet the majority) in the Turkish Parliament (1996), at the head of his Islamic Party, and was charged with the unforeseen responsibility to set up his coalition government, the time bomb of reversal began to tick towards a complete swing of the pendulum the other way.

The Stunning Events of 1989-91 and Their Consequences

The collapse of the Soviet Union and the Communist Bloc which accompanied the end of the Cold War that had governed the world since the end of W W II, had sharply reduced the importance of Turkey in the Western defense system (the "Northern Tier", a term borrowed in the 1950s from the northern border of the US with Canada, and referring to the allied countries of the US across the world which bordered and contained the southern borders of the Communist Bloc, like Turkey, Iran and the Balkans) and forced Ankara to reevaluate its standing in the world. It was perhaps no pure coincidence that it was in a meeting of Turkey's and Israel's foreign ministers in Moscow that both sides sought to mend their relationship and exchange ambassadors for the first time. The immediate causes were the outcome of the Desert Storm Operation that the Americans launched in Iraq and the subsequent Madrid Conference convened by President Bush I to try a breakthrough on peace between Israel and the Palestinians. But the *rapprochement* also stemmed from a clear realization by both parties that the new world order heralded by President Bush I to shore up his campaign against

Iraq which had otherwise failed to realize its declared goals (destruction of Saddam's troops, deep reforms in the Gulf states which America had rushed to rescue), had necessitated an upgrading of their relations. Israel, having long pursued closer links with the major Islamic country of the Middle East, which was also an ally of the US and a member in NATO, needed no prodding. But the prevailing opinion in Ankara was that the turn-about on relations with Israel, which had been until then held in low profile due to Turkish relations with the Arab and Islamic world, constituted one of the most important events in Turkish foreign policy in the preceding 50 years.[2]

There is always, of course, the question of whether any country has, or can have a "foreign policy" that can be decided and mapped in the back rooms of chanceries around the world. For, at least from the 20th Century onward, no country, even not great powers, could make such decisions and follow them through. Indeed, all the world events that determined the fate of humanity in the past hundred years, like the two world wars, the Korean and Vietnam Wars, the multiple eruptions of the Arab-Israeli conflicts, the massive American interventions in Afghanistan and Iraq, the disputes between India and Pakistan and any number of other local and regional disputes around the globe, were not chosen but forced upon the main actors in the international scene, compelling them to react and dragging them willy-nilly to respond to outside triggers or to foreign challenges to their interests. To embrace a "foreign policy", therefore, has become more and more of an illusion, and no longer only a deliberate implementation of schemes, dreams and blueprints of all sorts. So much more so in the case of medium and small nations which will always depend on the great powers and on the central empires- political, economic and cultural, who determine the fate

---

[2] Amikam Nachmani, "The Remarkable Turkish-Israeli Ties", *Middle East Quarterly*, June, 1998, p. 22

of the world, but are also restrained by the reactions, responses and capacities of their clients and of their rivals[3]. In that regard, the local Middle Eastern Turkish and Israeli powers cannot be endowed with any magic ability to make their "foreign policy" out of their own volition. Indeed, two of the three cited contingencies which allowed, or compelled, or at least directed, those two partners to make their choices, were external events that none of them controlled. They, like others, then acted on matters of evolving foreign relations, not of a foundational foreign policy.

As a result of the Second Gulf War of 1991 (if we count the much more inflammatory, prolonged and destructive war between Iran and Iraq in 1980-88 as the First), and the significant weakening of the defeated Iraqi Army, which was partly facilitated by Turkey allowing the Americans the use of its territory, Ankara felt reinforced by the fact that vast quantities of American weapons were left in Turkish hands, including armored vehicles, fighter aircraft and missiles. It also received billions of dollars' worth of export contracts, oil deliveries, customs concessions, canceled debts, grants and access to markets- all as compensation for its immense financial losses during the war.[4] Moreover, Turkey's support for the Western coalition against Iraq, which was probably calculated to gain favor with the US and the EU, paid off, at least in part in 1995, when Ankara concluded a customs agreement with the European Community- far short, admittedly, of the full membership that Turkey coveted, but a significant step (it looked at the time), in that direction. But it became apparent that the Gulf War had proved to the West that despite the collapse of the Soviet Union, Turkey remained a significant strategic asset. All those evaluations and calculations notwithstanding, the situation would be reversed when Necmettin

---

[3] R. Israeli, *Who is Right and Who is Left: the fate of Weak Nations Among great Empires*, Strategic Books, TX, 2018.

[4] Amikam Nachmani, "Turkey and the Middle East", in *Journal of Modern Hellenism, Vol. 15 (1999)*, p. 15

Erbakan, provisionally, then his disciple Tayyip Erdogan, continuously, came to power and metastasized Turkey from a staunch ally of the West, into an unreliable partner guided by doctrinaire Islam rather than pragmatic politics. In consequence, joining EU gradually faded away as a remote aspiration for Turkey, as the EU realized the demographic peril of 75 million more Turkish Muslims joining the 30 million recent Muslim immigrants, driving their rate in the half a billion European citizens to 15 or 20%, up from the present 5-7% (except for France with 10% or more).

Turkey's refusal to allow American troops to operate "against a sister Muslim state" (Iraq), from its territory under Erdogan's Islamic Party rule in 2003, followed by the rapid Islamization of Turkish society, soon reflected the sea change that Turkey was envisaging under its Islamic regime, which would have far-reaching consequences:

1. Turkish denial of its territory to facilitate the US onslaught against Saddam Hussein, was not a simple rejection of a Western blueprint while it served as a powerful member of NATO, but a blunt affront, and in fact an open sabotage of the Second (and this time decisive) American incursion into Iraq under George Bush II. For, had the Turks acceded to the American request, as they had done a decade earlier, that would have forced Saddam to split his troops between the south where the American troops were massing their forces for the offensive from Kuwait, and the northern frontier with eastern Anatolia. Instead, the Americans had to sail through Suez and add some of their crack divisions to the already overcrowded Kuwaiti territory which became the sole launching pad for the offensive. The Allies viewed themselves as let down, not to say betrayed, by their partner, and they rightly assessed the price that they had to pay, in human losses and in logistic complications as too high to contemplate.

2. Erdogan, as a result, would turn to other alternative partnerships, trying to crystallize around his Turkey the newly emerging Central Asian Muslim states and the awakening Muslim elements in the Balkans, a process that had started before him, but accelerated by his dream of Pan-Turkism or Pan-Turanism, which some of his critics have termed as Neo-Ottomanism, with himself regarded as the new Sultan in his new 1,100 room palace that he built in Ankara to substitute for the splendid by-gone royal precincts of Istanbul which had lodged the Sublime Porte for half a millennium. One of those alternatives, though not on the same grand scale, could have been Israel with its advanced technological capacities and its military and economic might combined. Later on, seeking hegemony, or at least a leader's position in Islamdom and Arabdom, he would turn to Egypt during the short tenure in office of Muslim Brother Muhammad Mursi (2012-13), and to Iran and Qatar.

3. As Europe was submerged under intractable waves of Muslim immigrants in the 2010s, mainly as a result of the Syrian Civil War, who passed through Turkey on their way as boat people from Turkish shores into EU territory, Erdogan was to use that human misery to extort more cash from the Union, as some sort of "protection money", to shield Europe from those human floods by retaining the migrating refugees in place. That did not prevent over a million migrants to flood Europe, especially Germany, causing major political and social disruptions there. That immense influx has not totally dried up, though it has substantially subsided, as Europeans turned against their leaders and demanded its stoppage.

4. The Madrid Conference convened by Bush I in the Summer of 1991, which was closely followed by the Oslo Declaration

of Principles (DOP, not Accords as they are customarily and wrongly dubbed), of September, 1993 between Israelis and Palestinians, helped solve another dilemma for the Turks and allowed them to draw closer to Israel for a while. For reasons more emotional (i.e. religious) than rational, the Palestinian cause enjoyed almost universal support among the Turkish citizenry, both before Erdogan and more emphatically under his rule. For example, the then Turkish Foreign Minister, Mumtaz Soysal insisted in late 1994, at the height of the honeymoon with Israel that what Israel called "Palestinian terrorism" was merely the Palestinians' attempt to defend their rights[5].

5. Domestically, the Erbakan government, which ruled for hardly two years in the mid 1990s and began its *rapprochement* with Iran and adopting an Islamic policy that, *inter alia,* would tempt him to reduce the extraordinarily close relations with Israel, especially on the military level, which had been cultivated by the previous civil governments, was removed by the military from office and his Islamic party was outlawed. When the substituting Islamic Party of Erdogan won the elections in 2002, it regarded as its first task the neutralization of the military from their constitutional role as the guardians of the Ataturk heritage, which had permitted them three military coups in the past, and the latest intervention in Erbakan's disfavor .Therefore, Erdogan embarked on a quiet, insidious domestic revolution which Islamized the school system and gradually replaced the pro-Western and pro-Israeli top military brass by his own people, chosen for their Muslim piety and not only for their military skill, so as to remove any threat of a military coup in the

---

[5] Nachmani, "The Remarkable etc…" p. 22.

future. That process, which took a decade, came to fruition when in one stroke the entire corps of generals and admirals was put under arrest, accused of subverting the state political leadership, and culminated in the 2016 counter-revolution, in which Erdogan purged the state system, especially the police and the educational hierarchy, from the Fethullah Gulen Islamic movement, which had been his ally before, but now became his enemy and it was imperative to eradicate it from the state machinery.

6. This whole process ended with Turkey shifting from a Parliamentary into a Presidential regime, with Erdogan taking over the reins of all branches of government, thus concentrating in his hands all the affairs of the state and putting an end both to the threat of the army to his rule and to the privileged relations with Israel. All dissidents who disagreed, either in the press or in the state machinery, were arrested or dismissed from their jobs. Thus the all-powerful Erdogan, backed by the popular vote of his ignorant and backward rural constituency, and resisted by the intellectuals and the middle class traders and urban bourgeoisie, the educated and sophisticated pro-Western population, can since the elections of 2018 which confirmed his prerogatives as the absolute head of state, to act as he sees fit. The net effect is that he no longer has to fear the military or anyone else when running any political course he chooses, including reducing and even cutting off when necessary the links with Israel.

Erdogan- Another Ataturk or a Sultan?

Turkey's population of close to 80 million, more than 60% of whom live in urban areas, is suffering from a severe identity crisis due to domestic and international developments. For a basically democratic country which saw three military takeovers before government returned to civilian hands, and later the removal of Erbakan by the military in 1997, and then an attempted *coup* against Erdogan's leadership in 2016, the rise of Islam presents a sort of paradox: As in Egypt, Pakistan, Jordan, Morocco and other Islamic countries where the process of liberalization, away from harsh doctrinaire authoritarianism, provoked a countercurrent in the form of political Islam, Turkey too has discovered that allowing all its people to express themselves freely often results in their choosing Islam as a focus of individual, communal and political identity, especially in the countryside which has been less exposed than the large urban areas to the West and its values, to international education and to cosmopolitan trends; and has conversely been shackled to parochial and traditional modes of thought, much guided by conservative and often ignorant and obscurantist *mullahs*. These are the audiences which were the first and easiest to yield to the Islamization campaign of the various Islamic parties of Erbakan and Erdogan, and regarded the Western subversion of the Ottoman Empire and then the contemporary Western inroads into Turkish civilization with horror, and now continue to provide the political and popular base for the authoritarianism of Recep Erdogan. Hence the growing sharp dichotomy between the urban and rural population of Turkey, between the old military who originated from the elite urban classes of the large cities and the poor Muslims of the countryside whose voice had been hardly heard during the civil governments which preceded Erdogan's. This also provides the tentative explanation for Erdogan's repeated decapitations of the old military top brass which was in league with the liberal middle class of merchants and intellectuals of the big cities, to replace them by pious Muslims from among the rank and file of his rural constituencies. This also explains why the failed coup of 2016 unfolded in Istanbul and was nipped in the bud there in a brief showdown between its urban leaders and the rural troops loyal to Erdogan. The later attempt by Erdogan and his underlings to accuse the *Fethullah Gulen* movement of the plot came as a pathetic move to justify and rationalize the massive arrests he unleashed against the bureaucracy, intellectuals and internal security forces whose lingering influence on the public might have hampered his plans for the authoritarian presidency that he was scheming.

This trend towards Islamization and authoritarianism, which went in par with each other, as shown by Matthias Kuntzel in the case of the Muslim Brothers in Egypt where they embraced that mode of government from the rising Nazis with whom they collaborated since the 1930[6], was put in its blaring context by Hay Yanarocak in his seminal article[7]. There he contends, that despite all predictions, Turkey's President Recep Tayyip Erdoğan, in power since 2003, won a landslide victory once again in the first round of the snap elections that were held on June 24, 2018, and that with this triumph, and short of extraordinary circumstances, he will continue to lead his country during the centenary celebrations of the Republic in 2023. This will enable him to break the record of the Republic's founder – Mustafa Kemal Atatürk – who was in office, *de-facto* and *de-jure*, for 18 years (1920-1938). Yanarocak pursues his argument:

> Similar to Ataturk, Erdogan now rules the country with unhindered power. Thanks to the … state of emergency as well as the 2017 referendum victory that turned Turkey into a presidential system, Erdogan has begun to enjoy a sultan's power, blunted only by cosmetic checks and balances. This has inevitably served his agenda of concentrating more power into his own hands, and has significantly contributed to his success in the recent

---

[6] Kuntzel Matthias, *Jihad and Jew-Hatred, Islamism, Nazism and the Roots of 9/11*, TElos Press, New York, 2007.

[7] Hay Yanarocak, "TURKEY'S ONE-MAN SHOW", *Turkeyskope*, The Moshe Dayan Center, Tel-Aviv University, Summer, 2018.

round of elections. Notably, during the last election campaign [of 2018], the President and his rivals did not fight on equal terms. While Erdogan enjoyed the full power of the state apparatus and absolute media cooperation, his adversaries suffered from the lack of media coverage. Kurdish People's Democratic Party candidate.... [for example], was even barred from meeting with his constituency as he has been imprisoned since 2016.[8]

Predictably, Erdogan's growing concentration of power in his hands and his need to project on others his own deficiencies, gained even more momentum after his reelection in 2018 to the presidency, and his growing paranoia, just like Stalin in his time, which prompted him to arrest journalists and intellectuals, officials and army officers and to find scapegoats for his purges and verbal calumniations which are popular among his ignorant anti-establishment crowds, who delight in the bombast of their adored leader and cheer him the more fault he can detect in Jews and Israel, like the broadcast show he mounted on the 24th of July, 2018 before hundreds of his party members where he treated the Israelis, as "fascist, racist and revivers of the Hitlerian spirit in their midst". The Israeli Prime Minister responded by asserting that the murderer of Kurds and Syrians and the dictator of the Turks, who dismisses innocent thousands from their jobs and throws in prison hundreds of others, is certainly in no position to sermonize others about democracy and murder. In fact, his expanding popularity has been edging toward canonization like Atatürk, and drawing criticism from his detractors or rivals rather suggests a comparison to Hitler or Stalin, although the immediate successors of Atatürk, namely Ismet İnönü, and Ednan Menderes, had also ruled Turkey without relying on coalitions. Having been challenged by his previous allies,

---

[8] Ibid

namely former Turkish President Abdullah Gül and former Prime Minister Ahmet Davutoğlu, Erdoğan no longer trusts his comrades in his Justice and Development Party (*Adalet ve Kalkınma Partisi* – AKP). His recent choice of nominating technocrats to his new cabinet, beyond the few AKP officials who already proved their loyalty to him, indicates a new phenomenon of keeping the executive body of the state distant from his own party. By doing so, Erdoğan will most likely eliminate the chance that a charismatic rival might emerge from within his own party to challenge his rule in the future.

Turkey's Uneasy Identity with The Middle East

The removal from power of Necmettin Erbakan by the military in 1997, in view of his perceived tilt towards Islam during his short tenure in office, and in order to preserve the secular heritage of Ataturk of which they were the Curator[9], and the close military partnership with Israel, only constituted the breaking of the thermometer, but did not cure the insidious fever which was growing under the surface, especially in the countryside where the successive civil governments that had preceded Erbakan, had lost contact with the realities of their forgotten contituency. There had been a slow process of a return to Islam in the rural areas, with new mosques being built, women going back to the veil, and other Muslim customs being revived among the neglected poor and backward population which saw itself sidelined and bypassed in the modernization and development processes that the well to do and pro-Western classes of intellectuals, professionals and merchants were pursuing in the big cities, which were the centers of power and prosperity while the rural areas seemed to be kept in the dark as if they lived on a different planet. The bigoted and anti-Western Islam that was

---

[9] A. Shmuelevitz, "The Attitude of the Islamic Press in Turkey Toward Israel" (Hebrew). in *Hamizrah He-Hadash* (The New East), 1997-8, pp. 114-24

being peddled to them by Erbakan and his disciples, including Erdogan, Gul and others, as the solution to all their problems and as the sole valid panacea to their marginality, found an attentive ear among them. But the bourgeois of Istanbul, Izmir and Ankara, together with their Western partners and allies, were too complacent to listen or to believe that the secularism of adored Ataturk was reversible, and they were stunned and frightened to discover that it was. Thus, the military *coup* of 1997 that took the liberty to remove the elected government of Erbakan and to outlaw his party, exacerbated the Islamic challenge by spawning extra- parliamentary movements on the Right and the Left which resorted to violence and threatened to undermine domestic stability.

Former President and Prime Minister, Torgut Ozal (1927-1993) was often cited as having affirmed that "Turkey is a secular state. I am not. I am a Muslim". He was the most prominent Turk who differentiated between his fealty to the Ataturk heritage and to his Western orientation, and his personal piety as a devout Muslim, a typically Western attitude toward the modern state which has been rejected by Erbakan, Erdogan and their likes. This comment had reflected at any rate the inherent tension between the identity of most Turkish individuals as Muslims who followed Islamic practice in various degrees, and their role within a state that had officially divorced itself from the faith. While in the West the separation of the sacred from the secular has been effected relatively painlessly and seems to work, no Islamic country has been able so far to come to terms with such a separation; and even modern Turkey, which was always cited as the successful case of secularization, proved under Erdogan to have been unable to effect that revolution at the grassroots. For no Islamic political theory has ever been enforced that distinguished between mosque and state, politics and their conduct being an integral part of the holy law (*shari'a*). Indeed, after visiting Turkey in the Summer of 1996, under Erbakan's tenure as Prime Minister, the daughter of Iranian President Ali Akbar

Hashemi Rafsanjani, noted similarities between the situation in Turkey and that of Iran at the end of the Shah's reign[10]. At that time, almost no one of consequence (except this author) heeded this warning, which turns out in perspective to have been a writing on the wall in capital letters, and a blinking and shrieking alarm red light. Maybe that was what also marginally alerted the Turkish military who sent Erbakan packing and appointed Mesut Yilmaz in his stead in June,1997. The paradox was set then which kept recurring ever since: on the one hand, the West has repeatedly condemned military *coups* which removed from power elected Muslim governments (It also happened in Egypt when in 2013, Chief of Staff Sisi toppled the Muslim Brother President Mursi who had been elected one year earlier). The West also welcomed the measures taken by Erdogan to cancel the prerogative of the army to remove elected governments. But when Muslim governments were elected, like in Turkey and Egypt, which were hostile to the West, even supported Muslim terrorist movements (like Mursi and Erdogan's sympathy for the Muslim Brothers, Hamas and Hizbullah), and ran processes of Islamization of their countries which necessitateed oppression, limitations of civil liberties and of the rights of non-Muslim minorities, the West always rushed to condemn those regimes, and in the case of Turkey to further alienate it from Europe and from its dream of joining the EU.

While the blunt intervention of the army in the political process always called into question Turkey's (and Egypt's for that matter) maturity to become a liberal-democratic state, there was also no doubt, before Erbakan and Erdogan, that it also reflected Turkey's determination to align itself with the West, including Israel. But with Erbakan and Erdogan it became equally evident that Islam had insinuated itself into the heart of Turkey's outwardly secular political system, and it was clear therefore, even before the Erdogan take-

---

[10] *Haaretz,* December 22, 1996.

over, that the Muslim identity of the Turks will again come to the fore and militate against a *rapprochement* with the West and Israel[11]. One has to remember that as a Muslim country and a prominent member of the Islamic Conference/Cooperation Organization, Turkey has always had to walk the tight rope between its interest in maintaining a relationship with the West and Israel, and its cultural, religious, economic, historical and emotional commitment to Islam. Therefore, for most of the period preceding the Turkish-Israeli close relationship of the 1990s, Ankara tilted toward its Islamic neighbors[12], and its foray towards Israel during those few honeymoon years has been the aberration, not the rule. When one watches the delirious crowds who greet with applaud Erdogan's words of libel and condemnation against Israel, one understands why. An additional element of the anti-Israeli bias, which is backed by the fervent but irrational and emotional support of Turks to the Palestinians, has been related to the neo-Ottomanism that Erdogan has been striving to revive. Until the humiliating Ottoman defeat in W W I, both Jews and Arabs in Palestine had been at the mercy of the Porte, while both were relegated and marginalized in the backwater that was Palestine under their rule. Erdogan cannot bear the idea that erstwhile *dhimmi* Jews who had repeatedly sought shelter in the Ottoman domain when expelled and persecuted elsewhere, should have the *chutzpah* (affront) today not only to subtract themselves from Turkish hegemony but even to challenge it in the open. Therefore, while constantly vilifying and accusing Israel of all the *malaise* of the world, he always emphasizes that Turkish Jews, those who have resigned to his rule, will be protected as they had always been.

Nonetheless, the worldwide process of globalization and sus-

---

[11] Hakan Yavuz,"Turkish-Israeli Relations Through the Lens of the Turkish Identity Debate", *Journal of Palestine Studies,* vol. 27, no 1, 1997, pp. 22-37

[12] Walter Weiker,"Turkey, the Middle East and Islam", *Middle East Review* Spring 1985, pp. 27-32

tained development that followed the collapse of the Soviet Union and the Gulf Wars, drew Ankara and Jerusalem closer together. Other Arab and Islamic countries and societies, however, remained fearful of such all-encompassing changes and distanced themselves from their erstwhile Turkish ally. Turkish President Suleyman Demirel's (1993-2000) declaration that "Israel and Turkey have decided on regional cooperation for increasing the economic welfare of the region and curbing terrorism", contrasted sharply with the continuous attacks on Israel by intellectuals and policymakers even in Arab countries that have signed peace accords with Israel [13]. The question of counterterrorism was of particular interest in this context, because Israel and Turkey both found themselves in boundary disputes with Syria (over the Golan and Alexandretta, respectively) and opposed Syria's effort to establish hegemony in Lebanon. What is more, Damascus also supported and sheltered terrorist groups directed either against Israel or against Turkey[14]. Considering that Israel had backed the Kurdish rebellions in Iraq in the 1970s and 1980s, it must have been difficult for it to collaborate with the Turks in their own struggle against Kurdish insurgents. But Israel's interest in thwarting Syria meshed well with Turkey's campaign against the Syrian-supported Kurdistan Workers Party (*Partiya Karkeren Kurdistan*- PKK) and evidently outweighed points of principle. As for the Turks, their simultaneous pursuit of relations with Israel and the Arabs was liked to a man who had both a wife and a mistress: He may feel a special attraction to his mistress who possesses certain charms his wife lacks, but in public he must appear a dutiful husband and cannot even officially acknowledge the exis-

---

[13] Cited by Meltem Muftuler-Bac, "Turkey and Israel: an Evolving Partnership", Ariel Center for Policy Research, *Policy Paper* 47, 1998. See also R. Israeli, Arab and Muslim Anti-Semitism", Ariel Center for Policy Research, April 2000.

[14] George Gruen, "Turkeys' relations with Israel and its Arab Neighbors:The Impact of Basic Interests and Changing Circumstances", *Middle East Review*, Spring, 1985,, pp. 33-43

tence of the mistress. This is all the more true if the wife comes, as do the Arabs, from a large and prominent family and has brought a big dowry to the marriage[15].

To be sure, Israelis resented this analogy because their country had never demanded that Turkey divorce itself from its Arab and Muslim neighbors, for Israelis have always only sought what the Turks were reluctant to grant them: a full and openly acknowledged relationship. But Turkey's long rebuff of Israel owed also much to its mistreatment by the West, for it had realized since the 1960s that in spite of its secular regime, loyalty to NATO, and attempts to emulate the West, its security was ignored during the 1962 Cuban missile crisis and the subsequent crisis over Cyprus. Indeed, far from enjoying US support at that time, Ankara watched as the Americans rushed to support Greece, "going so far as to supply the Greek Cypriots with arms for their campaign against the Turkish minority and the British in Cyprus"[16]. The Turks considered this a stab in the back and therefore pursued Muslim solidarity in the wake of the OPEC embargo in 1973. Then, commercial relations between Turkey and the Arabs picked up, especially in the domain of Turkish oil imports. But after the mid 1980s the volume of that trade slacked off and its character changed as Turkish exports increased and its oil imports decreased, diminishing considerably Ankara's dependence on those ties.[17] Remarkable in this web of Turkish relations with the Arab world was its love-hate relationship with Iraq. Both countries struggled against the Kurds, who constituted about one fifth of their respective populations. Moreover, Baghdad's ability to sustain its long war with Iran (1980-1988) depended on the flow of its oil across Turkish territory and the

---

[15] Cited in Amikam Nachmani, *Israel, Turkey and Greece: Uneasy Relations in the Eastern Mediterranean*, Frank Cass, London, 1987, p. 75.

[16] Amikam Nachmani, *Turkey and the Middle East*, BESA, Bar Ilan University, 1999, p. 3

[17] Ibid, pp. 4-5.

importation of food stuffs via Turkish ports. On the other hand, debt issues, conflict over water distribution, and Turkish support of the US during Operation Desert Storm, drove Turkish- Iraqi relations into new lows. As a consequence of that war, Turkey confronted not only vast economic deficits, but also hundreds of thousands of Kurdish refugees who streamed across the border with Iraq in search of asylum on its territory, just like the situation in the 2010s when Turkey became the most available shelter for millions of refugees from the Syrian civil war. At the same time, Turkey was also instrumental in implementing the oil-for-food program, which eased Turkey's economic pressures by allowing it to ship oil from, and foodstuffs to Iraq.

In sum, Turkey's ties with the Muslim world have been mixed indeed. But during much of the 1980s even that equivocal relationship was warm compared to the chill between Turkey and Israel[18], exactly as the almost hostile relations between Turkey and Israel in the 2000s under Erdogan's fanatic hatred to Israel and Jews, has made his resentful attitude to Egypt and Saudi Arabia, turned the main foes of his Muslim Brother allies, pale in comparison. After the passage in Israel of the Jerusalem Law in 1980, which in fact annexed East Jerusalem to Israel, the Turkish Consulate General in Jerusalem was closed down under the pressure of Erbakan's Islamic Party, while Turkish Airlines and Turkish Maritime Lines ceased transport between Turkey and Israel. It was not until 1986 that the level of diplomatic representation between the two countries was raised again, setting the stage for the *entente* that was to blossom in the 1990s. The swing of the pendulum between the two extremes, from intimacy to open hostility, depending on changing circumstances, interests and heads of government, will accompany the evolution (or deterioration) of these strange relationships over sev-

---

[18] Ekrem Guvendiren, *A Concise Report on Turkish-Israeli Relations*, Foreign-Economic Relations Board, Istanbul, 1990, p. 9.

eral decades thereafter. On the one hand, the stunning levels of cooperation, assistance, tourism industry and keen interest in the development of an extraordinarily close relationship, but on the other hand a degree of hatred, lie manufacturing, contempt and threats not found between countries which maintain diplomatic and trade relations at the highest level.[19]

---

[19] See R. Israeli, *Hatred, Lies and Violence in Islam,* Transaction,, NJ 2012.

Chapter One

From Empire to Republic, and Back?

Islam has undoubtedly not only shaped the history of the Ottoman Empire, the father of the modern Turkish state, but to a great extent is still forging the fortunes of the Islamic world, and increasingly so. We shall briefly tackle here the major aspects of Islam which are directly relevant to the attitudes of Islam towards Jews, Israel and Zionism. For it is important to remember that the millennial domination of the Jews in Islamdom, under the oppressive, humiliating and paralyzing status of *dhimmi*s that followed the history of the Prophet in Medina with the Jews of that first Islamic city, has been a major reason why modern Muslims cannot reconcile to the idea of a Jewish independent state whose fortunes had hinged upon Muslim goodwill, is now able to stand up and defy the much more numerous Muslims of the world, hence their adamant rejection of it lock, stock and barrel and refusal to come to terms with it, in spite of the short periods of accommodation with it which include modern Turkey when it was ruled by a civil administration which elected national interest over religious commitments. The loss of the Ottoman Empire, the last firmly established Islamic Caliphate with an *Amir al-Mu'minin* (the Commander of the Faithful) at its head,(if we ignore the fleeting existence of ISIS in the 2010s), and the institution of the Turkish Republic in its stead, constituted not only an admission of defeat of Islam in its determining confrontation with the West, but also that the universality of Islam as a global *umma* had revolved and been replaced by modern nation states that encompassed different ethnic and national groups like Turks, Arabs, Indonesians, Pakistanis and what have you. After 80 years of the secular Turkish republic founded by Ataturk, where it was thought that the founder's heritage was there to stay, due to the definitely removed Islamic hegemony from the politics of the country, Erdogan's revolution of the 2000s seems to strive to turn back the wheels of history. This is done by breathing life into the bygone Imperial Ottomanism and reviving Islamic universalism, and by associating with the contemporary trends of Islamic renewed vigor, that has been preached by the Muslim Brothers in the world (and their CAIR extension in America), and by such radical preachers as Yussuf Qaradawi. After all, it was the Turks of Central Asia who had injected into the weakened post- Abbasid Islam of the 13th Century the new vigor which enabled the Ottoman Dynasty to overwhelm the Byzantines and gain world dominion and supremacy with the establishment of the new Islamic Caliphate under the Ottoman sultan.

As a Muslim Dynasty, the Ottomans were bound by the traditional Islamic attitudes to non-Muslims in their realm, which were governed by the institution of *dhimma* (protection), which spelled out deep contempt of the infidels and the need to humiliate them, side by side with the obligation to protect them and their property as long as they paid the debilitating poll-tax (*jizyah*) of which Muslims were exempt. When one consults the historical and legal documents relating to the mistreatment of *dhimmis* in general, the Jews in particular, and specifically the cruel, sadistic and inhuman punishments meted out to the "Infidels", under a pressing psychological need to persecute, oppress and humiliate them, one finds that this stands in stark contradiction to the Jews emerging as a sovereign nation which is able to defy their Muslim masters of yesteryear and stand up against them, in spite of its being tiny, widely dispersed, stateless and vastly outnumbered. That condition of revival and resurgence is perceived as an illogical deviation from the constantly expansive, dominating rule and victorious pattern of medieval Islam, which had subjugated Jews (and Christians) to its dominion. The mistreatment of Jews under Islam, especially in North Africa and in Spain, has been firmly established despite the claimed interregnum of the "Golden Age", whose imagined myth under the independent western Umayyad Dynasty in Iberia has been shredded to pieces recently[20]. The same attitude toward Jews in different parts of the Middle East, either under the Mamluks of Egypt, or in the Persian kingdom further east, or later under the unifying Ottoman Empire, has been a matter of some controversy but as a rule it has applied throughout Islamdom with slight or severe deviations for the better or the worse. But the negative image of the Infidels in the eyes of the Believers has persisted to this very day and certainly guided the policies of Muslim governments and the convictions of their populace around the world.

It became evident once and again, that Jews depended for their very existence on their sycophancy towards absolute and corrupt Muslim rulers, who legislated, enforced their cruel laws and punished ruthlessly, all at once. Jews became unfailingly aware, every day anew, of their misery under this kind of oppressive rule and of the hazards of sitting atop a bubbling volcano which could burst at any time, without warning or transition. In the year 1680, for example, while everyone was asleep, the king of Morocco decreed that all the inhabitants of the Fez *mellah* (Jewish *ghetto)* had to be pulled out of their beds and sent to the surrounding fields. The reason was that a sword set with precious stones had been stolen from his palace. The horrified Jews, with their praying elderly, yelling infants and helpless sick, lay on the cold and barren earth, not understanding either of what they were guilty, or when that collective punishment

---

[20] See Dario Fernandez-Morera, *The myth of the Andalusian Paradise*, ISIS Press Wylmington, 2016

would be terminated. Only when the Jews were permitted to go back to their homes, and when they realized that nothing was stolen from their property in their absence, did they burst into celebration of the "miracle" which was done to them, for they were able to remain alive, while the torment, the terror and the menaces heaped on them in the middle of the night were considered "normal". Moreover, that inhuman ruling king, Mulai Isma'il, was considered "benevolent", and when one day, the news was released that he had just escaped from falling prey to lions, they celebrated the happy occasion in great pomp and ceremony, abstained from work, decorated the streets of the *mellah* (Jewish *ghetto*) with silk materials, and donned their most festive outfits. On that day they could even visit the royal palaces and enter the mosques with their shoes on, as they jubilantly reported in their records of 1699. But, in the same breath, they reported of Mulai Zaydan from the royal house in Tefilalt, who stormed the *mellah* of that city, taking as booty anything he and his underlings found of worth, and imposed a fine of two hundred and fifty gold coins on that impoverished community. These were the two poles of Jewish existence, which implied that the more the helpless Jews submitted and bent their heads down, the more mistreated and humiliated they were bound to be at the hands of their rulers. Just for the "privilege" of remaining alive, they would hold themselves grateful to their oppressors for the "generosity" from which they had benefited. That was, in essence, the status of "*dhimma*" which we will have to elaborate upon.

From the onset of Islam in the 7th Century AD, as the new religion was expanding rapidly through quick conquest of the entire Mediterranean basin and beyond, where ancient and exhausted nations were disintegrating, Islam divided humanity into three categories and the earth into two kinds of territory. At the center, of course, stood the Muslims, the humans closest to the ideal, due to their submission (*Islam*) to the will of Allah. The second category were the Scriptuaries (*ahl-al-Kitab*), namely people like Christians and Jews, who possessed a holy scripture, which was recognized by Islam until it was "distorted" and "forged" by its holders, and subsequently "amended and updated" by the revelations of Allah to the Prophet Muhammad. As the years wore on, and as the conquests were expanded further afield, other people too, like the Manicheans and the Hindus, were recognized as Scriptuaries. The outermost circle included the pagans who did not know one God. The lands where all those peoples dwelt were differentiated as either the Islamic Dominion (*Dar al-Islam*), or *Pax Islamica*, that is the territory ruled by Islam, regardless of the composition of its population (for instance, the lands still populated by a majority of non-Muslims, like Andalusia, were still part of this category, as long as they were ruled by Islam); and the Dominion of War (*Dar al-Harb*), namely the land that was yet to fall under Islamic rule. Evidently, for practical reasons, these categories are not effectively operational in modern times except for territories won over by radical Muslims such as ISIS, the Taliban and others, for otherwise the entire system of international relations and international rules of conduct would be chaotic, if every nation determined for itself its attitude towards others as it pleased. But in pre-modern Islamic countries, there was no public opinion, and the rules of conduct were determined by *Shari'a* law, exactly the way some revolutionary Islamic movements are attempting to revive them today. That law is immutable and not open to reform, pressure or whim of the ruler, even as some of those same rulers have occasionally deviated from those severe rules, depending upon whether they were personally more fanatic puritans or more open-minded and benevolent beings. Under the more puritanical Hanbalite and Malikite Schools of Law (and Shi'ites for that matter), where *shari'a* implementation was the strictest, the suffering of the Scriptuaries reached its peak.

The status of *dhimma* (protection or dhimmitude) has gained considerable treatment in the Muslim judicial treatises of the Middle Ages. To be a *dhimmi* not only signified the inferior class of the tolerated peoples, in contrast with the privileged Muslim subjects of the Caliphate, but meant also a lesser judicial stature (e.g. the evidence provided by a *dhimmi* was worth half of the Muslim's, and the *dhimmi* was legally incapacitated to bear witness against a Muslim; an inferior economic and social position (certain dirty jobs and occupations were reserved to the *dhimmis*); a submissive political rank (Jews and Christians had no political rights and could not be trusted to serve in the government or the military); and a cultural handicap (Jews were always suspected of plotting schemes or mirroring Satan). When Muslim children were disciplined by their parents for their misconduct, the "threat" that the Jews would be brought upon them was often used. That was understandable because the Qur'an instilled the idea that they were "the descendants of monkeys and pigs", and discouraged any amicable relations with them or with Christians. Many of the limitations imposed on Jews (and Christians) were crystallized in what came to be known as the *'Umar Regulations*, which expressed the ambivalent attitude of Muslims to the Scriptuaries: On the one hand they were supposed to be tolerated and protected due to their holy Scriptures and to their payment of the humiliating *jizyah*; but on the other hand, they were to be debased and tormented due to their "forgery of the Word of Allah", unless they complied and converted to Islam, as most conquered peoples did under duress. But one has to emphasize that those regulations were often violated, for the better or the worse. In Muslim Spain, where Jews attained temporary grandeur, served among the highest bureaucracy of the state, and distinguished themselves as professionals and intellectuals of the first degree, their actual stature was a huge improvement on their official status of *dhimmi*; but in Almohad North Africa and Mamluk Egypt, Jews knew worse periods of genocide of entire communities, massacres and extortions, persecutions and pogroms, even after they paid their poll tax and filled their obligations under the *dhimma*.

The most insidious aspect of *dhimma*, however, beyond the

humiliation and institutionalization of discrimination in the judicial, social, political, economic and cultural domains, has been the state of mind of fatalism and submission of the *dhimmi*s, born out of centuries of inescapable persecution and oppression, on the one hand, and the mood of sycophancy and identification with the oppressor, which has turned this state of affairs into a "natural and immutable" situation, on the other. In other words while it has been possible to extricate Jews and Christians from the *dhimma*, it is next to impossible to extricate the *dhimma* mentality out of some of those who had suffered it. We have already mentioned the mood of submission and sycophancy that had characterized Jewish (and Christian) conduct during the dark ages of their existence in the various *mellah*s (Jewish ghettos) of Morocco. For even after their exodus from that backward society in modern times, and their rootedness in the tolerant and advanced societies which absorbed them, where liberty and safety are guaranteed, there is among some of them a lingering habit of praising the Muslim rulers for their "benevolence" towards the *dhimmi*s; it is as if the Jews owed their right to exist to those absolute and corrupt rulers who held thousands of political prisoners in jail without trial. This typically Jewish parochial outlook of judging rulers only based on their conduct towards Jews, and not on the basis of their universal and human rights records, is what distorts the thinking of those Jews today, who erect monuments in Israel to Moroccan kings, or praise Moroccan monarchs, and participate in their funerals, only because they were thought to be "pro-Jewish", or accepted bribes to let Jews leave their bondage there, or had otherwise collaborated with Israel. Furthermore, the *dhimmi* outlook has insidiously penetrated the domain of international relations, inasmuch as the political correctness cultivated by the media, academics and diplomats, has imposed rules of conduct which prohibit criticizing anything Islamic, including their repressive regimes, their backward societies, their corrupt leaderships, or their aggressive and discriminatory policies. We have been surrounded by a sub-culture of legends and lies, which holds Islam as "the religion of peace", in the face of the rampages of *Jihadi* Islam across the world, at the same time that it is the more militant trends of Islam which prevail today. The Rushdie syndrome, the hiding of European politicians in their own lands from the wrath of Muslim attackers, the kowtowing of European countries before the masses of Muslims, under the excuse of multi-culturalism[21], who threaten to submerge them and to change Europe to their tune, the violence used by Muslims across the world, the fear of western media and publishers from giving vent to anything critical of Islam, and the wimpy supplications of the West for Iran to desist from its nuclear program, are all manifestations of this malaise. And if one dares to resist this *dhimmi* doctrine, one is dubbed "racist" or "Islamophobe".

After the first Muslim dynasties of the Umayyads and the Abbasids, the earlier from Damascus, the latter from Baghdad, and the Mongol ravages in the Middle East, it was the Turks who emerged from Central Asia and converted to Islam, who injected a new vigor into that faith and empire which seemed to dissolve into small rival sultanates. The Turkish takeover by the Seljuks and then the Ottomans, extended their dominion over most of the Islamic world during their half a millennium rule which also encompassed most of the Arab Middle East. The latter was to occupy a special place in the Ottoman heritage and sentiment, due to the fact that the holy Qur'an, the Word of Allah, was revealed to the Prophet and then written down in Arabic, whose script was adopted by the Ottoman Turks for their official language of the Empire, which also came to incorporate a vast Arabic terminology in the political, cultural and literary domains for which there had been a dearth of words in the nomadic Turkestan of Central Asia. The multi-century rule of the

---

[21] See R. Israeli, *Retreating from the Mirage of Multi-culturalism: the Cases of Holland, Britain and Israel,* Strategic Books, TX, 2018

Arabs by the Ottomans also created a special emotional link between the rulers and the ruled, beyond the Islamic nexus which was the unifying theme of the Empire in the first place. Hence the lingering feeling of guilt in modern Turkey for the Ottoman failure to defend and preserve the Arab world from Western colonial powers and especially its inability to scuttle the Balfour Declaration of 1917 which provided the legal underpinnings for the establishment of modern Israel thirty years later. Hence the special sense of responsibility for the fate of the Palestinians, whose nationhood has been overshadowed by the creation of modern Israel.

For that reason, Palestinians and other Muslims, often backed by other countries, including even from the Christian West and UNESCO, refuse to admit any historical link of the Jewish people to that ancient land, against all historical and archaeological evidence, and to recognize Israel as a Jewish state, or Jerusalem as its capital city, positions that are today wholeheartedly backed by Erdogan, in spite of the standing official recognition of Israel by Turkey. In the meantime, based on that historical precedent, Arabs and Muslims live in expectation of a new Saladin who might emerge to lead them into the battle of destiny against the Jews. When the hugely popular Gamal Abdul Nasser led Egypt (1952-71), he was often designated by many as the new Saladin who would unite all Arabs and bring them salvation; after him, the Saladin mantle was passed to Saddam Hussein (1976-2003) and then to Osama Bin Laden (killed in 2010), but none of them lived to implement the dreams of their delusionary fans. Some Arabs, and many Muslims, have come to believe that Recep Erdogan, due to his charisma and might domestically, and mounting international stature externally, is emerging as the likely successor to the mantle of the next Muslim savior. Hence, among both supporters of Erdogan and his detractors, and totally independently of him, many Turks, whether members of religious or nationalist parties, right-wing or leftist liberals, cannot detach themselves from that sense of obligation towards a favorable solution of the Palestinian issue, which in turn conditions public Turkish attitudes toward Jews, Zionism and Israel in accordance with the fortunes of this insoluble Middle Eastern dispute.

During the rule of the Shi'ite Fatimid Dynasty in Egypt and part of North Africa, contemporaneously with the domination of the Seljuk Turks in Iran and the Fertile Crescent, the Mongols ravaged the Abbasid Empire and set Baghdad and its riches aflame, before they were acculturated into Islam and founded their khanates which extended from the European borders to China. Then, followed the harsh days of the fanatic Mamluks, (slaves who took over the rule of their masters), who also ruled much of the Islamic world. The Ottoman Turks came to power at the end of the 15th Century and expanded their vast empire from the Anatolian Plateau. The Turks themselves had encroached from Central Asia since the previous two or three centuries into the entire Arab and most of the Islamic world, in the process embracing Islam, and re-baptizing Constantinople into Istanbul since its takeover from the preceding Byzantine Empire, as the hub of their sprawling domain, establishing Islam as the dominant faith of the realm and the Ottoman Sultan as the Caliph of all Muslims, until the Empire's demise during W W One (1914-18) and the rise of modern Turkey and nationalism. The Ottoman Empire began its downward spiral towards demise in the 19th Century, as it was considered the "Sick man of Europe", after its advance into the Balkans had been arrested at the gates of Vienna (1683), and it emerged as a rival to the rising European powers for Palestine. For precisely at that time Arab nationalism, including its Palestinian branch, was making its first steps, *inter alia* in Arab and Muslim-majority Palestine under Ottoman rule, and also under the impetus of the newly revived Jewish nationalism in the form of Zionism. As the authority and prestige of the Sublime Porte (as the Ottoman Empire was dubbed after the compound of buildings in Istanbul which housed government offices) was dwindling, and its hold on its territories was becoming precarious, it grew squeezable enough to yield, since the advent of the 19th, to the pressures exercised against its rule both domestically and externally. At home, it was Muhammad Ali, the governor of Egypt who rebelled against the Sultan's rule and took control of his governorate to advance his own program of rapid modernization, especially in the military domain, and ultimately led to the creation of a new dynasty which took over much of the Levant under its jurisdiction and brought reform and progress to it. Under Western pressures, the Ottoman regime also announced far reaching reforms in its own regime, administration and the governance of the various provinces of the empire, known as the *Tanzimat*.

The modern history of the Ottomans, especially since the beginning of their demise, had generated so many concessions they had to make to the West, and sometimes also to the fledgling Zionist movement, that their sense of guilt for allowing the Jews to settle in the land, though in a thin trickle, and thus causing a travesty of justice to the Palestinians, continues to haunt many of them to this day. Due to the overwhelming role of the Ottomans in shaping the modern Middle East, including the fate of the Palestinians, let us delve briefly into the main stations of the Ottoman rise and fall along the more than four centuries of its rule and try to understand how did they affect the modern developments of the region. It all started, one should always remember, with the newly Islamized Turks who re-invigorated their new faith, after the demise of the great Sunni Abbasid and Shi'ite Fatimid dynasties in the late Middle Ages, in one of the greatest Jihadi wars of expansion Islam had known. Indeed, since the 13th Century, Turkic tribes were pushed westward by the Mongol conquests in Central Asia and some of them were posted by their Seljuk masters to the border of Byzantium to wage their *razzias* against the Christians as *ghazi* (raiders) or *murabitun* (border garrison guards) in the service of *Jihad*. But as the Seljuk rule dwindled, various Turkish speaking groupings headed by local *amirs* rose in Anatolia, who pursued the Jihad war. One of them was 'Uthman (1259-1326) in Anatolia who gave his name to the 'Usmanli (bastardized as Ottomans) illustrious dynasty of mighty Islamic rulers, who produced 36 Sultans over more than six centuries (1300-1922). The Dynasty is accounted for "only " during the latter four centuries, because in the first years of its rule, far from being an Empire, it was a mere local grouping vying for power, whose *raison d'etre* was to maintain the *jihad* against the Christians and gradually nibble from the latter's grip on Anatolia until they were pushed to their great stronghold of Constantinople, which was to fall into Ottoman hands only in 1453 and renamed Istanbul, with all its major Christian sites, including the imposing *Hagia Sophia*, converted into Muslim mosques.

Externally, one of the most important developments which hastened the disintegration of the imperial capacity to control its vast territories, was the system of Capitulations imposed by the European powers, which in fact legitimized the direct intervention of the foreign consulates in Palestine in the domestic affairs of the country, and monopolized their jurisdiction over their many nationals in the land, who were in fact extricated from Ottoman rule and no longer subject to its control. Previously, all non-Muslim communities in the realm had been organized autonomously under the system of the *millet* (creed) which in fact meant that all religious minorities (Jewish, Catholic Christian, Orthodox Christians, Druze, Alevis etc.) were recognized as autonomous entities which retained the rights for self-government in matters of personal status (marriage, divorce, inheritance, adoption and religious affairs)) and the management of their own religious affairs under a recognized head appointed by the Sultan. For the Jews, it was the *Hakham Bashi*, the Chief Rabbi, who was invested with both the spiritual and temporal authority to lead (and supervise) his flock, and at the same time was a respected figure who had access to the Court and served as a two-way avenue for communication between the community and the central rule in Istanbul. Long after the Ottoman empire had vanished, some countries of the Middle East, including Israel, still retain this system of autonomous religious communities, with this time Islam becoming one of the religious minorities in Israel whose communal affairs (like the *waqf* and the *Shari'a* courts) are tackled autonomously, and the personal status affairs (like marriage and divorce) are delegated by the state to the various religious minority communities (Muslim, Druze, Christian) as they are with regard to the Jewish majority, where the rabbinical authorities and courts preside over the implementation of the religious rules.

After the defeat of Ali's armies and navy (under Ottoman command) by the European powers during the Greek war of independence from the Ottomans (1827), he turned his attention to the Middle East in which he and his successors were to play a major role. That meant that he internalized the lesson of not confronting directly the European powers who proved stronger, and turning his militant energies into the affairs of the Ottoman Empire which he knew was starting to unravel. His next target was Greater Syria where he knew he could match the dwindling power of Sultan Mahmud II, and which was seen as the vital land-bridge between his firmly held possessions in the Nile Valley and the Anatolian Plateau, the very heartland of the Sultan's rule with Istanbul at its apex. In preparation for his endeavor he expanded his relations with local chieftains in Syria (including Palestine and Lebanon) while the Sultan himself was licking his wounds after his defeat by the Europeans, and was deeply involved in reforming his armies and dissolving the famous Janissary elites into the new army. Soon, Syria became the battleground between the two parties, namely the all-Powerful Sultan and the rebellious Pasha of Egypt, who had successfully subtracted his domain and his forces from Istanbul's jurisdiction. He took as a pretext the desertion of Egyptian conscripts who had ensconced into Syria in order to dodge the draft into Ali's armies, and invaded Syria in 1831, under the command of Ibrahim, Ali's son, heading for Acre. But now, due to the new reformist trends in Istanbul, which inoculated the bureaucracy there with a sense of a renewed self-confidence, Muhammed Ali was officially declared a rebel while his son was laying siege around Acre, which finally capitulated in May, followed by Damascus in June. Ibrahim then defeated the Ottoman army in Homs, then conquered Aleppo and got to the Anatolian border near Alexandretta. He even advanced further into Kunya, defeating the much larger Ottoman army under the command of the Chief Wazir of the realm. That humiliating rout of the Ottoman troops meant that Ibrahim could continue his rapid advance towards Istanbul where he would have declared his father as the new Chief of the Empire. But Muhammed Ali was more hesitant and more cautious than his fiery son and he ordered him to arrest his rapid sweep, probably fearing that deposing the Sultan would have precipitated European intervention. Instead, he indulged in psychological warfare against Mahmud II "the fool", who had relinquished the old Islamic customs in favor of the European way. Ironically, Muhammed Ali who had paved the way to modernization and reform was now repudiating and ridiculing the Sultan who followed in his reformist footsteps. Once again, the intervention of the European powers, this time through the new Russian-Ottoman alliance, brought the Russian fleet into the Dardanelles, raising the concern of both Britain and France. The latter exerted pressure on both the Sultan and Muhammed Ali, bringing about Ibrahim's withdrawal from his conquest in Anatolia at the cost to the Empire of recognizing Ali's rule in Greater Syria, including Palestine. This territorial unification of Egypt with Syria will not have been without precedent or without a continuation in later history. Saladin had accomplished this unity before he subjugated the Crusaders in the 12th Century, then the Mamluks ruled that territorial continuity for almost three centuries (13th 16th centuries), until the Ottoman conquest in 1516, which once again incorporated the entire area under the Sultan's rule. In contemporary times, Gamal abdul Nasser, the ruler of Egypt and the champion of Arab nationalism and unity in the second half of the 20th Century, again attempted unification with Syria under the United Arab Republic (1958-61), which was short-lived. However, Ibrahim Pasha, who was appointed by his father as the governor of the newly conquered territories, set out to apply in earnest the style of government and reform that had been enforced in Egypt by Muhammed Ali, thus forcing it into a modernization process that aspired to go far ahead of what the Ottoman Empire would have initiated in that far remote Syrian province. However, serious opposition from the local populations slowed down his initiatives.

In 1839 Mahmud II died and his place was taken by Sultan Abd al Majid, who wished to pursue his struggle against Muhammed Ali, with the support of the European powers which were reluctant to see the Ottoman Empire dissolved. They imposed on the two rivals the London Agreement (1840) which assured the inheritance of the Egyptian territory in perpetuity to Ali and his descendents, as well as the Palestinian city of Acre only for Ali's lifetime, provided Ibrahim's conquests in Syria were given up. But when Ali dragged his feet on implementation, Western navies took Beirut and shelled Acre in 1840, compelling Ibrahim to abandon Syria altogether, but signaling the end of both Muhammed Ali's preeminence as well as the downward spiraling of the Empire. However, due to the centralized government Ibrahim established in Syria, including Palestine, the local notables whose hold on the populations had been disturbed, caused unrest in the country. These troubles were coupled with their dissatisfaction from the European's increasing presence in the land, generating the "Fellah's Rebellion" in 1834 Palestine, which was directly triggered by the mandatory conscription to Ibrahim's army on the one hand, and the collection by the authorities of the private guns that were held and owned by the local population. Twenty thousand farmers gathered around Jerusalem and raised the banner of rebellion, laying siege on the Egyptian garrison in town, but they were soon joined by Hebron and Nablus, Jaffa and Acre. It was not until the aging Muhammed Ali arrived at the head of reinforcement from Egypt that the rebellion was quelled. At the same time that Ibrahim quelled the Muslim rebellion, he was accused by the local population in Palestine as an apostate, sunk in debauchery, in order to protect his Christian *protégés*; so much so that when he finally crushed the Farmers' Uprising around Jerusalem and Bethlehem he took good care to secure the Christians' safety. That conformed to the old time on-again off-again protection that the Ottomans afforded to their minorities.

The post-uprising reforms (*tanzimat*) were also applied to Syria and Palestine, which were back under the grip of the Ottomans after the decades of Muhammed Ali and his son Ibrahim's interregnum. At the time, that Arab area was still divided administratively between the three provinces (*vilayet*) of Damascus, Aleppo and Saida, the latter including most of Palestine, with the districts (*sanjaks*) of Jerusalem, Nablus and Gaza enjoying special privileges due to their religious, ethnic and historical backgrounds. Jerusalem in particular, where a special sensitivity developed due to the foreign Powers' interest in it, was now brought directly under the central government in Istanbul. This entire area was targeted for more advanced reforms due to its control of the road to Mecca, Damascus being the starting point for the pilgrims' annual journey, which was central to Islamic worship throughout the Empire, and was constantly pleading for its Islamic nature and for the prestige of the Sultan as the *Amir al-Mu'minin*, the spiritual as well as temporal Head of all Muslims. The more the grip of the Ottomans on its Balkanic domains became precarious, the more the value of its Middle Eastern territories increased, particularly Syria and Palestine, which rose in importance due to their immediate proximity to Anatolia and their importance as the bridgehead between the Euro-Asian landmass and the North African Muslim countries in which Ottoman interest was still noticeable despite the French takeover of

Algeria in 1830. This theme was put to the test during the battles of W W I which concentrated on the expanse between Beersheba and Gaza, and into Jerusalem and finally Syria. In effect, one of the five armies into which the newly reformed Ottoman military was restructured, was dubbed the "Arabistan Army" that was based in Damascus (and from 1848 with a secondary command post in Baghdad), and meant to defend the entire area of the Arab Middle East. Simultaneously, this army undertook to fight domestically the rebellious forces of the Druze on the mountain ridges of the Horan, the tribal rebels in Mesopotamia, the Alawites in Western Syria and the Bedouins in the Syrian desert and east of the Jordan, where the Hijazi railway ran.

In the *sanjaks* of Palestine, the Ottomans tried to play local chieftains against each other, as part of the corrupted administration over which they presided, in spite of the lip service paid to the benefits of the reforms, but only in the 1850s did they partly succeed, through a system of official appointments to positions of power and to respectable sinecures, in reducing the authority of some tribal leaders and enforcing the primacy of their troops militarily and of their bureaucracy administratively. To project power onto the remote areas of their vast domain, they constructed chains of desert strongholds, and manned them with Ottoman garrisons under Ottoman commanders, in their vain attempts to thwart the Bedouin raids on both the commercial routes and on the path of the annual pilgrims to Mecca. They tried to achieve that, partly by collecting the "illegal" weapons owned by every tribe and clan, in defense from the Bedouin and other robbers' *razzias*; but that custom of possessing weapons and using them either in attacks against others or in defense from such raiders, has not receded in the entire Arab areas down to our days, as we watch entire countries, like Syria, Iraq, Yemen, and Libya, succumbing to the armed chaos that has broken those countries apart during the Arab Spring of the 2010s, or even in more orderly Israel as its 20% Arab population has been stocking "illegal" weapons for criminal activities, and partly also for subverting the state of Israel. As has been their wont, they do not, like in the US, relinquish their "right" to hold weapons, arguing that the state of insecurity and the requirements of personal safety oblige them to keep armed to the teeth.

The massive Ottoman investment in the reforms in Syria and its Southern part – Palestine, in addition to the basic Islamic link that had existed all along, has naturally created a very tight feeling of common fate between the Syrians (including Palestinians) and their Imperial masters who at that point did not even dream of relinquishing their rule over the land. And when the Ottomans were forced to leave that area after W W I, they took with them the lingering feeling of failure to meet their responsibilities both towards their fellow Muslims, but especially toward their former subjects who were abandoned before their lot was settled and their future ensured. This sort of feeling, sometimes unconsciously, helps explain the centrality of the Palestinian issue in Turkey's politics and in particular Erdogan's obsession with appearing on the world and Islamic scenes as their sponsor and protector. Hence his hostility toward Israel as the power which scuttles his plans to play that role. Additionally, in his quest to lead the Muslim world, as the new Sultan of the revived neo-Ottoman empire that he aspires to lead, he also feels bound to lend his protection to the most radical Muslim groups, such as the Muslim Brothers and Hamas, but only as long as they do not turn against Turkey, as ISIS and al-Qa'ida had occasionally done, and as long as they give the appearance of playing the democratic game by running elections, as he also does scrupulously, while at the same time limiting civil freedoms and dismissing opponents and throwing them into jails.

One has to remember that with all their drawbacks and their inability to implement the *Tanzimat's* positive goals, the Ottomans have nonetheless succeeded in introducing the principle of "elections", replacing the rule of hereditary notables or armed violent thugs with local councils (*majlis*) for each urban area, though the autonomous system of the *Sheikh*, or *Sayyed* in tribal areas remained valid to this very day. For despite the "elections", it was the traditional, wealthy, powerful or religious leaders in place who were "elected" and destined to continue to predominate in their locations or regions. To this day, including in Israel's functioning democracy, Arab villages and townships pursue their traditional test of force between the various clans and tribes, under the façade of "elections", which everyone knows are run only to conform to the law, but in effect it is the rapport of forces between the powerful families which determines the composition of the town council. This rule of clans rather than public service bureaucrats who owe no allegiance to any one, of course made for nepotism and its related corruption, which plague until today the Arab local governments in the entire Middle Eastern space, including Israel, and has certainly also infected Erdogan's rule. The Ottomans also imported in the 1870s Circassian Muslim refugees who ran away from the Russian expansion into the Caucasus, and posted them in the garrison strongholds on the Golan and in Transjordan, where to this day they constitute a loyal and peaceful minority both in Jordan and in Israel. The opening to the West in the major commercial centers of Beirut, Damascus, Aleppo and the like, also allowed the rise of a new Western-educated elite which will pave the way in the long run to the emergence of Arab intellectuals. The influx of a trickle of Jews to Palestine from Europe, will shape, in parallel, the new Zionist elite in the land, who would in time lead the Jewish *Yishuv*, old and new, under the Ottomans and then the British Mandate, into the birth of Israel. In Jerusalem for example, the number of Jews doubled from 5,000 to 10,000 during the decades of the 1840s and the 1850s, which will ensure a firm Jewish majority of 100,000 in that key city when Israel was born in 1948 and in which Erdogan has been trying today, a little too late, to reestablish a Turkish foothold.

In 1908 the "Young Turks" Revolution occurred in the leadership of the Ottoman Empire, when under the impact of modernization and Western influence the new military top brass began to think of the state from a specific Turkish modern national perspective, a departure from the previous Islamic universal and Caliphal point of view where Islam was the main focus of identity. That view was based on the Turkish language, history and culture that were specific to the Turkish ethnicity. That thought precipitated the same ideas among the non-Turkish subjects of the Empire, the most prominent of whom were the Arabs, who also rallied around Arab ethnicity (real or imagined) and promoted the Arab tongue, culture and history, all defined within a vast territory, from the Atlantic to the Persian/Arab Gulf. Arab identity and nationalism were to acquire a sharper focus when concretely and bloodily confronted with the parallel rise of Jewish Nationalism –Zionism, which was to grow into the State of Israel in 1948. Paradoxically, the idea of Arab nationalism started burgeoning among the Christian Arabs of the Levant, who imported the idea from their coreligionists in Europe, precisely under the impact of the *Tanzimat* reforms which installed a new spirit of opening, change, modernity and Westernization. The *Tanzimat* had brought up the idea of equality among all subjects of the Empire, and the Christian minority who knew how much was the awakening Arabism connected to Islam, naturally wished to ensure its position in the overwhelmingly Islamic world amidst which they lived. They were the spearhead in the Arab world of the literary Arabic language and they pioneered some of its modern masterpieces, at the same time that they were terrified lest the rebirth of Pan-Islam might revert to the classical discriminating attitudes of that dominant faith against the minorities. While in the Balkans it was the national awakening of the Christians that helped dissolve the Ottoman Empire, in the Arab world it was the Christian minorities who helped boost the emerging parochial Arab nationalism that, by definition, ran counter to the universal Islamic faith which had united all parts of the Empire. Indeed, in medieval times, it had been the convergence of faith and empire which had defined nations, regimes and international relations: Christianity in the Byzantine Empire, Zorostrianism in the Sassanid Empire and then Islam in the Arab Kingdom of the Umayyads, the Muslim state of the Abbasids and also the Caliphates of the Fatimids, the Mamluks, the Ottomans, and even the Moghul Empire of the Indian Sub-continent. Erdogan today, after having extirpated most Christians out of Turkey, has been showing signs or reverting to that pattern of rule in his Muslim state.

Erdogan's rise to prominence unfolded in an ambience of Islamic revivalism around the globe as many Muslims started to believe that Western hegemony in the world was giving way to the mounting influence of Islam. The Rushdie Affair which exploded in Tehran (1989), soon found popular support in the wide-range boycott of the *Satanic Verses* in Islamdom and in the *fatwa* sentencing its author to death and forcing him to hide. To show their loyalty to Islam and their protest against the *démarches* that their host countries took publicly in favor of Rushdie, thousands of European Muslims demonstrated against him and for the *fatwa* in Paris and New York on February 26, 1989, as the Rushdie Affair picked up steam and became a worldwide *cause célèbre*. On the same day, William Nygaard, the publisher of the *Satanic Verses* in Norway, received a death threat, while Iran severed its relations with Denmark for not banning the book. This was a sign that the Muslims wished to impose their terrorizing standards on international diplomacy too, under the threat of cutting off relations with any renegades. Iran's closest ally, Syria, soon joined the ban of the book on February 28, while several American bookstores and the New York Times offices were bombed for supporting Rushdie's novel. The next day, a large demonstration was held in Dhaka, Bangladesh, to protest the book while the US Senate passed Resolution 72, condemning the threats against Rushdie by Islamic countries, organizations, and bodies.

Muslim-populated countries, such as Kenya, Lebanon, Indonesia, Tanzania, and the tiny kingdom of Brunei banned the Satanic Verses, while violence erupted in Islamic Kashmir, where one person was killed and eighty-four injured. Even non-Islamic countries, such as Thailand, who feared the reaction of their Muslim minority, felt obliged to ban the book. In the heart of New York, bustling Fifth Avenue was blocked off due to a bomb threat to a large bookstore that carried the *Satanic Verses*. The amok that signaled the new mood that was imposed on the world following the Iranian Revolution, climaxed on March 16, 1989 when the fifty-seven member Organization of the Islamic Conference (later re-baptized Cooperation), including the most "moderate" and pro-Western among them, convening in Riyyadh, banned the book and lent to Khomeini's *fatwa* a spectacular success that even he never dreamt to gain across the Islamic world. The universal ban across Islamdom proved that the *fatwa* was not only the act of a fanatic regime in Iran, but was shared by the entire Islamic public, and that the arrogant and aggressive mood imposed by Muslim radicals was gaining ground. Even Muslim minorities in the West were further swept into that wave of extremism, as two Muslims were killed in Belgium on March 29 after speaking out against the *fatwa* on television. A measure of the popularity of the Islamic uprising worldwide was revealed in the results of the election in pre-Spring Tunisia in April 1989, where 15 percent of the electorate, some say even up to 30 percent, lent their votes to Muslim parties, though the Ben Ali regime quickly annulled those scores. But in retrospect, that turned out to be the precursor of the Arab Spring, turned Islamic Winter, on Xmas Eve of 2010.[22].

In the battlefield of terrorism in the path of Allah, the world has watched with amazement nineteen adepts of al-Qa'ida committing

---

[22] R. Israeli, from Arab Spring to Islamic Winter, Transaction, NJ, 2013.

three collective acts of *Islamikaze*[23], within one hour of each other, on American soil on 9/11. Al-Qa'ida and Taliban fighters in Afghanistan and Iraq and then ISIS in Iraq and Syria, have defied death in the face of American and international air power, like Hamas and Islamic Jihad operatives in Gaza or the Muslim terrorists of *Lashkar-e-Tayiba* in Kashmir or in India proper, who slay their own compatriots with the same senseless and blind zeal as they attack foreigners. This universalization of Muslim terrorism also carried with it a heightened daring in the operations, yet it was becoming routinely banal in its frequency, diffusion, and beastly cruelty. Not only have the massive attacks of 9/11 left their mark, but the almost daily attacks on Israel and its civilians during the 1990s and 2000s by Hamas, Islamic Jihad, and even PLO-related Palestinian terrorists, and by adepts of al-Qa'ida and ISIS in Europe, have rendered these harrowing acts current and "acceptable", to the point that they became "part of life," as if they were God-ordained and impervious to human prevention. Even though Israel had become accustomed to the horrendous sights of Muslims celebrating over the spilled blood of their victims, it was shocked anew each time ecstatic crowds indulged in jubilation after news broke of "successful" attacks against Jews, Israel, or the United States. After the US retaliated in Afghanistan and Iraq, those worldwide Islamic terrorist attacks were universalized and one could expect new blasts with thousands of victims in Asia, Africa, the Middle East and later in the heart of Europe itself. With no one in sight to rein them in, what followed in those orgies of killing in the cities of the world were of processions of Muslims distributing sweets, dancing in the streets amid cries of "Allahu Akbar!" as if to attribute to Allah their

---

[23] *Islamikaze* is a term coined by this author, combining Islam and Kamikaze, due to the resemblance of the so-called "Muslim Suicide Bombers" to those self-sacrificing Japanese pilots in the Pacific War against the American warships. See R. Israeli, Islamikaze: Manifestation of Islamic Martyrology, Frank Cass, London, 2003.

great feats of murder against their sworn enemies, and then went again into the repetitive ritual of burning the flags of their enemies or trampling them under their feet. Since the demonstrators were not usually participants in the real terrorist events themselves, where the perpetrators had perished as *shahids*, they reenacted the horror symbolically to share it with the public, praising Allah for His intercession on their behalf. Outsiders paid little attention to the makeshift stages and structures erected at the terminal of those processions. Often, the actual target of the operation, for example, an Israeli bus loaded with civilian passengers or a restaurant where entire families sat to enjoy their lunch, was meticulously reconstructed in paper, cardboard, and cloth, collated and painted so as to imitate the original, and then set ablaze, to the sadistic delight of the watching crowd. All the while, any perpetrators of the original act, if any had survived it, or more likely their successors, who wished to cultivate the heritage of the deceased *Islamikaze*, ran around the stage in frenzy, shouting blood-chilling war-cries, repeatedly invoking the power of Allah, smashing the burned "carcass" of the bus or the restaurant, and stabbing with their bayonets the remnants of their slain "victims", whom they or their fellow *Islamikaze* had maimed or murdered. Muslim crowds worldwide, including in Turkey, could not remain indifferent to that universal Islamic frenzy, which was constantly fed by Imams in mosques, whose rural audiences were otherwise ignorant of world events.

How persistent were these trends in the vast Islamic world? We have observed that when part-time processes of liberalization are adopted, like in Algeria, Jordan, Egypt, and lately Libya and Tunisia, and especially when liberties are accompanied by a sustained campaign of incitement and indoctrination, like in rural Turkey during the years which preceded the rise of the Islamic Party; namely when people are given the opportunity to express themselves freely, it is almost invariably political Islam that gains votes, and since this is popular vote, it cannot be said to represent radicals, exactly as it cannot be claimed that the more than 60 percent of Palestinians who voted for Hamas in 2006, or the 70 percent who voted for Islamic parties in 2012 in post Mubarak Egypt, were all Muslim radicals. If, as some claim, there is a certain percentage of Muslims who are "radical," "fundamentalist," or simply "Islamists," while the majority are the good brand of "moderate" Muslims, which politicians like Bush and Blair have simply (and wrongly) called "peace-loving," then how are we to take those vast crowds, which seem to represent the local majorities, in every place where Muslims burst out in violence—be it in Cairo, Gaza, Quetta, Tehran, or Kabul—as during the Rushdie Affair in 1989, the Twin Tower event in 2001, or the Cartoon Affair in 2006? What happened to those supposedly peace-loving majorities who are not represented by the violent crowds? And when Western-educated Muslim columnists wrote in the mainstream journals of the Muslim world, including in "moderate" and "pro-Western" countries, such as Egypt, Saudi Arabia, Turkey or Jordan, anti-Western broadsides or expressed blazingly genocidal wishes against Jews and Israel, and expressions of joy after 9/11, or every time a bus or a restaurant blew up in the West or in Israel causing dozens of victims, are those necessarily representatives of radical Islam? Or so-called Islamists?[24]. Those referred to as Islamists regard themselves simply as Muslims, who are perhaps more zealous than others and wish to fulfill Muslim ideals. All religious Muslims venerate the great masters of radical Islam, such as Hassan al-Banna, Sayyid Qutb, Abu 'ala' Mawdudi, and Yusuf Qaradawi, even if they do not fit into the category of "radicals." Such were the simple Believers of rural Turkey that the Islamic Party of Erbakan and Erdogan had worked surreptitiously to win over during the long years of patient and persistent *da'wa* that ultimately brought them to power.

---

[24] See R. Israeli, *Islamikaze: Manifestations of Islamic Martyrology*, Frank Cass, London, 2003, chapter 1, pp. 11–32.

Matters get further complicated in Western minds by the paranoia and conspiracy theories that are widespread in the Muslim world[25], whether Muslims are modern and Western-educated, or traditionalist and obscurantist. Those theories, that are rampant even among Muslims living in the West, insist that world leaders who support Israel are Jewish (like presidents Reagan and Bush); that the United Nations, of all places, is the mastermind of the Jews, who utilize it as a tool for their world dominion; and that the major violent acts that shook the world in the past, like the world wars, the world revolutions, and 9/11, are all the fruit of Jewish imagination and execution. Their minds are so permeated with these nonsensical theories that they become impervious to logical, rational debate that is open to argument, discussion, and persuasion. Therefore, the difficulty of dealing with Muslim minds consists not only of removing the mountains of pure delusion that choke their free thinking, but also of persuading them that the very attempt to counter-argue those futilities is not necessarily part of the world conspiracy that is being woven against them. It is possible to explain their imaginary concept of the world by their need to project on their enemies the analytical shortcomings that bewitch them, but it is impossible to move them out of the illusory scenarios that they have constructed and then cling to with a tenacity that defies and contradicts Western standards of logic and conduct. Recep Erdogan has proven in his inexplicable outburst of delusionary fury, that he excels his country's Muslims in this domain. The result is that even when Muslims initiate and launch an act of violence, they accuse the West or Israel, or both, of it and dub it, or what led to it, as an act of aggression leaving them as the eternal victims deserving of indemnities and of a chance at retaliation against the enemies-that-be.

---

[25] See e.g. R. Israeli, *Paranoia, Inferiority Complex and Fanaticism: Muslim Attitudes to Jews*, Strategic Books, TX, 2018.

Symptomatic to all these eruptions of violence—whether provoked by the West, like the Cartoon Affair, or by Muslims themselves against the West, like 9/11, or by Muslims against Muslims, like the ongoing carnage between Shi'ites and Sunnites in Iraq—is that they are all imputed by Muslims to the Jews in general, to Israel and *Mossad* in particular, or to Western "subversion" of Islam. As 9/11 was widely attributed by the Muslim world to Jews,[26] the cartoon controversy that began in Denmark was ascribed by the spiritual leader of Iran, and others following his example, to Israel and the Jews, "the only ones to benefit from the rift between Islam and Europe."[27] However, blaming the Jews for 9/11 did not stop Muslims from simultaneously praising bin Laden for the attack. Furious Iraqi Shi'ites, who demonstrated against the wanton destruction of their holy site in Samara by their fellow Sunni countrymen, were persuaded in their depositions to the world media that it must have been the Jews or the Americans who wished to cause civil war between the two factions of Islam in Iraq.[28] What was particularly tragic for future generations of the Muslim society was that they too were coached from their childhood to disown any responsibility for their actions, since others can always be blamed: the West, imperialism, Jews, Israel, Christians, Zionists, anybody and everybody, just not Muslims. The rationale is clear: Islam is a religion of peace, harmony, and love (never mind the Muslim infighting around the globe and its self-inflicted fatalities), and any wrongdoing must be attributed to those most likely to benefit from it: invariably Jews or their allies in the West, especially the Americans. It is a tragedy because with this state of mind there is no incentive to improve their puerile thinking, for, as any child soon learns, it is much easier to accuse others than to amend oneself. In

---

[26] See R. Israeli, *Islamikaze: Manifestations of Islamic Martyrology*, London, Frank Cass, 2003, especially chapter 8.

[27] In a public speech by Ali Khamenei, February 20, 2006.

[28] CNN World News, February 22, 2006.

that shame-based society, anything is better than admitting a mistake or a misdeed, but if it happened and cannot be denied, then attributing it to others is the only way out. Muslim Turkish leaders, notably Erbakan and Erdogan, as we have explained above and will do more in the coming pages, have become models to their populace in launching some of those delusionary stories about Jewish conspiracies, which often sweep the minds of the ignorant rural population which supports them.

The medieval Jewish chroniclers, Abraham ibn Dawud, and the poet Abraham ibn Ezra, depicted in harrowing detail the events under the authorities of the Almohads in Spain and North Africa, who had forced Jews to either Islamize or to die as martyrs. Those who converted were kept under close supervision lest they reneged and secretly abided by their faith. Their children were taken from them and submitted to Muslim education, an exact antecedent to what was to happen three centuries later by the Spanish Inquisition. Maimonides himself was the most famous victim of that policy, when he fled Ahmohad's conquest of Cordova in 1148, found a temporary shelter in Fez, Morocco, sometimes posing as a Muslim, until he found a permanent refuge in Cairo, under the Fatimid Dynasty, which afforded a more hospitable shelter for Jews of Islam. Jews were always proud of his heritage for they had all heard of his greatness, but never asked why he fled, or had to hide and to run away from one Muslim place to another. Only later did they understand that Moroccan Jews were themselves stateless and in constant search for a permanent turf, which always eluded them, because Christian Europe was worse to them than was Islamdom; therefore they could seek refuge only in other Muslim lands. Maimonides was unique in his learning of Hebrew and Arab culture, and was also a renowned doctor, so he could find a permanent shelter for himself, not as a persecuted Jewish refugee but as a skilled and extremely learned and gifted individual who easily spanned Arab and Jewish cultures, western and Islamic. The great paradox is often cited in that the giant and unique Maimonides, who is often brought up as the paradigmatic example of the product of the Andalusian Golden Age of Islamo-Jewish coexistence and cross-fertilization, had also himself become the archetype of its failure, and the most debunking manifestation of that utopian myth, which has been cultivated by many politically correct politicians and scholars, but, as a whole, as Fernandez- Morero has convincingly demonstrated[29], had no leg to stand on. That Arabs and Muslims needed to cultivate this utopia for their self-image and propaganda needs, one can understand if not accept. But when Jews themselves fall into this trap, it is pitiful and self-defeating, and can only be explained as the paradigmatic expression of *dhimmi* behavior. Maimonides, who knew and understood the situation better than any of his contemporaries, said that "the Ismai'lites (Muslims) have per-secuted us and discriminated against us, and no other nation has humiliated and hated Jews more than them". The hellish and night-marish Jewish existence under the Almohads, which remains incrusted in the memory of Moroccan Jewry, was not amended or made up for thereafter, and no effort was exerted by later dynasties to erase those atrocities completely. Quite the contrary, that dynasty lives among the most glorious in Moroccan history on account of its expansionism and religiosity. Moreover, even under the current Moroccan Alawite Dynasty which is supposed to be benevolent and generous, there were very dark days of massacres and cruelty towards its Jews. Namely, one does not have to take the Almohad period as an extraordinary aberration to an otherwise benevolent rule, but, on the contrary, as a yardstick to what would come after them. For, during all the periods when wars of succession raged in North Africa, it was always the Jews who paid the price, and the brief periods of let-up were the exceptions rather than the rule in the long, sad, dangerous and ultimately destructive existence of

---

[29] Op. cit.

Jews in Islamdom in general and in North Africa in particular.

The scenes of horror and fear which every Jew experienced since his or her childhood in Islamdom, were not temporary and passing episodes, but a permanent feature in his or her psychological and behavioral make-up. For Muslims, Jews were considered inferior ("the descendants of apes and swines") and, therefore, were condemned to eternal misery and subordination. Thus, their very claim to independence and equal status with other nations contradicted the Shari'a, the most perfect of legal systems that originated from divine inspiration. *Prima facie*, this looked and sounded like a classic case of unfairness and oppression, when the strong and dominant Islam demanded and practiced institutionalized discrimination, and the submitted Jews had to live as "tolerated people" at best, and most of the time as much less than that. Until recently, it was Muslim historiography and judicial literature which described dhimmitude as a gift from "Islamic tolerance" to the Jews and others, and expected the *dhimmi*s to count their blessings and be grateful, and could not even imagine that anyone could possibly compete with their generosity towards the tolerated minorities in their midst. And since this was a divinely-inspired condition, one could not expect or aspire to its improvement, far less to its alteration. The Jews kept lamenting their fate, as in the *Fez Chronicle*, but their complaints were turned inwards, for making them public could only attract more reprisals and suffering. Only when Jews of Islam were liberated, first by the colonial powers, and then by creating their own country in Israel and migrating there, was Jewish writing also liberated and the sorry story of dhimmitude was recounted and analyzed in all its complexity and ugliness. But as we have seen, even then, the *dhimmi* mentality kept many Jews indebted to their oppressors long after being liberated.

The Muslims could have changed their minds when they realized that liberated Jews can be successful and even challenge them in open societies; however, they elected to ignore Jewish success and to continue to look down upon them, for otherwise, how could they continue to feel superior to them? Hence the massive return of Muslims to the fundaments of their glorious past, for only there can they revive their pride in their culture and their dominance of the *dhimmis*. The Jews' decision to leave Muslim lands was, thus, a disengagement from a situation they could not bear, but which they could not alter either. They were yearning to live in a new world where they would no longer need to cater to Muslims and act sycophantically to please them in order to ensure their continued existence. But Jews could not imagine that the status of *dhimma* would pursue them to their old-new country. In effect, Muslims in conflict with Israel still consider Jews as rebels who did not accept their due place of submission under Islam, and thus they transformed their anti-Jewish hatred into anti-Zionism and anti-Israelism, which amount to the same. For them, Zionism and Israel mean that the rebellious *dhimmi*s have invaded a Muslim territory in a quest to make it their base to battle Islam. Hence their yearning to return the Jews to the condition of "eternal misery" allocated to them by the eternal and immutable Qur'an, and that proposition is not negotiable. Islam does not recognize Jews as a people, therefore Jews do not deserve a state, and their movement of national liberation – Zionism, is discarded as "racism", Allah knows why. The end result is that the vicious circle of persecuting the Jews as *dhimmi*s, first in the lands of Islam and then as rebels who need to be subjugated anew, has been closed when modern Israel came about. For now, for every attempt to humiliate Jews, the latter can, in turn, cause more pain and more humiliation to whomsoever attempts to harm them. For modern Jews, better to be accused of humiliating others than be the victims of humiliation themselves, though it would have been better if one could avert humiliation to either side.

As Muslims see it, the world is replete with hatred towards them, as evidenced today by the widespread claims of Islamophobia; and plots are constantly woven against them, hence their backwardness.

They are the innocent victims who are never at fault, while all their woes and deficiencies are others' faults. Therefore whenever Muslim honor, or that of their Prophet seems to be hurt, like in the Rushdie affair of 1989, or the cartoon affair of 2006, or the *Charlie Hebdo* event of 2015, their vengeance is called for which justifies killing, rampaging and destroying the perpetrators. Usually, believers of any faith who are firm in their convictions, do not force them on others, nor are afraid to compete in the public square with different faiths. But when reality does not conform to Muslim belief about the predominance of Islam, Muslims resort to violence to redress the situation. In other words, they do not live by the firmness and spiritual strength of their religion, but by watching what the others say about it to denigrate it, and they burst in violence when anyone wishes to contradict it.

CHAPTER TWO

Turks and Jews in History

In the lifetime of Muhammad, his conflicts with the Jewish tribes of Medina, typically following each of his fateful battles of Islam : Badr, Uhud and the Battle of the Trench, had occasioned a gradual expulsion (ethnic cleansing) of the Jews from the city: first the Banu Qaynuqa', then Banu Nadir; and ultimately the execution (genocide) of Banu Quraiza's adult men, and enslavement of their women and children, including their forced conversion to Islam. Since the Prophet was the most perfect of men in the eyes of Muslims, he could do no wrong and commit no fault, therefore in Islamic tradition it was always the fault of the Jews which caused their expulsion and execution, an approach which was to be adopted by the Nazis who accused the Jews of their holocaust. Indeed, in the wake of the first significant victory of the Prophet against the Meccans in Badr (AD 624), he felt strong enough to move against his enemies in Medina, namely the Jews who had humiliated him both by refusing to join his teaching and by ridiculing him for his misquotations of the Biblical stories that he had heard from Jews and Christians and made his own. Thereupon, he turned against the weakest of the Jewish tribes- Banu Qaynuqa', who were allowed to leave Medina unharmed with some of their possessions, only thanks to the intervention in their favor by Arab tribes who had been allied with them prior to the coming of the Prophet, and headed to Syria. That was a relatively soft forced migration. But the defeat of the Muslim army at Uhud in AD 625, as the Prophet was apparently desperate for some other victory to regain his tarnished reputation, he turned against the Banu Nadir who were one of the smallest and weakest Jewish tribes. They were accused of failing to come to the Prophet's aid, hence causing his defeat, during the battle of Uhud, a claim that would be heard again and again by Muslims throughout the generations, accusing Jews (and others in general) of all their failures, refusing to take responsibility for their own errors and misdeeds. But this time the Jews had at least a plausible excuse: the battle took place on Sabbath and they Jews could not violate their laws.

But the Prophet had no use for excuses, and the emulation of his conduct during the following generations of Muslims, who regarded him as the infallible Messenger of Allah, sanctified not only his own acts but also justified any Believer who acted likewise after him. Since the Prophet was determined to pursue the expulsion of Jews out of Medina, he simply charged Banu Nadir of plotting against his life, and had no need to even prove his accusation since he could do no fault, and he therefore ordered them out, and they acceded to this demand if they were allowed to take their movable property with them, save for their arms. They departed to the Jewish oasis of Khaybar with an impressive caravan of 600 camels, an indication of their wealth, while proudly parading through Medina playing their music pipes, and their women showing their unveiled faces which were famously beautiful, to flaunt their Muslim persecutors. But two years later, all the men of Nadir paid for their pride when they were executed when the Muslims took Khaybar, and their women and children were enslaved, meaning that Muhammad's initial idea was not merely to ethno-cleanse Arabia from them, but to annihilate them and force their families into adopting Islam, contrary to the Qur'anic verse that the Muslims hail repeatedly to the effect that "there is no compulsion in religion". The lands of Banu Nadir were distributed among the *muhajirun* (the emigrants who had accompanied the Prophet in his *hijra* from Mecca in AD 622, and who became favorites in Islamic tradition). Incidentally, the Palestinian participants in their first intifadah in the West Bank and Gaza (1987-1993) distributed a leaflet in the streets which ended with the summons: "*Hanat Khaybar*" !!! (the time for Khaybar has come !!!), which has no other meaning than "the time to eliminate the Jews and enslave their families has come; rise up and annihilate them!". This hateful phrase also demonstrated that contrary to Muslim propaganda that they had nothing against the Jews, only against Zionism, the call for vengeance against today's Israelis as a continuation of the Khaybar event against the Jews of 14 centuries ago, only proved how deeply incrusted in the Muslim mind is the burning need to exterminate Jews as such.

Even after these cruel and inhuman measures against the Jews, a major problem remained for the Prophet, namely the presence of the most important Jewish tribe in Medina, who challenged his rule : the Banu Qurayza. His decision to eliminate them, part of them with his own hands, simply brought to light his previous genocidal intentions against the Jews. In self-justification, Muslim tradition claims that the last Jewish tribe had made a contract with the Prophet to contribute work tools to the Prophet's army for the defense of Medina during the Battle of the Trench (627), but when the Meccans laid siege to it, it remained neutral in its forts which made their "loyalty" to him questionable, since they "sinned in their hearts". So, when the siege was lifted, Muhammad turned against Banu Qurayza, and following a long siege against them, and after appointing another Muslim to "adjudicate " between the rivals so as to appear "objective" and "just", the "mediator" condemned all the Jewish men to death and their unfortunate women and children to slavery, which Muhammad himself sanctioned as "an act of Allah". The 600-900 men of Qurayza were beheaded in the central place of Medina and their bodies thrown into trenches, except for 2-3 of them who chose to convert to Islam. The infallible Prophet needed no pretexts and no justifications since his deed were Allah-inspired and sanctioned. Muhammad and his followers went even further. He never forgot or forgave the fact that many of the expelled members of Nadir had settled and prospered in Khaybar. A Jewish delegation went unarmed to him for negotiations to prevent future clashes, but it was murdered by Muslims. In 628, the Muslims advanced compellingly against Khaybar, forcing its Jews to surrender and to commit half of their farming revenue to the Muslim treasury, in return for keeping their lands and houses, in effect becoming the serfs of the Muslim state and the prototype of the future *dhimmi*s under Islamic rule. An important clause allowed the submitted Jews to remain in place only as long as the Muslim state agreed; and they were kept in place temporarily only due to their farming skills which were crucial and irreplaceable in Arabia. However, later Arab expansion brought in many skilled farmers as prisoners of wars, making the Jews disposable. The Jews of Kahybar then spread all around, many of them settling in Palestine. In effect, Caliph 'Umar (634-644) later ejected all Jews from the entire Hijaz, and this settlement with Khaybar was also applied to other Jewish oases in Arabia, but did not include the tribe of Nadir which was killed or exiled for the second time, and became the model for treating Jews and Christians as the Muslim state expanded after the death of the Prophet in 632. Then, Islam picked up those horrible precedents as law and to this very day, Jews are prohibited from living in Saudi Arabia, though the other countries on the periphery of the Peninsula have had some Jewish populations, either permanent (like in Aden, Yemen and Bahrain) or transitory (as in the Arab Gulf Emirates).[30]

The death of the Prophet, which some of the Muslim sources attributed to poisoning by Jews (like Yasser Arafat's death in Paris

---

[30] Norman Stillman, *The Jews of Arab Lands*, The Jewish Publication Society of America, 1979, pp. 3-21. See also Michael Lecker, *Muhammad and the Jews* (Hebrew), Jerusalem, 2012.

in 2004), did not alleviate the plight of Jews under Islam, which was from the start modeled after the Prophet's and 'Umar's mistreatment of the Jews of Arabia and especially in Khaybar. Those precedents, which made Jewish living under Islam virtually untenable, were summarized in the 'Umar regulations which put into practice the Prophet's judgments as incorporated in the Qur'an, regarding the treatment of Jews (and Christians) as *dhimmis*, i.e. "protected people" or Scriptuaries. Those prescriptions, though assuring theoretically protection by the Islamic state in return for their payment of the humiliating *jizyah* poll-tax "out of hand", as mandated in the Holy Book, have imposed over the years an almost continuous stream of either forced conversions or expulsions, or campaigns of physical annihilation, in what would be termed today genocidal or religio-ethnic cleansing.

During the formative period of the Ottoman Empire, Jews became gradually part of the wide array of minorities that became included within the realm. Therefore, the settlement of Jews in Palestine under the Ottomans (what is known in Jewish history as the Old *Yishuv*) can be seen as the precursor to the rise of the Zionist settlement in the land since the 19th Century, and then the modern Jewish-Zionist state after W W II. The first Jewish synagogue linked to Ottoman rule was *Etz ha-Hayyim* (Hebrew for Tree of Life) was founded in Bursa which passed to Ottoman authority in 1324 and was the Empire's Capital in the years 1335-63. The synagogue is still in use, although the modern Jewish population of Bursa has shrunk to a tiny vestige of the old Jewish presence in Anatolia. During the early Ottoman period the Jews, together with most other communities of the empire, enjoyed a certain level of prosperity, and compared with other Ottoman subjects, they played an important role in commerce as well as in diplomacy and other high offices. In the 16th century especially, the Jews rose to prominence under the *millet* system, and to the apogee of Jewish influence which was crowned by the appointment of Joseph Nasi (literally

President Joseph in Hebrew- 1524-79) to the high position of San-jak-bey (literally Province Governor), a rank usually reserved to the Muslim high officials of the Empire, of the island of Naxos. That promising era was marred in the 17th Century by the upheaval that was caused when Sabbatai Zevi (1626-76) proclaimed to be the expected Jewish Messiah. He was eventually caught by the Ottoman authorities, and when given the choice between death and conversion (another proof of Islamic tolerance), he opted for the latter. His remaining disciples converted to Islam too. Their descendants are today known as *Donmeh* (the Returning people)[31]. After Sultan Mehmet II's Conquest of Constantinople (1453) he found the city in a state of disarray and in order to revivify it, he ordered that Muslims, Christians and Jews from all over his empire be resettled in the new capital. Within months most of the Empire's Romaniote Jews, from the Balkans and Anatolia, were concentrated in Constantinople, where they made up 10% of the city's population, a move that was sometimes taken by Jews as another forced resettlement in their long history of wandering.

Thirty Jewish communities had existed in Ottoman Palestine, such as Haifa, Nablus, Hebron, Ramleh, Gaza, Jerusalem, and Safed, the latter in the 15th Century becoming a spiritual centre for the Jews where the sacred *Sulchan Aruch* ("set table", the corpus of Jewish practical tenets that was compiled there by Rabbi Joseph Caro), as well as many Kabbalistic texts compiled by other rabbis. At that time, a number of Jewish subjects or citizens of the Islamic Empire achieved high rank in power, great financial influence, and significant and recognized intellectual attainment; (and the same could be said of the Christian minorities). But there were also persecutions, arbitrary confiscations, attempted forced conversions, or pogroms as part of the landscape. For the status of Jewry in the

---

[31] Incidentally, the Muslims of China are also called "Hui", also meaning "returning", but not necessarily pointing to the same source of the name.

Ottoman Empire often hinged on the whims of the Sultan. So, for example, while Murad III (1546 –1595) ordered that the attitude of all non-Muslims should be one of "humility and abjection" and they should not "live near mosques or tall buildings", (and other limitations known in other lands of Islam)[32], or own slaves, other Ottomans in other times or places were more receptive, respectful and tolerant towards the minorities. Under the *millet* system, the non-Muslims were organized as autonomous communities on the basis of religion, alongside the other *millet*s (viz. Orthodox *millet*, Armenian *millet*, etc.). In the framework of the *millet* they had a considerable amount of administrative autonomy and were repre-sented by the *Hakham Bashi*, the Chief Rabbi. There were no restrictions in the professions Jews could practice, analogous to those common in Western Christian countries, but there were some restrictions in the areas where Jews could live or work, as there were similar limitations on Ottoman subjects of other religions. Like all non-Muslims, Jews had to pay the *harac* ("head tax", the equivalent of *jizyah* [*Cizye* in Turkish] in other Islamic lands) and faced other restrictions in clothing, horse riding, army service etc., although they could occasionally be waived or circumvented. Jews who reached high positions in the early Ottoman court and administra-tion included Mehmet II's (1451-1481) minister of Finance (*Deft-erdar*) Hekim Yakup Pasa, and his Portuguese physician, Moses Hamon; also Murad II's (1448-1451) physician Ishak Pasha; and Abraham de Castro, the master of the mint and tax farmer under Suleyman the Magnificent (1520-66). De Castro was a Jewish refu-gee from Portugal who was credited with having warned the Sultan when one of his subordinates planned a rebellion against him.[33]

In one of the most catastrophic events in Jewish history prior to

---

[32] See R. Israeli, *Paranoia, Inferiority Complex and Fanatical Religion*, Strategic Books, Tx, 2018.

[33] Simon Sebag-Montefiore, *Jerusalem, the Biography*, WEidenfeld and Nicolson, London, 2011, p. 351

the *Sho'a*, when the royal couple of Spain, Ferdinand and Isabella, decided to force the Jews of Spain to convert to Catholicism and to expel the rest, about two hundred thousand of them sought asylum in other countries, one of them being the Ottoman Empire under Suleyman. That illustrious ruler needed them both to boost his economy and to castigate Christendom for having denied the Jews their heritage. By contrast, Suleyman's generous move had caused the center of gravity of the dispersed Jews to move eastwards and to bring about significant Jewish populations into Istanbul, the Balkans and Ottoman Palestine. It is said that in 1553 the Sultan's Jewish doctor introduced him to Joseph Nasi who fled conversion in Spain by immigrating to Istanbul, where he won the Emperor's trust and became the confidential agent of his son and heir, so much so that he was known to the Europeans as the Great Jew. He also ran a very successful international business and was appointed by the Court as its envoy to special diplomatic missions in the West. Since he was a precursor of Zionism, believing in the eventual return of the Jews to their land, he also won an appointment as the local Lord of Tiberias where he settled Italian Jews, rebuilt the town and fostered its silk industry. Thus, though the powerful Sultan promoted the superiority of Islam, Joseph managed to patronize Jewish scholars in the land.

Under Selim II, Jerusalem's fame as a resettled Jewish place attracted caravans of Jews from Egypt to the annual Jewish festivals, and Jewish scholarship was enhanced by the four *Sephardic* synagogues built there, though there was also a thin trickle of Jews from Eastern Europe (*Ahkenazis*) who flowed continuously there. The great mysticist, Isaac Lurie, who was born in Jerusalem engaged in *Kabbalah* in the mystic ambience of Safed. But the Ottoman Governor of Jerusalem closed down the popular Ramban Synagogue at the demand of the Muslim *ulama'* who resented its popularity, and those sumptuous precincts were converted to a warehouse. But when in 1648 Sabbatai Zvi, the mystic from Smyrna, proclaimed himself the Jewish messiah and a forthcoming Judgment Day in 1666, he was expelled from his city, first to Cairo and then to Jerusalem, performing everywhere outlandish acts of piety and prayer. He could have been declared as a miserable unbalanced maniac if not for the messianic ambience around which made many Jews receptive of his strange manners and conduct had assembled. But Jewish rabbis put him under a ban in Jerusalem, forcing him to move to Gaza and then to Aleppo. But when Sabbatai's ambition to replace the Sultan became apparent, he was arrested and forced to convert to Islam or renege his Judaism. He took the fist option.

A new era dawned on Ottoman Jewry, right before and more so after the expulsion of Jews from Spain and Portugal (1492), when the number of native Ottoman Jews was soon bolstered by small groups of Jews who immigrated to the Empire between 1421–1453. Among these new *Ashkenazi* immigrants was Rabbi Yitzhak Sarfati (Sarfati, meaning "French" in Hebrew), a German-born Jew whose family had previously lived in France, and who became the Chief Rabbi of Edirne in Anatolia, and wrote a letter inviting European Jewry to settle in the Ottoman Empire, in which he stated that the living for the Jews of the Empire was superior to living in Christendom. It is said that Sultan Bayezid II (1447-1512) dispatched his personal emissary to save the Sephardic Jews of Spain from the Spanish Inquisition and expulsion in 1492, and granted them permission to settle in the Ottoman Empire, and many of them moved to the European cities in the Empire: Istanbul, Sarajevo, Salonica (later Thessaloniki) and Adrianople, but also within the Ottoman heartland like Bursa, Izmir, Jerusalem, Safed, Damascus and Egypt. The Jewish population of Jerusalem increased from 70 families in 1488 to 1,500 at the beginning of the 16th century. That of Safed increased from 300 to 2,000 families and almost surpassed Jerusalem in importance. Damascus had a *Sephardic* congregation, while Istanbul had a Jewish community of 30,000 individuals with 44 synagogues; and Egypt, especially Cairo, received a large number of the exiles, who soon out-numbered the pre-existing community. Gradually, the chief center of the Sephardic Jews became Salonica, where the new-comers soon outnumbered the pre-existing Jewish community. All in all, Jewish existence within the Ottoman Empire even prior to the rise of modern Zionism seemed to provide a consistent and continuous demographic pool, both in the Holy Land and the surrounding environment, which not only demonstrated the permanent Jewish presence in the land, but also served as the base for the added accretion of Jewish immigration into the land from the 19th century on. One of the reasons cited for the encouragement of Jews to settle throughout the Empire was that they satisfied various needs in the Ottoman Empire. For the Muslim Turks were still largely uninterested in those times in business enterprises, and accordingly left commercial occupations to members of minority religions. But since they also distrusted their Christian subjects in the Balkans, whose countries had only recently been conquered by the Ottomans, it was natural to prefer Jewish subjects to whom this consideration did not apply, at least until Istanbul adopted the *devshirme* system, under which they "levied" young Christian boys from their families, raised them as Muslims back in the Capital, and then incorporated them into the Janissary corps, when their loyalty to both the Sultan and the predominant Islamic faith were assured. When they returned to their native lands as devout Muslims, they served the Empire as Ottoman officials and their privileges were accorded to their families. So, the Slavic inhabitants of Bosnia, for example, who used to be either Serbs or Croats, once converted under the *devshirme*, became Bosnian Muslims with their unwavering allegiance to the Ottoman Sultan. Although the Ottomans have been gradually ousted from the Balkans since the 19th Century, their Muslim vestiges have survived to this day, occasioning such independent Muslim entities as Bosnia and Kosovo, and large, and growing, Muslim minorities in the Sanjak (southern Serbia), Macedonia and Montenegro. The Bosnia War (1992-5) where Muslim Jihadi volunteers from the outside, mainly Iran and other Middle Eastern countries played a part, has remained an open sore as a result, followed by the Kosovo War (1998-9) which gave rise to yet another Islamic independent entity.

On the life of the Jews in Ottoman Palestine of the 17th Century, directly, and on the exclusivity to Muslims of its holy shrines, especially in Jerusalem, thus denying any others' attachment to those sites, especially to Jews, we possess several rare documentaries, among others, which reveal several intriguing features. Those sources may be cited today to counter the litany of Turkish (and other Muslims') claims geared to disinherit Jews and Israel from their historical, religious and cultural links to the land.

a. *Excerpts from the travelog by Evliya Tshelebi* of the years 1648-50[34], which depict the Islamic shrines of Palestine (Kana'an or the Vilayet of Tabaristan/Tiberias in his parlance) as well as the Jewish communities of Safed and Jerusalem. Being a pious Muslim, he naturally emphasized the Muslim holy places and his own worship there. There is mention of *Yahuda* (Judah) and all of Ya'qub's (Jacob) sons as Prophets, and he cites the region as being "the Country of the Children of Israel". Safed was founded for the Children of Israel by Shem, Noah's son, and was the place whence the Children of Israel had originated. They had their Temple there, which is like the Ka'ba to them, and their numbers amount to 80,000. According to their "vain belief", any Jew is considered a black Jew unless he visits Safed at least once in his lifetime. The Jews were more numerous than the Muslims. The capitation tax (*Jizyah*) from all the seven Jewish quarters was "paid in the amount of nine thousand". In the past, 70,000 Jews

---

[34] Evliya Tshelebi, *Travels in Palestine (1648-50)*, Translated from Turkish by St H. Stephan, Arield Publishing House, Jrerusalem, 1980

had lived there, but now they have all moved out to Thessaloniki. In the past, Safed was known for its 3,000 felt factories, of which only 40 survived.

The description of al-Aqsa[35], contrary to Islamic historiography which attributes its construction to the Umayyad King Abdulmalek, or to Islamic legends about its descent to its emplacement straight from Heaven, the story was told of a plague which had broken out among the Children of Israel under King David, which passed after he prayed, and he thereafter built al- Aqsa Mosque. But before its completion, he died and it was left to King Solomon to complete it. The latter was leaning on his royal staff when ordered to return his soul to the Lord. Thereafter, during the time of Asif Berakhya- a wise man of Solomon, his vizier and keeper of the Privy Seal, who used to dismiss all the spirits and imprison them near Damascus Gate, the divine order came down which declared al-Aqsa as a first *Qiblah*(direction of prayer). Only after the Prophet's migration to Medina (AD 622) was he ordered to shift the *Qiblah* towards Mecca. In short, the al-Aqsa not only replaced the Jewish Temple in a consecutive historical development in this tale, but it supplanted it from its inception, since it had been built by David and Solomon who were assuredly Muslim Prophets. That was the version of history acceptable to Muslims worldwide and no place was left to the historical attachment of Jews to the place, the myth of "Muslim tolerance," and the recognized continued settlement of Jews in the land notwithstanding.

With reference to the Dome of the Rock, this report hails Abdul Malik for having begun to build it and Ottoman Sultan Suleyman for having spruced and upgraded it as a result of a dream he had where the Prophet appeared to him and urged

---

[35] Ibid. pp. 69ff

him to do so and especially to reinforce the Citadel in its proximity so that the Unbelivers who would try to conquer it in the future be thwarted. To further confirm its Muslim function, the author describes every architechtural detail of the structure and its ornaments and stresses that it used the be the *Qiblah* for Adam himself, and that contrary to the accepted belief that the Prophet had simply come from Mecca to Jerusalem on the back of al-Buraq, [in what is known as the *Isra'*], he arrived there only after all his multiple souls had preceded him in order to welcome him there, and then he saw the Holy Rock suspended in Heaven by the edict of Allah, meriting the description as the "Hanging Stone", ending up as one of two stones that had descended from Heaven, the other being the Black Rock in Mecca. This, and further detailed descriptions of the sites and of the Rock make them an equal of Mecca and immunize them, as it were, from any claim by non-Muslims.

b. In a booklet published by the Hebrew University in Jerusalem in 1970[36] it is suggested that the importance of Jerusalem was not recognized by the Central Ottoman government in Istanbul until the middle of the 19th Century, because in the previous centuries the region was of little import due to its scanty resources and population and its small contribution in terms of income and military potential to the Empire. Its primary importance was in terms of its holy places: the Christian places due to their relevance to the Ottomans' relations with the Western powers, and the Muslim holy places, especially those in Jerusalem, Hebron and Nabi Musa because they attracted Muslim pilgrims on their way to and from Mecca and Medina. But after the 17th Century, the growing military pressure of

---

[36] Moshe Maoz (ed),*Palestine Duringthe Ottoman Period:Documents from Archives and Collections in Israel,* The Institute of Asian and African Studies, Hebrew University, Jerusalem, 1970.

the European powers, especially Russia, intensified by internal decline, the corruption of local governors, the neglect of public works, and the Bedouins breaking into the cultivated areas, turned large areas into a backwater wilderness. Trade and security were severely damaged, the population was oppressed and impoverished and the suffering of Jews and Christians increased. The devolution of power caused local chieftains to seize the actual rule in vast swathes of the country. Only Jerusalem was exempted from this chaotic situation because Ottoman rule was directly imposed there by the Ottoman Governor who was directly subordinated to the Wali of Damascus. For a decade, Ottoman rule ceased totally with the takeover of the land by Muhammad Ali, when it was opened to development and to granting rights to the Christians and to European powers. But divisions between various groups of the half million strong population, which pitted Sunnites against Druze and both against Christians and Jews, hardly contributed to the stabilization and welfare of the country.

Following the reconquest of Palestine by the Ottomans, and the immigration of Jewish exiles from Spain, the Jewish community had recovered after the years of depression under the preceding Mamluks. Leading the resurgence were the Jews of Safed and Tiberias who had enjoyed prosperity and security in the 16th Century and became centers of Jewish learning. But since the end of the 16th Century, those Jewish communities started to decline as a result of the deterioration of Ottoman rule and the general disintegration of both security and economic condition of the land. This saw the center of Jewish activity moving to Jerusalem, where the majority *Sephardic* population was growing together with its spiritual creativity in spite of the sinking economic and security situation. Jewish communities also existed then in Hebron, Gaza, Nablus and several settlements in the Galilee. In Jerusalem the Jewish population doubled in 20 years and numbered in 1850 around half the total population. Zionist immigration since the 1880s increased the Jewish population and established Jewish agricultural settlements, together with Jewish urban centers in Jaffa and Haifa.

c. These rapid changes included the beginnings of the Zionist estalishment in Palestine which proceded under the open eyes of the Ottomans in their waning years in the entire country, especially in the Jordan Valley, indicating the far reaching designs of the Zionists, despite the official opposition of the Porte to the establishment of a Jewish home in the land[37]

d. Summaries and photographs from the end of the Ottoman rule in Palestine depicting the Zionist enterprise in all Palestine, urban and rural, provide documentary proof of the extent of Jewish settlement throughout the land, which in fact served as the solid base and point of departure of the future state of Israel. Today's reelings by Ankara against the Jewish state can be rightly countered by the openness (or helplessness?) of the Ottoman authorities to facilitate (or obstruct?) the rebirth of the modern Jewish nation.[38]

Jews in Turkey in the eighteenth and nineteenth centuries are principally a chronicle of decline in influence and power, for they lost their influential positions in trade, mainly due to the Greeks, who were able to capitalize on their religio-cultural ties with the West and their trading brethren across Europe. However, the rise of

---

[37] Y. Ben-Arieh, *The Changing Landscape of the Central Jordan Valley*, Scripta Hierosolymitana, Jerusalem, 1968.

[38] Y. Rafaelovich, *The Land of Israel and its Moshavot* (Hebrew and German), Ariel Press, Jerusalem,1979, a Reproduction of the First Albumof the settlement in the Land of Israel, dated 1899.

Daniel de Fonseca, who was the chief court physician and played a certain political role, must be noted as a prominent exception. He was mentioned by Voltaire, who spoke of him as an acquaintance whom he esteemed highly. Ottoman Jews, just like European Jewry then and American Jewry today, held a variety of views on the desirable role of Jews in the Ottoman Empire, from loyal Ottomanism to Zionism. Emanuel Karasu of Salonica, for example, was a founding member of the Young Turks, and believed that the Jews of the Empire should be Turks first, and Jews second. Concurrently with the rising dissent among the various Jewish communities in the Empire, there is no doubt that their general condition worsened since the 19th Century, as it did throughout the entire Islamic world. Some scholars attribute that change to the rise of Arab nationalism in the 19th century, when the Ottoman-Islamic focus of identity began to dissipate and the Arab-ethnic alternative started to emerge under the impact of European nationalism. Christian Arab nationalists, who injected European anti-Semitism into the Arab awakening, also caused the rise of anti-Jewish sentiments when it became apparent that Jewish nationalism was also a competing actor in the Middle Eastern scene. However, another newer well-documented view suggests that the hatred of Jews in and by the Islamic world had accompanied the existence of Jews within Islamdom since the times of the Prophet and for the following millennium and a half [39].

At any rate, a succession of major pogroms against the Jews was noted in the Muslim countries of the Middle East under the vanishing Ottoman Empire, which greatly, though unwittingly and ironically, contributed to the growth of the Zionist sentiment. For,

---

[39] See, e.g A. Bostom, *The Legacy of Islamic anti-Semitism*; R. Israeli, *Paranoia, Inferiority Complex and Fanaticism: Muslim Attitudes Towards Jews*; P. Fenton and David Littman, *Exile in the Maghreb*; Dario Fernandez, *The Myth of the Andalusian Paradise*; and Robert Spencer (ed), *The Myth of Islamic Tolerance : How Islamic Law Treats non-Muslims*, Prometheus, NY, 2005

exactly as the Arabs started awakening when the yoke of Ottoman rule was seen and felt as easing, so the Jews who had felt oppressed under their *dhimmi* status throughout Islamdom, began to see the promise of Zionism, which meant Jewish independence, as the light at the end of the tunnel. The onslaught on the Jews, which was every bit as severe as that incurred by the Jews of the Baltics and Eastern Europe, was less publicized due to the communications restrictions in the Islamic world, but no less worrisome and no less auguring the new era of Jews shaking off finally the yoke of two millennia of subjugation, persecution, expulsion, oppression and slaughters, to emerge as an independent nation on its ancient land, as the only way to escape being the Jew among the world nations. In fact, there was a massacre of Jews in Baghdad in 1828, in Barfurush (Iran) in 1867, a blood libel in Damascus (1840), followed by more blood libels in the Egyptian Delta[40]. Even in 1865, when the equality of all subjects of the Ottoman Empire was proclaimed, a high-ranking official observed that whereas in former times, in the Ottoman State, the communities were ranked, with the Muslims first, then the Greeks, then the Armenians, then the Jews, now all of them were put on the same level though some Greeks objected to this, arguing that they rejected being put together with the Jews, and they would have been more content with the supremacy of Islam, which left the Jews at the bottom of the pile of nationalities. Throughout the 1860s, the Jews of Libya were subjected to punitive taxation, and in 1864, around 500 Jews were massacred in Marrakech and Fez in Morocco. This compares to the infamous pogroms of Kishinev, Bessarabia (today's Moldova) in 1903, where a "mere" 49 Jews were slaughtered, but its reverberations sounded throughout the entire civilized world, occasioning the publication of the poem "The City of Death" by national poet Chaim Nachman Bialik, which became a classic. In 1869, another 18 Jews were killed

---

[40] R. Israeli, *The Blood Libel and its Derivatives*, Transaction, NJ, 2012.

in Tunis, and an Arab mob looted Jewish homes and stores, and burned synagogues, on Jerba Island. In 1875, 20 Jews were killed by a mob in Demnat, Morocco; elsewhere in Morocco, Jews were attacked and killed in the streets in broad daylight. In 1891, the leading Muslims in Jerusalem asked the Ottoman authorities in Constantinople to prohibit the entry of Jews arriving from Russia. In 1897, synagogues were ransacked and Jews were murdered in Tripolitania. In all those places the one symbol of Jewish degradation was the recurrent stone-throwing at Jews by Muslim children, a phenomenon experienced by this author in Morocco in the 1940s, and today in the West Bank and Gaza during the three Palestinian *intifadah*s (1987-93, 2000-3, and 2016 onwards). Since the overwhelming majority of Ottoman Jews lived in the European-provinces of the Empire, these Jewish communities found themselves under Christian rule as the empire lost control over its European provinces in the late nineteenth and early twentieth centuries. The Bosnian Jews for example came under Austro-Hungarian rule after the occupation of the region in 1878, while the independence of Greece, Bulgaria and Serbia further lowered the number of Jews within the borders of the Ottoman Empire. But the plight of the Jews who remained under Islamic majorities in the Middle East and North Africa continued unabated until British and French colonial rule abolished their (and the Christian minorities') *dhimmi* status at the beginning of the 20th Century.

Towards the end of the Ottoman rule, and slightly thereafter, several eyewitness travelers in the land of Palestine came up with various remarks about the condition of the Jewish community there:

a. Sven Hedin, the famous Swedish explorer of Central Asia who visited Palestine in the heat of W W I, which signaled the end of the Ottoman Empire, wrote":

We are walking around [the Old City] streets. It is *Bajram* today, but the city is not adorned for the feast, as the Muhammedans are only a seventh of the inhabitants. They sat now on small stools in front of their stalls, playing cards and tricktrack and smoked *nargileh*. Arabs had come in from the neighbourhood, and Bedouins sailed past in their always airy and beautifully white or brown gowns and fluttering headgear.

[about Rischon le Sion, one of the first Jewish settlements]: Through wise maintenance of the Land [the Jews] hoped to win dwelling places and livelihood for increased [Jewish] immigration. Djemal Pascha [One of the three Triumvirate rulers of the Young Turks] had given the population rights to keep the marshlands, though they dried them up. Their relations to the Turkish Government afford the Jews with a difficulty. One cannot blame the Turks that they do not see how the previously weak and pliable people grow to the same strength and demands as other foreign nations under the Crescent. The Turks are entitled to fear that the Jews, when they feel strong enough, will strive for national and political independence. But the Jews claim that those fears are groundless and absurd. They do not have a desire for the political party wars and the risks that would follow independence. What they desire is the right to freely develop their national peculiarity and their language. The Turks would beyond doubt in many aspects win great advantages from expanding Jewish immigration. Already now the Jews have given birth to several industrial companies, and manufacturing methods, and massively increased the wine and orange production in the land. They have introduced the planting of Eucalyptus trees that have drained the marshes and made the desert bloom. All their enterprises are on a higher level than the local population's . They have increased the tax revenues on the Land. If the Turkish Government would give them the same protection and advantages that other peoples enjoy under the Crescent, they would all become Ottoman subjects, and the knowhow that now must be called in from Europe for industrial and technical projects would be available within the borders of the Land.[41] Such thoughts, if precise, would have certainly enhanced the opinion of the ruling Ottomans on the Jews at a time when they felt betrayed by many of them who spied for the British, and many others were incarcerated or expelled from the land.

b. Another traveler, Erik Stave, recorded his memories from a trip to Palestine, in Spring 1891. He reminisced that:

At Abu Dis, a village to the right of Betania, we received a Bedouin who introduced himself as our escort, bearing an antique shotgun over his shoulder. He was to protect us, who, save our porter, had no kinds of weapons! He was rather a guarantee, that we had bought our freedom from robbery from his Sheikh. The Sheikh of Abu Dis enjoys such a prestige among the Bedouin tribes in the Judean Desert, that one man from his subjects is enough of protection for the travelers. The

---

[41] Sven Hedin *Till Jerusalem* (Swedish), Albert Bonniers Forlag, Stockholm 1917, pp. 258, 205, 486, 491.

Government has thus given him the right and responsibility to escort those who visit this area, without which a traveler will not venture from Jerusalem to Jericho, without falling into hands of robbers, just as the man in the parable of Luke 10.

Since the hostilities against the Jews in Russia and in the Balkans during recent years have taken greater dimensions, many of the persecuted Jews have been forced to immigrate to Palestine, and in unison with the flow of immigration many new organisations, richly supplied by many parties, were established to increase the ability of the Jewish population to sustain itself. Yet the efforts have not shown to be successful. The Jews in all of Palestine are more or less poor. This is because of the Turkish Government's reluctance so far to grant more immigration permits. Another reason for the Turkish Government reluctance to allow the increase of Jewish elements in the land, is the circumstance that the immigrants thus far have chosen European protection, through which they enhance their power and hurt the rule of the Land. Those who immigrated thus far have been obliged to become Turkish subjects. How the Jews make themselves lords over Jerusalem may be worth mentioning. The head of the *Sephardic* community asks for the keys of the city, in order to fulfil the commands of the elders, of not carrying burdens on Shabbat. As the Jews are now only half of the population of Jerusalem, this ceremony presents a happy solution to their dilemma. When the Turkish Governor presents the keys, it gives them the right to consider it theirs, and the right to carry light objects during Sabbath. The passing of the keys ensures a treaty for a period of 15 years, to be renewed, should a new Sultan ascend to the throne. The keys are kept for a few hours, overnight, in the leading Jewish man's possession, and are then returned to the Governor, who at this time is expecting a gift from the Jewish community.[42] This procedure implies, on the one hand, a concession to the Jewish community, but also, on the other hand, the Governor's desire to maintain the peace at the price of this symbolic gesture to over half the population of the city.

Since the Christian minority in the Ottoman Empire was much larger than its Jewish counterpart and at times its rival in seeking the favors of the Porte, Jewish fate under the Turks was often related to that of the Christians. On the one hand, both were *dhimmis* and they theoretically shared the same despised status, but there is no doubt that constituting a much larger proportion of the population in the Empire, and its original native population to boot, the perceived danger they posed to the Ottoman Turkish rulers seemed much more salient, concrete and immediate than any dissidence which might be evinced on the part of the small refugee nation of the Jews. In fact, while Jewish refugees from Spain were welcomed and absorbed throughout the Empire in the 16th Century, it was the Christians of the 20th Century who were relentlessly and cruelly expelled or physically eliminated in the realm: first the Armenian genocide during W W I, and then the expulsion of Greeks after that war under the euphemistic headline of "exchange of population". The Jews who watched those developments were naturally alarmed by what they observed was being done to other *dhimmis* (they were either exterminated or "exchanged") while they had nowhere else to go and were doomed to remain all alone at the mercy of the Muslim rulers. The alarm originated from the fact that not only the Turks, as Muslims, had occupied and destroyed the Christian culture of Byzantine Anatolia, but they made sure that almost all the vestiges of Christianity were eliminated over the years, and they have credited their Sultan Mehmet II, who subju-

---

[42] Erik Stave, *Genom Palestina- Memories from a trip, Spring 1891*, (Swedish)P.A. Norstedt & Soners Forlag, Stockholm,pp.125, 204-5

gated the glorious Christian Capital of Constantinople, as "the Conqueror", for ever glorifying his name. But no other feat of the Muslim conquerors has shaken the Christian world as the re-baptizing of Constantinople as Istanbul, and the greatest structure of Christianity, the immense *Hagia Sophia* Church (the Greek for "Holy Wisdom"), into a mosque. That shock, which modern Turkey had been trying to assuage since the end of the Ottoman Caliphate after World War I, by converting the structure into a museum, has emerged once again since Tayyip Erdogan came to power in 2003, and Muslim pressure has been building up to revert the structure to its Islamic glamour by returning it to Muslim usage as a mosque.

Before that outrageous conversion by force, a practice that has been embraced in the entire Islamic world, where conquered great Christian churches or Jewish synagogues have been converted into mosques, thus demonstrating who was the sovereign in place, the *Hagia Sophia* had been for almost a millennium Christianity's greatest cathedral. Built in AD 537 in the heart of the Christian Empire, in Constantinople, the largest and most glamorous city of the Middle Ages, it had been also a stalwart symbol of Christian strength and defiance to the advancing Islamic troops which gnawed at its periphery until it succumbed in 1453. Finally, when it fell to the Ottomans, the city was ransacked, churches and crosses were desecrated, and icons were defaced. Minarets were added to the majestic structure of the Cathedral in order to convert it irretrievably to the new dominant faith of Islam. In the 2000s, according to the *Hurriyet Daily News*, a parliamentary commission was considering an application of Turkish citizens to reconvert Hagia Sophia into a mosque once again, and reopen it to Muslim worship. Other great historical cathedrals have known the same fate. For example, in the northern city of Trabzon, a 13th Century church, also called *Hagia Sophia*, which had been converted into a mosque, turned into a museum under the secular government of post-Ottoman Turkey, and now the local authorities have decreed that its original frescoes, which had been restored under the civil governments, would again be covered and the structure turned again into a mosque.[43]

Studios Monastery, a 5th Century Christian structure, dedicated to John the Baptist, as well as the other 5th Century *Mor Gabriel* Monastery, are at risk of turning into mosques, although the latter is a functioning institution, with a few dozen monks dedicated to worship and scholarship, but it was sued for pursuing "anti-Turkish" activities, such as occupying lands that belong to Muslim villagers. Expectedly, the Supreme Court in Ankara ruled in favor of the Muslims, saying that the Monastery's possession of those lands for a millennium and a half, is no proof of ownership, and that the structure had been built on the ruins of a mosque, at a time when there was no Islam and no Muhammad, and certainly no mosque, in existence yet. The Orthodox Patriarch, whose dwindling power and authority are much in painful evidence for the vestiges of the Christian minority, is naturally protesting these land grabs, but apparently in vain, as the de-Christianization and Islamization of Turkey continue at full pace, while the Christian West is looking on indifferently and showering favors and benefits on Erdogan, in spite of his annihilationist intolerance. The even smaller and weaker Jewish community in Turkey, which is, on top of all that, suspected of supporting the cause of Israel and Zionism, the *nemesis* of Tayyip Erdogan, cannot naturally find solace in his mistreatment of the Christians. A report by *Reuters* in 2012 reflects on this state of affairs in NATO-affiliate and American-allied Turkey, which could not help but augment the level of anxiety of Christians and Jews:

> Thousands of devout Muslims prayed outside Turkey's historic *Hagia Sophia* Museum on Saturday, May 23, 2012 [in Istanbul] to protest a 1934 law that bars religious

---

[43] Raymond Ibrahim, *PJ Media,* June 18, 2013

services at the former church and mosque. Worshippers shouted:" Break the chains! Let *Hagia Sophia* Mosque open again! Allahu Akbar!", before kneeling in prayer as tourists looked on. Turkey's secular laws prevent Muslims and Christians from formal worship within the 6th Century monument, the world's greatest cathedral for almost a millennium before invading Ottomans converted it into a mosque in the 15th Century[44].

It is evident, that with its active 3,000 mosques, Istanbul is not in want of places to pray, but that the whole of Turkey has been swept by the Islamic zeal that Erdogan and his government have enforced since 2003. The ambience they have created, which glorifies Jihad and Islamic conquests, also produced the massive staged prayers marking the 559th anniversary of the Ottoman Mehmet the Conqueror, who decimated the Byzantine Empire and generated the Islamization of Istanbul and the entire Anatolian heights. His followers who still adore him and are proud of his heritage, believe it is their legitimate right to rededicate *Hagia Sophia* as a mosque. Not only do they not repent or apologize for their outrageous confiscation of that glorious cathedral and conversion into a mosque, but they consider that it is an insult to the 75 million Islamic majority in the land, that Western unjustified pressures are keeping that mosque closed to Muslim worship. This is also an oblique warning to the growing Muslim communities of Europe that, wherever and whenever they achieve local majorities in their diasporas, they will be apt to advance "legitimate" demands of this sort. Erdogan himself expressed this skewed view of history by declaring in May, 2012, on the anniversary of the fall of Constantinople to the Turks, when countless Christians were slaughtered, raped and

---

[44] Ibid.

enslaved that, "that was the true time of enlightenment".[45]

The sweeping victory of Erdogan and his party in the October, 2015 new elections, which were a corrective to the previous election of June 2015 in which he had lost his absolute majority in Parliament, may render things still worse for Christians and Jews in the country, all the more so since Erdogan's acquiring the authoritarian powers of the executive President of his country since 2018, as he has already relaunched his onslaughts and accusations against the state of Israel and his persecutions of the Christians. His paranoia has increased since the 2016 attempted *coup* against his rule, of which he accused the *Fethulleh Gulen* movement and some Christian clerics. For now Erdogan will be able to change the constitution and turn his regime from republican-parliamentary to presidential and Sultanate-like authoritarian rule where he would reign supreme and no constraints would check his power, enabling him to pursue his campaign of Islamization vis-à-vis the Christians, and Turkification vis-à-vis the Kurds and the Jews that won him his latest victory. So, from his new 1,100-room palace in Ankara, from which he can impose awe, he will pursue his terrorism towards indocile media, intimidation of political and ethnic rivals domestically, and a high handed policy towards the Kurds and the Jews which even his international critics in America and Europe would not dare to contradict.

The oppression of minorities and the catering to Muslim radicalism has created some contradictions in Erdogan's policies that he himself has difficulties to handle, as long as he continues to subject his Islamization program to his personal power and make it conditional on his ability to keep it under control. Take al-Qa'ida and ISIS, for example, which have been pursuing their propaganda in Turkey, while often being at odds with the Erdogan administration. The author of this most updated analysis claims that since the out-

---

[45] Ibid.

break of the war with Syria, Erdogan's Turkey became one of the most influential actors, since it was allowed to become a gateway through which tens of thousands of Muslim volunteers worldwide who penetrated into Syria and Iraq to join the Jihad there[46]. Thus, while Turkey assisted the jihadi elements among the rebels in Syria, it was not immune against them. Turkey became a recruitment base of fundamentalism and sectarianism for those who sought to fight in the combat zones of Syria and Iraq against Assad's regime. Yet the more extremist elements within the Salafi-jihadi movement continue to regard Turkey as an "infidel and illegitimate entity". This perspective interpreted Turkey's cooperation with Russia and Iran as an effort to protect the interests of the Assad regime contrary to the image of the great sponsor of radical Islam that Erdogan has been trying to project. The author covers a number of online platforms and jihadist groups identified with al-Qa'ida, the main among which is *İlim ve Cihad* ([religious] Knowledge and Holy War) – a website that promotes the jihad in Syria as part of its global jihad worldview. This site, like others, often expresses its adulation of former and present heads of the organization. Expectedly, Turkish Jihadi propaganda is aimed at Turkish-speaking individuals worldwide and also has an audience in Syria, and certainly in Germany where the Turkish population of several millions predominates among the Muslims immigrants. No wonder then that Turkish fighting groups were identified in Syria, who had been subject to al-Qa'ida propaganda. Indeed, the war in Syria and Turkey's "open-door" policy towards jihadists provided an opportunity for Turkish jihadists who wanted to participate in a violent jihad. However, the cooperation between Turkey, Iran, and Russia in Syria created a situation in which jihadists, while enjoying the protection of Turkey must also face the anger within the global jihad

---

[46] See Ariel Koch, "Al-Qaeda's Propaganda in the Virtual Turkey " in *Turkescope*, Tel Aviv University, October 15, 2018

movement towards rebel organizations in Syria, which are blamed for cooperating with an "atheist", an "Ikhwanji" (a derogatory term referring to a member of the Muslim Brotherhood) and a "Majus" (A derogatory term referring to Iranians as idolaters). These terms have frequently been utilized against Vladimir Putin, Tayyip Erdoğan, and Hassan Rouhani in order to express the hostility of the Salafi-jihadists to the "Russian-Shiite-Turkish axis", which was perceived as part of the Western (and Jewish) plot to save Assad and destroy the Sunni dream of a Sharia-controlled emirate, the like of which ISIS has tried to erect in Syria and Iraq, and the Taliban had previously experienced in Afghanistan.

In view of these developments in the Syrian arena, argues Koch, most of the allegations of cooperation with the Russian-Shiite-Turkish axis are now directed against *Tahrir al-Sham* (the Liberation of Syria) organization, which has inherited the mantle and title of *Jabhat al-Nusra*, the erstwhile branch of al-Qa'ida in Syria in order precisely to shed that identity, while trying to stop the desertion of fighters to other organizations. It also appears that the influence of Turkish jihadists on the Syrian arena is growing; they can help smuggle fighters, money, and weapons into Syria, and they can also help jihadists out of the war zone. In light (or rather obscurity) of the above, it seems logical that global jihadists such as al-Qa'ida are trying to recruit Turkish speakers, as reflected in the increase in the jihadist propaganda in Turkey. This phenomenon can also be seen, among others, in the *İlim ve Cihad* website. If the Salafi-jihadists will manage to establish their power in Syria near the border with Turkey, some day they may turn their wrath against Turkey as well. In addition, al-Qa'ida may exploit the social networks to infiltrate weapons or terrorists into Europe. Regardless, the matter of Turkish fighters and jihadist propaganda in the Turkish language will remain relevant issues in the near future and constitute a thorn in Erdogan's side[47].

---

[47] Ibid

CHAPTER THREE

Civil Governments and the Honeymoon with Israel[48]

When the new Central Asian Republics and Azerbaijan have all established diplomatic relations with Israel upon the disintegration of the Soviet Union which had banned such links before, this had also impacted on the lukewarm attitudes of Turkey with Israel. This was especially noteworthy since, apart from Turkey, Egypt, Jordan, Mauritania and Senegal (and Iran prior to the Khomeini Revolution of 1978), the rest of the fifty-odd countries with large Islamic populations had as yet been reluctant to commit themselves to full diplomatic relations with Israel. For even after the breakthrough of peace with Egypt (1977) and Jordan (1994) only Israeli "interest offices" were permitted to open in North Africa and some countries of the Arab/Persian Gulf. That showed the potential appeal of Israel to those nations, on different levels that will be discussed below. These points of convergence not only attracted to Israel Western and Third World countries in need of aid and development, but also Turkish interest that also meshed well with Ankara's aspiration in the pre-Erdogan era to forge a moderate, secular and developed Central Asia on the model of Turkey itself. However, unlike great powers that may make their assistance to those countries hinge on

---

[48] This chapter is mainly based on this author's "The Turkish-Israeli Odd Couple", in *Orbis*, January, 2001, pp. 165-179.

their own global corporate interests, or use their power to exert political pressure for regime change and civil rights amendments domestically, small Israel cannot impose such conditions, therefore it offers its aid without demanding any collateral price. Consequently, Turkey recognized the value of Israeli cooperation for both its own needs and in shaping the future of Central Asia. It was ironic in this context that the infamously forged anti-Semitic "document" concocted in Czarist Russia at the turn of the 20th century should reemerge again in the following decades, not as a mischievous and vicious tool to libel the Jews and make them an easy prey for attacks and pogroms, but as a benevolent and naïve myth to aggrandize and praise Israel and the Jews beyond measure. Indeed, it is true that though in some circles, especially Islamic and Arab, the *Protocols of the Elders of Zion*[49] are still cited in their old anti-Semitic context, some well-meaning people who never knew anti-Semitism, like the Japanese, the Chinese and other Asians, praise the Jews for their alleged world influence. At any rate, they are viewed in Turkey, Central Asia and many developing countries as the key and conduit for access to the United States of America, naively assuming that the road to Washington leads through Jerusalem.

This belief derives in part from the fact that Israel enjoys a privileged relationship with the US, and in part from the myth of America's "redoubtable" and "omnipotent" Jewish lobby. Occasionally, it still engenders outbursts of anti-Semitic remarks, such as the Malaysian Prime Minister's consistently blaming financier George Soros and Jewish bankers for the collapse of the Asian money markets in the 1990s. To the allegedly magical prowess of Jews in world economics and American domestic politics one may add the perception

---

[49] See R. Israeli, *Absence of Evidence and its Consequences in Travesties of Justice*, Cambridge Scholars, Cambridge, 2018. See also the Charter of the Hamas which contains references to the Protocols. See R Israeli, "The Charter of Allah: The Platform of the Hamas", in Y. Alexander (ed) *The 1988-9 Annual of Terrorism, NIjhoff, Boston, 1990.*

that Jews also control the world media, enabling them to propagate any belief or rumor that suit their interests. And yet, in the assessment of some Turkish and Middle Eastern policy makers, the very belief in Jewish world power also underscores the value of good relations with Israel. Zvi Elpeleg, the former Israeli Ambassador to Ankara has noted that "it is helpful that Turks believe in the *Protocols of the Elders of Zion,* for this leads them to think that Israel has vast powers[50]. Similarly, Ilhan Selcuk,[51] a Turkish intellectual observed that Muslims, Arabs, Greeks, Kurds and Armenians and their respective lobbies in America would all like to see Kemalism vanish, concluding that

> We have nobody but Israel … and the Jewish lobby to depend on for support. Thus, it is in the Turks' national interest to collaborate with Israel, because the latter could relieve their isolation and balance the Greek and Armenian lobbies in American politics.

Of all the complex issues affecting pre-Erdogan Turkey's relations with Israel, which encompassed security and commerce, the concerns about strategy and military and technological collaboration were the most acute for the military top brass which closely monitored their country's foreign policy and internal politics. Not only did the military, as the guardian of Kemalist heritage, initiate the *rapprochement* with previously alienated Israel, but it also forced Erbakan's government to accept that line of thinking and then ousted him as soon as he refused to pursue it further. The Islamic press in Turkey went as far as accusing Israeli Ambassador Elpeleg of acting as "the confidant of the generals who were intent on toppling the [legally elected] Erbakan's government"[52]. It is therefore

---

[50] *Haaretz,* September 30, 1997.

[51] *Cumhuriyet,* November 5, 1994.

[52] *Haaretz,* Sep. 30, 1997.

no wonder that the most striking and rapid advance in the relations between the two countries was in the military-strategic domain. Turkey has in effect purchased advanced Israeli weaponry and electronics, engaged in joint military maneuvers, cooperated in intelligence gathering, allowed the Israeli Air Force training in Turkey's air space and exchanged high level visits with the Israeli Defense forces. These nitiatives had rested on the assumption that Turkey, surrounded by hostile, authoritarian, unpredictable and anti-Western regimes, would be foolish not to cooperate with the only other power in the region that is democratic, stable, strong and pro-Western. Israel, for its part, continued to believe, as it had since the 1950s, that it must forge ties with the strong, stable and pro-Western and non-Arab peripheral states surrounding the Arab world, thereby leap-frogging past the hostile ring of front-line Arab states. Iran and Ethiopia had also played this role for decades, but by the end of the 1970s the Islamic Revolution in the former and the Marxist takeover of the latter had eliminated those two pillars of the long- haul Israeli strategy, leaving Israel to rely on Islamic Turkey alone. After the peace accords between Israel and Egypt in 1979, it became all the more imperative for Israel to counterbalance its most formidable enemies in the north (Iran, Iraq and Syria) with Turkish power. Syria, in particular, had maintained a long-standing territorial dispute with Turkey, and the latter, merely by deploying troops on the Syrian border, could force Syria to split its military power between two fronts, thereby paralyzing any military threat emanating from Damascus against Israel. This indeed helps to explain why Syria had kept quiet on the Golan issue for the preceding three decades, and why Turkey was left free to quash the separatist Kurdish bases within its own borders. Hafez al-Assad (the founder of the present day Assad dynasty) could simply not afford to provoke Turkish ire as long as he was locked in a struggle with Israel over the Golan and Lebanon.

The Turks likewise worried about the Kurds in Iraq whose

demands for autonomy, if realized, could prompt similar agitation among the Kurds inside Turkey. Still another concern was Iran's perceived hostility to the civil government of the time by dint of the latter's anti-Islamic radicalism and competition for influence in the Central Asian Republics which had just thrown off the yoke of the Soviet Union.[53] Add to that the growing fear in Israel and Turkey of Iraqi (under Saddam) and Revolutionary Iran's development of mass destruction and delivery systems, and it is evident that Turkey's and Israel's respective interests converged along many avenues. It was for that reason that the resumption of negotiations in 1999 between Israel and Syria (a close ally of Iran) under American auspices, caused deep concern in Turkey, for if Syria achieved peace with Israel and regained control of the Golan, it would have become much freer to challenge Turkey with Iran's support, a menacing prospect for Ankara. Therefore, although both Israel and Turkey sought to appease international fears by stating that their alliance was not directed against any third party, everyone understood that Iran and Syria may have been its primary target. Incidentally, the combination Iran-Syria has remained a threat to both Turkey and Israel throughout the Syrian Civil War (2011-8) though separately and for different reasons.

As mentioned before, the strategic cooperation between Turkey and Israel was most evident and visible in the close and intimate relations between the two militaries, although in those years another strategic aspect to that collaboration emerged with regard to water supplies. For, on the one hand, Turkey enjoyed a vast surplus of water mainly from the large rivers of the Tigris and Euphrates before they flowed down to Syria and Iraq, and there was talk of Israel importing water tankers by sea from the Anatolian coast before it later embarked on a large scale project of water desalination. If that were to be implemented, Ankara could not only control a huge

---

[53] See Muftuler-Bac, op. cit, pp. 10-11.

leverage on Israel and at the same time exercize pressure on its Arab rivals downstream. Due to the water needs in the area, exactly when due to consecutive years of drought and the rise in population, those needs increased considerably, water had become, like oil, a political weapon in the hands of countries and statesmen. Another arena of cooperation between Turkey and Israel, second only to military collaboration in importance during the peak years of the 1990s, was the purely civilian domain of economic development, investments and trade. The huge volume of Israeli tourism to Turkey (notably to the region of Antalya in southerm Anatolia) has long been acknowldeged, but in areas such as investment, construction, manufacturing, environment, water and land conservation, technical cooperation and joint enterprises, these domains were extensively expanded during the peak period of the 1990s. For example, from a measly $54 million in 1987, trade grew to one billion by the end of that period and was expected to reach the two billion mark by 2001, the largest flow of commerce between any two countries in the Middle East, all thanks to a 1997 free-trade agreement that opened new vistas for business between the two countries.[54]

Put in perspective, one can say that the political *détente* between Turkey and Israel in the 1990s had initially prompted the intensification and diversification of economic activity, but then the process acquired a dynamic of its own. The vast and growing markets of Turkey are a powerful lure to Israeli investors and exporters, and Turkey's relatively low labor costs (at about one third of Israel's at the time) encouraged the flow of Turkish goods as long as the political arena seemed inviting, friendly and beneficial to Israelis. However, due to the limitations of Israel's tiny market, Turkish aggregate trade with Arab countries still surpassed by far the volume of bilat-

---

[54] See Fil Feiler, "Economic Relations Between Turkey and Israel" (Hebrew) in A. Shmuelevitz *(ed.)*, *Turkey and Israel in a Changing Environment*, BESA Center for Strategic Studies, Bar Ilan University, 1996

eral Turkish-Israeli exchanges, and the nature of that trade was and remains very different. For while Turkey needed Israeli electronics, high tech products, military and communications hardware and software, and welcomed hundreds of thousands of "all included" Israeli tourists to Antalya, Israel imported mainly agricultural products and building materials from its commercial partner. Moreover, remittances from millions of Turkish workers employed in Arab countries ensured the continuation of a balancing act by Ankara between its Israeli and Arab partners. Since Israel discovred its vast gas reserves in its off-shore Mediterranean waters, in the 2000s, new prospects emerged for growing Israeli exportation to Turkey in the field of energy of which developing Turkey has been a voracious consumer. There was even talk of an Israeli-Turkish gas- supply line that would have a pipeline carrying the precious fuel via Turkey to Europe. But after the *mavi marmara* event of 2010 was used by the hostile Erdogan government to cool off his relations with Israel, the ambience of partnership between the two has also all but vanished. After more than a decade in office, Erdogan had been able to purge his military top brass, using the palatable pretext to Europeans of ensuring his civilian control over the military, replaced it by his loyalists who no longer threatened to overtake power as his military rivals had done in the past, and toughened his attitude and dealings with Israel.

On the eve of the Jewish Passover and Festival of Freedom in April 2000, Israeli newspapers stressed the need for a greater humanitarian thrust to international politics. The Israeli government and public responded to the famine in Ethiopia with the same energy they showed at the time to the great earthquake that devastated Turkey's Aegean coast, where Israeli rescue teams were the first and the most massively pumping aid, like temporary dwellings for the homeless, a medical field hospital, bottled water and medicine supplies, which were all a dramatic and moving manifestation of the intimacy and concern that had developed in their relationship,

and produced an outpour of Turkish popular gratitude to the enormous effort invested by Israel in that huge rescue operation. But
when the Israeli left-wing Minister of education, Yossi Sarid,
announced in a ceremony commemorating the Armenian massacre
that the Israeli school system would henceforth included that Turkish atrocity as part of the curriculum, protests poured in at once
from the Turks, for whom the Armenian tragedy has been an
extremely sensistive issue and a subject of blatant denial.[55] Only a
few years earlier Ankara had refused to accredit a respected Israeli
scholar, Ehud Toledano, a great expert on Ottoman history, as
Ambassador because of an allegation that he had voiced accusations
against the Turks and had sympathized with the Armenians' plight.
Predictably, all elements of Turkish society, not just the mounting
Islamic parties, wiewed the Armenian affair as "proof" of the "unreliable" Jewish state's tendency to side with Christians against Muslims. Diehard nationalists in Turkey also seized upon the on-again
off-again negotiations between Israel and Syria, which was at the
time considered a direct foe of Turkey, as a sign that Israel would
always subordinate Turkish strategic interests to its own (as if that
was not the usual norm throughout the world, and as if Turkey
would be ready to sacrifice her own strategic goals for Israel's). Israel's explanations to the effect that it could maintain its growing
relationship with Turkey even as it evoked the Armenian massacre
(just as it does with Germany, despite recurring references to the
Sho'ah), fell on deaf ears in Ankara. For unlike Germany, which has
recognized its past and accepted responsibility for it, Turkey continues to treat the Armenian massacre as taboo and does not officially acknowledge any guilt, though some self-flagellating good
souls may in their inner selves sense the remorse that constantly
gnaws at them from within. At any rate, the perennial disputes over

---

[55] See R. Israeli, *Ethnic Cleansing, Migrations and Population Transfers* (forthcoming).

Armenia and then the prospects of Israeli peace with Syria which loomed for a while in the horizon, continued to strain the relationship between Turkish and Israeli governments, even at the height of their honeymoon in the 1990s, their strategic and economic cooperation notwithstanding.

Before the breakup which developed under the aegis of fanatic and paranoid Erdogan, another element of incongruity has crept within this once happy couple, in the shape of a nascent détente between Israel and Greece- Turkey's *nemesis*. The nature of this relationship appeared to be reminiscent of what had occurred a decade earlier between Israel and Turkey: military coordination, sales of Israeli weapons and technology, upgrading of old-dated Greek military equipment, mutual visits by high officials, full diplomatic relations and a growing degree of intimacy between the governments, which also led to joint military maneuvers. A decade earlier it would have been inconceivable that either the Turks or the Greeks would have countenanced this sort or flirtation involving Israel with both of them at the same time. But, as the precedent had been established where both Greece and Turks could belong simultaneously in NATO, the much lesser engagement of each of them with Israel could do no worse. In fact, as the old enmities between them seemed to be easing, despite the ongoing intractable dispute in Cyprus, they both learned to contain these disparities and live with them. But it remained evident that both of them would have elected to be the only bride under the wedding canopy, and that any failure by Israel to take into consideration the sensibilities involved could have spoiled the links of Israel with any one of them, or both. In retrospect, one can definitely say that Israel's gamble did pay off, as Erdogan's hatred towards Jews and Israel continued to explode at his whim, and drive the honeymoon of yesterday into a scornful separation, almost brinking on a divorce. At least Israel found solace in the bossom of Greece and Cyprus, the trio forming a large base for both strategic and economic cooperation around the massive gas exploitation in the eastern Mediterranean. Erdogan is continuing to wander between Russia, Iran and Qatar, hoping to find a new satisfying love affair there, in the process spoiling the good relationship his country had once enjoyed with Washington under the pre-Edogan civil governments.

At that turn a further development was looming which might have had serious consequences for Israel's relations with Turkey, and that was Syria's slow turn back towards Iraq, (both were under the "brotherly" *Ba'ath* regime). Prior to the 1980s tensions already existed between the two "sister states" due to the competition for hegemony between the two branches of that nationalist Arab party to which both had claimed allegiance. The rivalry was also a matter of one-upmanship between Saddam Hussein and Hafez al-Assad. But in August 1980, just prior to the outbreak of the Iran-Iraq eight-year war, when Syria sided with Iran, the countries cut off their diplomatic relations. When Syria then joined, at least nominally, the US-led coalition during Desert Storm, the ties between them deteriorated even further. In 1997, however, Syria was desperate for cash, and Assad swallowed his pride and approached the Iraqis for contacts under the UN oil-for-food deal. By the Spring of 2000, the first signs of improvement emerged as Syrian goods found their way to Iraqi markets and Iraqi oil was illicitly ferried via Syrian (and Kurdish) territory. Diplomatic negotiations aiming at normalization between the two took place through third parties and there was even talk of growing economic exchanges between them.[56] Those two besieged and isolated Arab states, which were both members of the Arab League and of the Conference of Islamic Cooperation, then seemed to form a united front against the Americans, a joint defense against

---

[56] Leon Barkho, "Iraq Betting on Oil Wealth to End Isolation", *Associated Press (AP)*, March 1, 2000.

Turkish-Israeli collaboration, and a fallback position should the US-sponsored Israeli-Syrian peacetalks over the Golan come to naught, as they eventually did. Soon thereafter the US launched its incursion into Iraq and dislodged Saddam from power, but Syria gave refuge to the many Ba'athist officials and Jihadi fighters seeking shelter in flight from the US forces, to the point that the Americans openly threatened to chastise Damascus and the young Assad for his sponsoring the Iraqis on the run.

At the same time that the Syrian hurdle was removed, a more menacing Turkish trend against the Turkish-Israeli partnership in the shape of ultra-nationalist and ultra-religious parties started to agitate for a return to the Anatolian and Islamic roots, undoing the Kemalist heritage so jealously guarded by the military. An insoluble dilemma would then confront the US and Israel. Was the partnership with Turkey so vital that it was worth maintaining even under the bayonets of the Turkish military, by encouraging them to seize power again and prevent their purge by the mounting Islamic trends in country; or was it preferable to allow the popular democracy of the Muslim parties to prevail even at the cost of letting Turkey slip- as Iran had done two decades earlier and Algeria almost did one decade later- into the anti-Western (and anti-Israel) Islamic camp? The stepped up activity of the Turkish Hizbullah (apart from the name, it was separate from the Lebanese one) in the eastern confines of the country at the beginning of 2000, which generated arrests and killings on a massive scale, and were matched by the gains of the Lebanese Hizbullah against Israel, did not seem to augur well for the Turkish-Israeli relationships, which seemed to them as being enforced by the coercive power of arms rather than resting on the democratic principles they claimed to uophold. It turns out in retrospect that the popularity of "Islamic democracy" proved much stronger than Western and Israeli illusions that using soft power was much more conducive to collaboration than a tougher approach to international politics. According to Ofra

Bengio[57], the quiet (in fact not so quiet) revolution that Turkey has been undergoing under Erdogan, has had a particular impact on Israel and the Middle East Region, inasmuch as it comprised three crucial elements which determined its course:

1. The "mind" of Foreign Minister Ahmed Davutoglu, who laid the ideological underpinnings of the Revolution;
2. The "power" of the ruling AKP (the Justice and Development Party) led by Prime Minsiter (and then President) Recep Tayyip Erdogan which made it politically possible; and
3. The receptive audience of Turkish society which had been forged by years of quiet and subversive *da'wa* among the ignorant and poor rural populations, while the preceding civil and pro-secular governments had lived under the illusion that ruling the major cities, where the more prosperous and educated people sided with secularism and guaranteed that the Kemalist tradition, was irreversible.

As we learn from the sociology of religion[58], any established creed needs for its existence six elements: a theology, a founding father (real of mythical), a ritual based on a classical canon, a clergy to spread the message and lead the ritual, an audience of followers, and a place of prayer where the believers can congregate. Erdogan, who was the disciple of doctrinaire, disorganized and weak Erbakan, proved that he was a genius of organization, patient in working his way up, first by acceding to the mayorship of Istanbul, simultaneously working on Islamic *da'wa* in the countryside and tapping the neglected masses of rural Turkey for the conquest of power. In some ways, he acted like the Chinese Communists under Mao, who

---

[57] Ofra Bengio, "Turkey's Qiet Revolution and its Impact on Israel", in *The Israel Journal of Foreign Affairs*, Vol Four, No. One, 2010, pp. 15-21
[58] C. K. Yang, *Religion in Chinese Society*, U.C. Berkeley, 1967, Chap. XII.

could not rely on an unexisting proletariat to trigger a revolution from the top down in Lenin's style, which took over Peterburg before the revolution seeped down to the vast countryside of Russia; instead, he acted first among the farmers in the countryside, initiated reforms to their benefit while subverting the Chiang Kaishek regime which controlled the cities, and finally took Beijing by assault and declared the People's Republic of China in 1949. Having the masses on his side notwithstanding the energetic and contemptuous attitude of the urban intellectuals and businessmen towards him, Erdogan, similarly, has in fact assured his immense popularity and repeated re-election for the past decade and a half as these lines are written (2018).

Erdogan's revolution gradually took the shape of an uncompromising doctrine of Islamization and hatred towards Jews that had been launched by Necmettin Erbakan- his master and predecessor, while he himself has taken up the role of Paul - the actor and organizer, who had followed Jesus Christ- the spiritual founder (like Lenin and Stalin, Mao and Zhou Enlai or Deng Xiaoping, Muhammad and Caliph 'Umar, Moses and Joshua etc.). The adopted ritual has been the visibility of Islamic mores in the public square, like the return of the veil in public and glorification of traditional Islam, skillfully and adroitly managed by the Party cadres within the mosques, who addressed the vast audiences of the uneducated and parochially-oriented peasants. All the while, Erdogan provided a personal model of faith, Islamic rhetoric, his wife always appearing at his side fully covered from head to toe, a perennial condemnation of Israel as an enemy which battles Islam, a strong emotional link to other embattled Muslims in Gaza, China and other parts of the world, and a consistent support for Muslim radical movements such as the Muslim Brothers, or fraternizing with the countries that sustain them like Qatar. At the same time, Erdogan has been cautious to present to the world his democratic facet by scrupuloslly holding elections and referenda, his authoritarian and monarchical style of rule, his imprisonment of journalists and clampdown on political rivals notwithstanding. He even succeeded in pleasing the powerful businessmen class by pushing forward the country's economy. He also tried to settle the Kurdish issue domestically, much to the dismay of the military who felt capable of continuing to quell them by force. At any rate, that was another occasion of projecting a positive image to the West while at the same time dethroning the army from its decisive stance in domestic politics.

Externally, the prominent role given to Ahmet Davutoglu, first as a foreign policy adviser and then as Foreign Minister, in this not so quiet revolution, was reflected in his blueprint-laying book : *Strategic Depth: Turkey's International Position*[59], that was so popular among Turks that it won him many editions. His most salient criticism of foreign policy was the alienation from Arab and Muslim countries of the 1990s and its corollary, the years of the honeymoon with Israel. In return, he suggested that Turkey should vie for global, not just regional power, which may thrust it back to the Ottoman era of world impact, on the way achieving a "zero-problem" relationship with its neighbors, thus abandoning its security-oriented policy (which had been the rationale for the détente with Israel in the 1990) and resetting itself to an economic orientation, (which would naturally give precedence to the much larger Islamic and Arab markets than to tiny Israel). Hence the need to promote economic relations with Syria, Iran and Saudi Arabia, the latter being the sources of energy that Turkey could rely on in the future. The hope was that this blueprint would enhance Ankara's acceptance in the EU, and upgrading from asymmetry to parity with the US. While Israel was totally ignored in this scheme, it was immediately clear what its repercussions on Israel would be[60]. All in all, Turkey has soured its relations with Egypt, Israel, Syria and Saudi

---

[59] Ahmet Davutoglu, *Strategic Depth: Turkey's International Position* (Turkish), Istanbul, 2001.
[60] Bangio, op. cit.

Arabia, and turned the zero-problem of Davutoglu's vision into a multi- (and increasing)-problem affair. So much so that Davutoglu is gone and Erdogan is now compelled to deal with the ravages he has left behind.

Alon Liel, an Israeli *charge d'affaires* in Ankara in the 1980s and one persistent critique of anything Israel does, domestically and externally, in the Natanyahu era (since 2009), offers a slightly different perspective of the situation[61]. He imputes the extraordinary relations between Israel and Turkey in the 1990s to the Madrid Conference (1991) and the Oslo DOP (1993) which considerably relaxed the tensions between the parties and even produced in 1996 the Turkish decision to upgrade in Israel 170 of its combat tanks, besides the increase of Israeli tourism to the Antalya coast and a long and diversified series of trade accords, culminating in the unusually rapid and extensive aid brought by Israel following the devastating earthquake in the Istanbul area in the Summer of 1999. That was the era when Turkish popular sympathy to Israel had reached its peak, before it was turned around by the Erdogan change of mind and heart in the 2000s under Davutoglu's new geopolitical strategy. It started with Minister of Education Yossi Sarid announcing in 2000 his intention to teach Israeli children about the Armenian genocide, followed by the outbreak of the second (al-Aqsa) *intifadah* and the extensive acts of violence with the Palestinians which very much upset Turkey. When Israel eliminated two heads of the Hamas in Gaza (2004), the newly elected Prime Minister of Turkey, Tayyip Erdogan, exhibited his first explosion of rage when he accused Israel of state terrorism. In the same years, when PM Sharon in Israel rejected Turkey's offer to mediate beween Israel and Syria, as he did not show any enthusiasm for Turkey's offer to export water to Israel, stories started to circulate in Turkey's

---

[61] Alon Liel," Israeli-Turkish Retaltions under Strain", *The Israel Journal of Foreign Affairs*, Vol Four, No. One, 2010, pp. 23-26

media about alleged Israeli military aid to the rebelling Kurds in northern Iraq who lay in close (and dangerous) proximity to Turkish Kurds in northeastern Analolia.

The spiraling downward of Turkish anguish toward Israel was intensified in 2007 when the Jewish-American Anti Defamation League (ADL) announced its intention to denounce the Armenian genocide during W W I, *a demarche* that Ankara attributed, rightly or wrongly, to Jerusalem. But what really pushed the relationship to its breaking point was Israel's Cast Lead Operation in Gaza that followed weeks of unilateral Hamas shelling and bombing of the Israeli towns and villages of the area, and an extraordinary effort by the Israeli government to contain those attacks in the face of the Israeli public who resented that unnecessary and self-defeating self-control. Turkey, who was more attentive to Syrian-Israeli talks in Ankara, that ran under Turkish mediation, than to the plight of the bombarded Israeli population, brought about the end to the Turkish mediating efforts. That was when in the Davos Conference, shortly thereafter Erdogan left a panel with President Shimon Peres, accusing Israel of "killing Gaza Children". That incident, in which Erdogan showed his contemptuous and hateful attitude towards Israel, was the breaking point since he was unable to contain his infamous temper and at least be courteous and diplomatic in spite of his disagreement with Israel. Later on, he added fuel to the flame by pleading to oust Israel from the UN and for UN inspection of Israel's nuclear facilities. Israel was thereafter excluded from the annual military exercizes in Turkey after being disinvited, and Turkish state TV showed a *montage* of Israeli soldiers intentionally shooting Palestinian children, a manufactured lie that only the most sworn enemies of Israel had dared to propagate as a news item. Predictably, Liel put the onus of remedying the deteriorating relations on Israel which he charged with the task of re-launching the peace process with the Palestinians, as if it was she who deadlocked it. On the Syrian front, as Erdogan turned from an ally of Assad into its most bitter, vitriolic and hostile opponent, this only showed the fragility of the Syrian regime to which he wanted Israel to make major concessions in view of attaining peace and vindicate Turkey's "success" where the US had failed, only to end up qualifying the Syrian dictator as a murderer of his own people.

Renowned Israeli strategist Efraim Inbar[62] has tackled the issue from his professional point of view and evoked yet a different angle of the issue. While agreeing with the other analysts about the immediate triggers to the the turn-about of Erdogan's new orientation in his Middle Eastern and Islamic policies, he naturally stressed the strategic effects thereof. He mentioned that as part of the defense contracts worth hundreds of millions of dollars signed by the parties, Israel undertook to modernize Turkey's aging fleet of F-4 Phantom jets for the handsome sum of $ 700 million, and another equivalent deal to upgrade M-60 tanks with sophisticated new and advanced weaponry. In addition, Israel was permitted to conduct in Turkish air space complex maneuvers that the limited size of Israel did not allow, while a close and intimate relationship developed in the domains of intelligence and counter terrorism as well. So much so, that Israel's close relationship with Ankara was second only to the link with Washington. All this was demoted, reduced, diminished and shrunk under Erdogan, due to his new orientation to distance himself from the West and approach the Islamic world, especially his immediate neighbors, with the obvious consequence of holding Israel at arms length. The greatest manifestation of this reorientation was the new approach to Iran, the archetype of Islamic revolution, which had abhorred the de-Islamization and pro-Westernism that Kemalism had held as the foundation of the policies of pre-Erdogan Turkey. So much so that in 2008 the President of Iran visited Ankara, his first to any pro-Western country, and Erdogan

---

[62] Efraim Inbar, "Israeli-Turkish Tensions and Beyond", *The Israel Journal of Foreign Affairs*, Vol Four, No. One, 2010, pp. 27-35

announced that his country would not participate in any western sanctions against the Iranian effort of nuclearization. Moreover, in defiance of the US sanctions against Iran in the domain of refined oil products, Ankara joined Tehran in a joint venture to establish a crude oil refinery in northern Iran. Erdogan returned the visit to Tehran in 2009, where he stated the common views that he held with his Ayatullah hosts, and his renewed support for Iran's "pacific" nuclear program.

At that point, prior to the outbreak of Syria's civil war (2011), Turkey also defied the US hostile attitude toward Syria, that forced her, under a stringent set of threats to urge her to withdraw her military forces from Lebanon, and toward Sudan, by collaborating with Damascus and hosting war criminal Omar Bashir in Ankara. Moreover, Erdogan launched negotiations with Hamas which had taken over the rule of Gaza in 2007, again in defiance of the West which had labeled that rebellious movement against the Palestinian Authority (PA), as a terrorist group. Moreover, during the Israeli operation in Gaza (*Cast Lead*, 2008-9), Turkey publicly sided with Hamas at a time when moderate Arab states voiced their support to Israel and against the Hamas. In his typical and uncontrollable outbursts of hyperbole, Erdogan even announced that Israel had threatened to use nuclear arms against Gaza.[63] Turkey's view of itself as a great power, in accordance with Davutoglu's visionary blueprint, was bound therefore to see Israel as a lesser power, was trying to scuttle the American stature of mediator and brocker in the Middle East, and to prevent her dominance and hegemony in the Arab and Islamic environment. That was infuriating enough for Turkey to create a bitter resentment against that once –agreeable ally and now a redoubtable rival - Israel.

The *mavi marmara* event which was intentionally planned by the

---

[63] Robert Tart, "Iran is our Friend, Says Turkish PM Erdogan", *The Guardian*, October 26, 2009, cited by Inbar, p. 30.

Turks to show their mettle to Israel and to the vast audiences of Arabs and Muslims watching them, was the last straw and the breaking point of the once-privileged relationship between the two countries. The American efforts to bridge over the gap between its two allies whose rift embarrassed Washington, only proved, following Israel's shameful and unjustified capitulation to Erdogan's and Obama's demands, that there was no way back, for the break had become irremediable and the divorce final, despite the apparent patching up effort deployed by all parties to keep the appearance of some sort of normalcy in the relations.

CHAPTER FOUR

The Rise of Teyyip Erdogan: the Deterioration Process

Prime Minister Teyyip Erdogan, commenting in 2007 on the term "moderate Islam", to counter the Western elusive distinction between Islam and Islamism[64], as if those were two different doctrines, and to mock the way ignorant and politically correct politicians, scholars and journalists described his own AKP ruling political party, stated very simply and very accurately: "These descriptions are very ugly, it is offensive and an insult to our religion. There is no moderate or immoderate Islam. Islam is Islam and that's it"[65]. Erdogan's personal Islamic piety is well known, and his remark was certainly motivated by his attempt to show that any suggestion that he has departed from the image of moderation that Turkey had acquired over the years, was simply baseless. Andrew Bostom indeed pointed out to the 1990 Cairo Declaration that was drafted and ratified by all 57 member nations of the Organization of the Islamic [not Islamist] Conference (later re-paptized Cooperation) (OIC), under Erdogan's hand-picked Secretary General Ekmeleddine Ihsanoglu, as an added proof of the vanity of that distinction, since all 57 Muslim countries

---

[64] On that erroneous distinction, see R. Israeli, *The Internationalization of ISIS; The Muslim State in Iraq and Syria*, Transaction, NJ, 2016, Chap. One, pp. 1-48-
[65] http://www.thememriblog.org/turkey/blog_personal/en/2595.htm. Cited by Andrew Bostom, "Islam or Islamism? Islamist or Islamic?",posted on 12 November 2009.

reached a consensus about it as representing the world congregation of Muslims- the *Ummah*. The declaration's preamble affirmed the supremacy of Islam in that it cited the Qur'anic[66] assertion that Allah has made the Islamic *Ummah* the best nation. The fact that it was acknowledged in a world opinion survey as a confirmation of the Islamic striving for universal Jihad towards the establishment of a global Caliphate governed by Islamic law- the *Shari'a,* indicates not only that pan-Islamic sentiment is alive and kicking, but that it also encompasses most Muslims, regardless of whether Western elites treat them as moderate Muslims or radical islamists. It also indicates where Erdogan's heart lies.

Turkey consequent to the Ataturk revolution, which had forcibly converted the reduced remnants of the Ottoman Empire into a modern secular state, imposing on the population a western demeanor, divorcing modern Turkish from the Arabic script, separating the state from the mosque, and resolutely turning its orientation westward, was able to enforce its policy domestically and to project a uniform image of modernization, secularism and progress outwardly. To the extent that when NATO was constituted, and later when the Common Market and the European Union were implemented, Turkey was regarded, and viewed itself, as a natural candidate to join. The great leaders of modern and secular Turkey after Ataturk, like Inonu, Bayar, Menderes, Demirel, Ozal, Ecevit and Ciller, who were thoroughly westernized, gave the outside and irrevocable impression that Turkey had been indeed so thoroughly revolutionized that it had definitely placed itself in the Western-European camp. Except that they refused to see that the picture was much more complex, from many angles:

a. That the ideas of democracy did not penetrate deeply enough into Turkish society. Elections were held all right, for the

---

[66] Sura 3, verse 110

most part honest and fair, but the questions of civil rights, freedom of expression and of organization, independence of the press and the judiciary, the total subjection of the military to civilian rule, a fair treatment of the minorities, safety nets for the poor, the elderly and the like, remained problematic since. Enough to mention, that journalists are still arrested for their views and writings into the 21st century, civil demonstrations are still broken up violently, and until the Erdogan reform, in the 2000s, which broke the independent power of the military, as the "curator of the Ataturk's legacy", to interfere when it thought it was threatened, the generals did play a great role in politics.

b. Two parallel societies had been produced by the Ataturk Revolution: the bourgeois urban society, made up of politicians, intellectuals and businessmen, which dwelt in the large cities of Istanbul, Ankara, Izmir and the like, or those in the tourist industry who hosted the multitudes of tourists from Europe and Israel; that was the modern and secular Turkey known to the West. But the other half (or more) of society, namely the rural population, who stuck to Islam, was remote from the urban centers and remained alien to the West, was less educated, poorer and did not see eye to eye with the rest of the Turks who dwelt in the cities. There, the Revolution could not be strictly enforced, and it was there that Islamic parties were cultivated and nourished, by Prime Ministers Erbakan, Gul and Erdogan. It is also there that Erdogan recruits his big numbers of followers when he is faced by the urban demonstrators who do not accept his policies.

c. The image of "moderate Islam" of Turkey, that the Americans erroneously diffused around the world, especially after the collapse of the Soviet Union since the end of the 1980s, was geared to form an allied continuum of "manageable Islam" from Central Asia where the Islamic countries of the Caucasus and the former Soviet Union (Azarbaijan, Turkemenistan, Uzbekistan, Kazakhstan, Tajikistan and Kyrgyzstan), led by secular Turkey, had attained independence, to the Balkans, once the domain of the Ottomans, and now the territory where local Muslim populations (in Bosnia, Albania, Kosovo and Macedonia) have been asserting their presence and independence. Hence the foolish American and NATO support to the Muslims in the 1990s and 2000s (in Bosnia and Kosovo), which backfired on them, when they forfeited the millennial Christian territorial continuity from Russia, Central Europe, Greece and into the Mediterranian, and allowed so many Muslim wedges to be driven inside the heart of Europe.

d. A foreboding of things to come had unfolded in the 1996 elections when the Erbakan Islamic Party won the plurality and its head formed the government. When he started approaching Iran, the army moved in, removed him from power, banned his Islamic party (that measure was "democratic" in the eye of the military) and forced the formation of another civil government. But the writing was on the wall: Islam had not disappeared, it simply hid in the countryside, and sooner or later it would reappear. In the elections of 2002 it did, under Gul as long as Erdogan was incarcerated for his incitement, and then under Erdogan continuously, proving that the public opinion in Turkey had been impressively turned around, by the Islamic Party which mobilized the passive and timid rural population into the active masses which this time won the majority and crushed the urban *bourgeoisie* who had supported the civil governments. These are the masses that Erdogan threatens to assemble as his show of force every time he is threatened by his urban opposition.

e. As a rule, modern Turkish policy towards Israel, was one of a cold shoulder, even under the civil and secular governments, mainly due to its reluctance to create disagreements with its former Arab colonies which had been part of its Ottoman Empire, and to its Islamic sympathies with the Palestinians who alone remained as the one people among its former subjects that did not settle into an independent state. In the 1990s, however, an extraordinary shift[67] occurred in that policy, due to, among others,

- The pressures of the army, which was interested in a security pact with modern and pro-American Israel;
- The belief in Turkey that Israel was an efficient channel to improve Ankara's relations with the US;
- The shift in Turkey towards Pan-Turkism and Pan-Turanism, as the prospects of integrating into Europe diminished, on the one hand, and its expansion towards Central Asia increased;
- The internal upheaval of the Kurds which required close external allies;
- The tremendous intelligence collaboration between the security apparatuses of the parties; and
- The opening up of Israel as a new source for advanced technology, which did not demand in return any compliance with human rights requirements, especially before the takeover… when the takeover of the Islamic Party in 2002, the relationship between the two countries grew to a close alliance and true intimacy between the leaders, which even the

---

[67] R. Israeli, "The Odd Couple: Turkey and Israel", <u>Orbis</u>, January, 2001, pp 165-179.

rise of Erbakan in 1996-7 could not obscure. It was he who was pushed aside by the military when he tried to interfere in that close relationship.

Ever since the Ottoman Empire crumbled at the end of world war I, and the Ataturk reforms that ensued, the likelihood of an Islamic return there was constantly at the gate, much as the civil leadership of the Ataturk legacy and the West gave it little credence and tended to dismiss it as inescapably gone with the wind. However, the collapse of a 500-year old empire cannot be summed up by a sudden and cruel transition from an imperial religious regime into an utterly secular and anti-clerical one. Certainly, the vast empire had shrunk and that multi-ethnic, multi-cultural and multi-linguistic entity had melted into a modern nation state where one predominant group- the Turks- spoke Turkish, identified itself as Turkish and its country as Turkey. But the imperial culture and the imperial religion which made the empire glorious and world reputed, could not be wiped out at once as if it had never existed. Indeed, in the countryside which remained backward, illiterate and traditional even after the Ataturk revolution was imposed on the country, enclaves of puritanical Islam had survived, hidden from Western tourists and scrutiny, and from the spoiled *bourgeois* urbanites who boosted the growth of the civil culture which was to transform modern Turkey and push it to the arms of NATO and the European Union. In all those eight decades between the rise of the Republic in 1922 and 2002, when the Islamic government took over the country, the politics, the economy, the culture, modern education, intellectual life, and the opening to the world unfolded in the great cities, which continued to attract a constant flow of countryside migrants, while the rural areas remained backwater and unconcerned with world trends. The elections, which ran regularly unless interrupted by military takeovers, were mainly a business of the urban populations, and the successive civil governments were essentially made up of urban intellectuals, businessmen and politicians, and oriented towards the West.

In the atmosphere of aggressive secularism, where the military old guard permanently threatened to intervene if the secular heritage of Ataturk were to be endangered, the survival of religious tradition was ignored, considered as non-existent and non relevant, though it was still alive and kicking, albeit pushed to the sidelines. Even when such a great leader as Turgut Ozal was in charge in the 1990s, his total commitment to civil government and to his American allies, obscured the fact that he was himself a religious Muslim. An Islamic party was there most of the time, though it did not pass the threshold of representation in parliament, and when it did under Necmettin Erbakan, Erdogan's mentor, in 1996, it won the plurality for the first time and was entrusted with forming a government. That was a dramatic proof that all the western experts who had "killed and buried" Turkish Islam for ever, and did not believe that it could ever regain power in Turkey, had to swallow their hats and to adapt to a new reality of an Islamic-led government of a member-state of NATO, a candidate for membership in the European Union, and a close ally of the US and Israel. The US, as had been its wont under Obama, might continue to deny that Turkey has any Islamic inclinations, just as it continued to deny that the Muslim Brothers were undermining the Mubarak government in Egypt, or that they are presently infiltrating US government, but the truth revealed itself ultimately, after the Americans and their allies have paid the price of negligence and under-estimation of the new contours of the Middle East and of Islamic penetration into their own ranks.

At the time of successive civilian governments since the 1980's, the Turkish army had attained the conclusion that in matters of armament, security and strategy Israel was a close ally, and it imposed on the government in place to hold those relations in high priority. Relations were brought to the highest diplomatic level of embassies, business and trade flourished, arms deals peaked and training areas were made available to Israel in the vast Anatolian plateau, as well as water supply from Turkey in case Israel ran into drought years. Two difficult problems continued to mar the relationship nonetheless: Turkey's special sensitivity with regard to the Palestinian issue, which the Turks felt somehow responsible for, due to their inheritance of the Ottoman heritage. For while all other Arab countries established their own states, the Palestinian problem remained unresolved. The second problem was the slow revival of Islam in the heartland of Turkey, which those in power in the urban areas, and especially foreign observers who were persuaded that the era of Islam had revolved, never suspected would rise in such a dramatic fashion. But already in the 1990's and even before, the anti-Semitic poison was being spread in the countryside, under the chief mentor and ideologue Necmettin Erbakan, and with the help of his dedicated disciples like Erdogan and Gul. Side by side with that quiet and long-term revival, there were other Islamic movements of Turkish inspiration among the Turkish migrant population in Europe and Muslims in the west in general, such as the *Fethullah Gulen* and the *Milli Gorus*, which won a large audience at home and developed a growing one abroad, especially through "education". These movements would be the precursors of the Islamic Spring in Turkey one full decade before it rose in the Arab world, and will have pursued three or four decades of patient and dormant activities, just like the Muslim Brothers in Tunisia, Egypt and the rest, prior to the big bang of the Arab Spring.

Necmettin Erbakan, who was removed from power by the Army in 1997, and his Islamic party declared as illegal and banned, had also been the founder of the *Milli Gorus* which was the hotbed for the rise of Erdogan and Co, who would attain the highest positions of power after the elections of 2002. Before that, some of them had reached prominence in local government, like Erdogan who served as Mayor of Istanbul until he was tried and incarcerated for incitement. Erbakan's removal by the military was accepted as a matter of course, *inter alia* because during his rule the daughter of Iranian President Rafsanjani visited Turkey and declared to the press that the ambience in the country reminded her of the pre-revolutionary atmosphere in Tehran in the final days of the Shah, something that sounded as a threat on the civil government in Turkey, though (or perhaps because) its diagnostics could not be more precise. Erbakan did not hide his bigotry, exclusion of non-Mulims and anti-Semitic hatred, which he bequeathed to his disciples, and after Erdogan won the elections at the head of a new-old Islamic party in 2002, his mentor increased the pace of his anti-Christian and anti-Semitic propaganda and brought it to levels unknown since the Nazi regime. In the elections of 2007, he was interviewed by various television channels and spoke to them in terms reminiscent of the maddened remarks made by Erdogan himself against Israel when he decided to veer towards Islam, to embrace Iran and Syria as allies instead of Israel, and to send Muslim terrorists aboard the *mavi marmara* to Gaza in order to defy Israel and discredit it. Those interviews to the Turkish media[68] reveal the sources of his hatred towards Christians, Jews and Israel, whom he dubbed as "bacteria" and "disease", and he repeated that infamy in every city and town where he stopped. A selection from his outrageous remarks will make the point:

1. All Infidel nations are one Zionist entity; Jews want to rule from Morocco to Indonesia… These elections are about whether we will be, or we will cease to be. I'll tell you where this is coming from, and for this we have to first expose the infrastructure. […] The right path to the happiness of all

---

[68] TV Interview given by previous PM Erbakan to Flash TV on 1 July, 2007 as part of a pre-election program
Htpp://www.milligorusarsiv.com/videolar/file.php?f=5

humanity is our path, the *Milli Gorus* way. Our Prophet was sent with love and compassion, and our goal is the happiness of all six billion people in the world. We are Muslims, and our civilization has brought happiness to the entire world. This is the good, but there also is evil. Our religion says that the Infidels are one nation [*Millah*]. That means evil is run by one control center. When we look at the map of the world, we see about 200 countries painted in colors, and we think that there are many races, religions, and nations. The fact is that for 300 years, all these [200 nations] have been controlled from one center only. This center is racist, imperialist Zionism. Unless you make this correct diagnosis for the illness, you cannot find the cure to it. You will ask, 'What is this belief, this racist imperialism that destroys happiness in this world?'

2. This belief began 5,765 years ago, when the children of Israel were living in Egypt, with a book of magic that was written by someone called *Kabbala*. The author or authors of this book later claimed that they belonged to the tribe of Moses, but this is not true. They distorted the *Tevrat* [= Torah, Bible] of Moses and put in it the *Kabbala*. If you want to see proof of this, you can look at their *Tevrat* and then look at the *Kabbala*. What do these people believe in? Their belief has four principles that say: [...]

   a. You [the Jews] are the real people of God; all others are created to be your slaves; you were created as men and others [were created] as monkeys that later turned into men. This is what they believe and what they teach. They believe that they are the superior class.

   b. This superiority will be not only in thought, but will be materialized, actually realized. They will be the masters and the others will be their slaves.

   c. For all this to come true, they must perform three duties:
The first duty will be to gather all the exiled sons of Israel
into Quds [Jerusalem]; the second duty is to build
'Greater Israel' between the Nile and the Euphrates,
within these determined borders, and [three], to provide
for the safety of this Greater Israel.

3. Do you know what the safety of Israel means? It means that
they will rule the 28 countries from Morocco to Indonesia.
Since all the Crusades were organized by the Zionists, and
since it was our forefathers the Seljuks who stopped them,
according to the *Kabbala* there should be no sovereign state
in Anatolia. This is this people's [i.e. the Jews'] religion, their
faith. You can't argue or negotiate with them. This is their
religion, and it comes from the *Kabbala*. Why did this man,
Kabbala, write this book? Because he wanted to encourage
those who were oppressed by the Pharaohs, by saying that
they were superior and were God's true people. *Kabbala* says
that this people defeated even God – may Allah forgive. The
same line is found in the *Tevrat* as well.

4. They will destroy – Allah forbid !!! – Al-Aqsa mosque and in
its place build Solomon's temple. Only then will their messiah come and establish them as the rulers of the world. This
is what they believe in. To realize these goals and meet their
obligations, they [i.e. the Jews] have been working for 5,767
years! Their history begins with this *Kabbala*. They say that
they want to be the rulers of the world. This is a racist religion. If your mother is not a Jew, you cannot be a Jew. That's
why they cannot multiply and grow. Among six billion people they are only 30 million. [...] So how will they rule the
world? They say, "Wait a minute, we have conquered the
power of money within the capitalist order. As one can see in

the symbol of the 13 levels of a pyramid that is depicted on the American dollar, all peoples will serve us at the top. With the power of the dollar, we have established a world order where money and manpower are dependent on us. This is how we rule the world".

5. Now, let's come to us [the Muslims]. Thanks to our beloved Prophet, light and happiness came to the six billion people of the world. We became the masters. We [the Muslims] ruled for 11 centuries. But unfortunately, in the last three centuries the children of Israel have grabbed this material power. Now they control the world that we live in. What kind of a world did they build? Without understanding this, nothing can be comprehended. Ballots, elections are all details. The essence is this: Let's assume that you, as a Muslim, want to go to [Mecca for] the *haj* (=pilgrimage), and you want to fly on a Turkish plane. For an airline to get a permit to fly and land in other airports, it must be a member of the IATA. IATA is an organization of the children of Israel, of Rockefeller. To become a member, airlines must give them [the Jews] 9% of the ticket proceeds. You know what this means. It means saying to Israel, 'Take this money, buy guns, and kill me tomorrow, [so that you can] occupy Turkey.' This is the order that they have built and have implemented for three centuries.

6. Let's say that you, as a Muslim, want to send money to another Muslim country. Say you want to send money to Pakistan. You cannot send it, because you don't have the infrastructure to do that. You are living in their [i.e. the Zionists'] world. To send the money, you need to take it to a Turkish bank. Then the Turkish bank will give it to the American bank. The American bank will give an order to its branch [in Pakistan], and that branch will give the money to

the Pakistani bank that will pay out the money that you sent. But in all this, you will pay 1%. From wherever [and] to wherever the money goes, 1% is paid to the Jew. They have taken the world into their hands. That green dollar that you recognize is Zionist money. The owner is not the American central bank. The American central bank only rents this money, paying $500 billion a year for rent. They [the Zionists] print this green money, the paper, and they bring it to our *sheikh*s in Saudi Arabia and they say, 'Here, take this green paper and give us your oil.' And they take the oil with these pieces of paper. There are five trillion [of these] dollars outside of America.

7. And look at what else they do. I am telling you all this so we can all recognize this bacteria. What do they [i.e. the Zionists] do? They go back to the oil *sheikh* and tell him to return the green papers, and give him a yellow paper instead. What is this yellow paper? It is an American bond. There are bonds outside the U.S. valued at $5 trillion as well. That means they took back their green papers to use them again. Those bonds go to the central banks. And what does the American Central Bank do? It gathers all the central banks, to give them a white paper. So where are all the reserves of the countries? Our reserves are not in the safes of our central bank. They are in the safes of Rockefeller. He is using all this money. What do we have? The head of our central bank has a white paper in front of him. On this paper it is written that such and such a number of billions of dollars are in the banks [in the U.S.] What we have is only a piece of white paper.

8. They are crooks three times over. They suck [money] from everybody – five trillion with green papers, another five trillion with yellow papers, and they keep trillions with the

white paper they give you. Every child born should be told: 'Welcome to this house, my dear, but this house has an owner, and there is rent to be paid. The owner of this house – that is, this world – is the Zionist, and you must pay him $1,200 every month.' Every one of us has to pay this $1,200, because of those trillions of exploitation dollars. There's more: Say you go to a supermarket, wherever you are in the world. You [select] some products, and you pay for them. Say the cashier tells you the total is 300 lira. You pay 300, and you walk out with your sack. No matter where you are and where you buy, 100 lira of the 300 is interest. You buy bread. The tractor was purchased with interest. The flour mills, the factories were built with interest. We are made to pay for this interest [charges]. If you read the book we wrote on this, you would see clearly that one-third of the money we pay for a loaf of bread is paid out in interest.

9. My students and disciples [i.e. the current rulers of Turkey] must have thought, 'Since there is so much money going around, why shouldn't we have a share of it too?' But that money is exploitation money. It is not good money. Our students apparently have not understood what we have been teaching them for 30 years [in *Milli Gorus*]. Let's go back to the [Zionist] bacteria. About $22 trillion out of all the money we spend every year is paid to these racist imperialist Zionists. We, as a country, are paying $200 billion every year to the Zionists so that they can prepare their bombs, so that they can one day come and take our country. This is the world that the Zionists have built. [...] This racist imperialist Zionism organized 19 Crusades just to reach its goals. To organize the Crusades, it used the Christians. Why is it that the Christians are helping the Jews? A rabbi goes out on the balcony and tells them, 'Oh Christians, isn't it the Messiah

that you are waiting for? We too are waiting for the same Messiah.' What the rabbi is doing is *taqiya*,[69] of course. Then he goes into his synagogue and tells a five-year-old, 'What you heard me say outside is not true. Our Messiah is different. Jesus is someone whom we killed. He will not come or go anywhere. I told them that to deceive them.' These people tell the Christians: 'You are waiting but you have no guidelines as to how to make him come. Our *Tevrat* tells us what to do. Let's do it together and let's bring the Messiah.' And what were those guidelines? To bring the Jews to Jerusalem, to build and secure Greater Israel, and so on.

10. It was Zionism that established the sect of Protestantism. The capitalist order of today is the religious order of Protestantism. It's because the pope rejects the concept of interest, so as not to allow the exploitation of his children. That's why the Jews decided to change the [Christian] religion, and founded Protestantism. This way they can charge interest and make everybody work for them. That's also why they built the Evangelical sect in America, which now numbers 90 million members. Most people you see there [in the U.S.] belong to this sect. Take [President] Clinton: He said that he did not serve in the military for America, 'but for Israel' he said, 'I would take up arms, go into a bunker, and fight.' You ask him, "Hey, Clinton, are you a Jew? Why is Israel your business?' He says, 'Nooo. It is not because I am a Jew that I say this. It is because I am a good Christian that I think that way. It's because I want Jesus to come that I am saying this.' All this is because the Evangelical sect was built by the Jews for them to think that way. Bush belongs to that sect. Clin-

---

[69] *Taqiya* is an Islamic term that means concealing one's true beliefs to avoid repression

ton belongs to that sect. Anyone you know... Now look, when we look at someone we see his skin only; but behind it are all the muscles, bones, nerves. I am now giving you the anatomy of the world to show you what is behind the skin, behind the surface.

11. Without knowing all this, you cannot comprehend what is going on in the world. When we learn all this, we will know that there are no 200 countries in the world. There are only two. One is the world of Islam, and the other is all the others. Who uses these others? Racist imperialism [meaning Zionism]. The Zionists are holding the Christians in the palms of their hands, and using them. China's and India's industrial development is being carried out with Jewish capital. Japan's too. They control them too. Now, only Islam remains against them. The Jews say you will be our slaves. Islam says *la ilaha illa'Allah (*=there is no God but Allah, the first part of the declaration of faith and the rite of passage in Islam). We won't bow to anyone but Allah. Nobody will be slaves to anybody. So this is the clash between the two – the clash between good and evil.

12. These Jews started 19 Crusades. The 19th was World War [I]. Why? Only to build Israel. They used the Christians to build Israel. The Canakkale [Gallipoli] victory was only one of our battles. We fought on 30 fronts during the war. Then they had us sign the Treaty of Sèvres. They told us they would eliminate us and build Greater Israel and make us their slaves. No other nation could fight against them on 30 battlefronts like our nation did. After they made us sign the Treaty of Sèvres, the French came to Kahramanmaras [on the Syrian border], not to keep it but to give it out so as to make it part of Greater Israel. The English went to Palestine, not

to keep it for themselves, but to build Israel. They are doing all this just so that Jesus will return. If we do not see these realities, we cannot understand world affairs. What does Bush say? He says that Jesus ordered him to invade Iraq. He says that the most important factor in making his decision on Iraq was his being Christian. [He thought,] 'I will take Iraq. I will build Greater Israel, so that Jesus can return.' These people work with that kind of belief. If you don't know about these peoples' beliefs, you cannot understand why they do what they do. Our youth must learn all this." [...]

One wonders how this ignoramus, inhuman, anti-Christian and anti-Semite, full of hatred and steeped in fantasy, and bordering on mental derangement, could serve as Turkey's Prime Minister when his party won the plurality in the 1996 elections and served for nearly two years as the head of a coalition government, before his party was ousted by the military (and they still called that democracy), mainly due to his rapprochement to Iran and the cold shoulder he showed towards the alliance with Israel. He and his party were then outlawed and excluded from politics. His disciple, Erdogan, who was jailed for incitement while serving as the mayor of Istanbul, ended up as the head of the AKP, an Islamist party which won the majority for the first time in 2002, and dwarfed the civilian parties. Erdogan, who did not hesitate to attack in a very uncivilized fashion, Israel's President during a debate in Davos, and especially during the flotilla affair (summer 2010) when he sent Muslim terrorists to defy Israel in Gaza, was not far from the statements of his master, mentor and predecessor, hence his false accusations against Israel which pushed the relations between the parties to the brink. With his allies in Syria and Iran toeing the same line, that entire anti-Semitic bunch found itself reinforced until Ankara realized that Assad and Ahmadinejad were not exactly the sort of allies it needed to increase its reputation in the world, but he refrained from acting upon this realization. After he purged his army from the personnel who wished to maintain a good relationship with Israel, and placed his own men at the helm in their stead, he embarked on a campaign of hatred and lies, in order to occupy his place of leadership in the Islamic world, in replacement of the position in Europe that his allies in NATO denied him. It stands to reason that as long as Erdogan heads that party, and as his religious fanaticism and erratic conduct take the place of rational calculations, that man who knows no effrontery, will continue to manufacture accusations and encourage anti-Israeli hatred to justify his irrational policies.

On 28 December 2002, columnist Y. Bayer of the high circulation Turkish daily *Hurriyet* (Freedom) wrote:

> Did you know that in 1974, when Erdogan was President of the *Beyoglu* Islamic youth Group in Istanbul, which belonged to the Erbakan National Salvation Party, he wrote and directed a theatrical play called *Maskoyama*, and also played the lead role of the "bad son". Maskoyama stood for Mas--ko-ya, the acronym for Masons, Kommunists and Yahudi (Jews), which was built on the combination of the evil concepts of these three terms and the hatred towards them, and was staged all over Turkey.[70]

That was published after Erdogan won his landslide in 2002. But when one digs up the sources of his upbringing and political activity, one is reminded of his utterances as Mayor of Istanbul, for part of which he was incarcerated and ousted from politics until his release, whereupon his illegal and inciting deviations became the law of the land under his Islamic government. As mayor of Istanbul in the late 1990s, Recep Teyyip Erdogan publicly read a poem that included the lines: "The mosques are our barracks, the domes our helmets, the

---

[70] MEMRI, Special Dispatch No 916, 6 June, 2005.

minarets our bayonets and the faithful our soldiers." This radical Islamic message earned him a few months in jail from Turkey's military-backed secular government. A few years later, Erdogan re-emerged in politics as a "champion of liberal democracy" calling for sweeping institutional reforms and closer ties with Europe, when he became prime minister and led Turkey through a decade of prosperity and influence. Then, Mr. Erdogan has ticked back in the other direction, igniting weeks of protests from Turks who were concerned by what they saw as Erdogan's efforts to consolidate his power and Islamize public life. The shift has raised new questions among many Turkish voters about whether the then Prime Minister was democrat or autocrat. It was felt that how far Erdogan pushed his new agenda might determine the durability of Turkey's revival and undeniable economic prosperity. Massive protests were indeed kindled by Erdogan's development plans for an Istanbul park but quickly spread into a national crisis. On June 15, 2013 he restored order by ordering riot police to storm the park, sending protesters fleeing in a hail of tear gas and water cannons and consequences started to emerge. Germany, Turkey's largest trading partner, sought to block the start of new talks about Turkey entering the European Union. The U.S., which has called on Turkey to show restraint, was watching to see if the protests constrained Erdogan's ability to pressure the Syrian regime that President Barack Obama wanted to oust.[71]

When the US was presenting Turkey as the moderate Muslim country which might lead the Turkic bloc and the former Ottoman patrimony from the Balkans to Central Asia, its idea was to bring under control a moderate brand of Islam led by its ally in NATO and Europe; but when it failed, and realized the return of Turkey to an authoritarian Islam under Erdogan's rule, and his abandonment of

---

[71] Joe Parkinson, "Erdogan Tightens Grip on Turkey, Putting Nation at Crossroads", 27 June 2013.
http://online.wsj.com/article/SB10001424127887323300004578557693146971554.html?KEYWORDS=germany+turkey

the alliance with Israel in favor of a rapprochement with Arabs and Muslims, especially when he chose to align himself to Iran and Syria until they failed him, Washington began to present him as a "model" of Islamic democracy, who could combine Islam with all the trappings of liberal rule, to serve as an example to emulate in the rest of the awakening Islamic world. But the Americans were wrong again: it took them too long to wake up to the fact that although elections in Turkey were fair and democratic, and Erdogan won his sweeping majority, once and again, without the riggings of Mubarak or Assad, other aspects of democracy were sorely absent : harsh oppression of civilian demonstrations, an enforcement of Islam in the public square which gave it much more visibility than previously under the civil governments, more journalists imprisoned than in any country in the world, the failure to reconcile with its past, as Germany has done, by recognizing the massacre of the Armenians and paying them some damages; and especially the campaigns of incitement and lies against Turkey's former ally - Israel, which have practically frozen the alliance between the two countries and sent it back to what it was prior to the 1990s and probably worse.

How Erdogan navigates the next stages could affect other Muslim countries that have viewed his brand of Islam-infused democracy as a model. Turkey was quick to champion the "pro-democracy" uprisings that unseated dictatorships in Tunisia, Libya and Egypt in 2011, during the ill-fated Arab Spring, and to offer advice how to return the military to their barracks and put an end to their interference in civil politics. In Egypt, Turkey offered more than $2 billion to bolster the economy, and dispatched leading officials and business people to help short-lived President Mohammed Mursi's attempted reforms (2012-3), Turkish-style, in order to overhaul the country's secular-dominated institutions. But when Mursi was demoted by the Sisi military *coup* and the Muslim Brothers activists were imprisoned, Erdogan effected an immediate *volte-face*, poisoned his relations with Cairo and set out to embolden Muslim radicals in Gaza and elsewhere in partnership with Qatar to resist both Egypt and Israel. For Erdogan himself, the domestic protests seemed to hinder his effort to alter the constitution to his benefit so as to allow him to switch to presidential rule and so augment his authoritarian power. But ultimately he maneuvered resolutely and purposefully, all the more so after the aborted coup against him in the Summer of 2016, and succeeded in his policy to reinforce the divisions between the liberal, urban pro-democratic civil demonstrators, and his rural, religious and conservative rural supporters of the hinterland. His supporters openly denied that he was sliding toward a more religious authoritarianism, arguing that his "democratic records are impeccable", something that can be easily dismissed by his wild and uncivilized onslaught on Israel and incitement against its people; by his further restrictions on alcohol consumption and abortion; by his harsh measures against freedom of expression and his massive purges of government and military officials; and by his repeated calls for all women to have at least three children to boost Turkey's population. He has held forth on what citizens should eat at the family dinner table, and intervened to censor sex scenes in prime-time television series. His government has not only sought to muzzle the press but has jailed more journalists than Iran or China, according to the Committee to Protect Journalists.[72]

Following an adolescence steeped in religion and soccer, we are told, Mr. Erdogan entered politics in the 1970s as a follower of Erbakan's Islamic National Salvation Party. It was a violent period. More than 5,000 people died in the daily street violence, mainly at the hands of armed left- and right-wing militants. Two of Mr. Erdogan's close friends were killed—one in a bombing, the other shot. "Religion was the only source for the ideas that Mr. Erdogan and his friends shared at the time", says Mehmet Metiner, a fellow

---

[72] Ibid.

member of the youth wing of the National Salvation Party at the time. "We opposed radical secularism in a country where most of the population was Muslim." Mr. Erdogan gained nationwide attention when, campaigning for an Istanbul Municipal Council seat, he canvassed for votes in a licensed brothel. But he remained very conservative. In a 1992 speech, he said Turkey's armed forces "should not be a slave to NATO," and that "The EU's real name is Union of Catholic Christian States." Amid broad discontent with political corruption, Mr. Erdogan won election for mayor of Istanbul in 1994 on a populist platform to fix the city's ailing infrastructure. His views were said to have changed when he was jailed for four months in 1999 following his recitation of the poem deemed an incitement to religious hatred. He used his time in prison to read up on history and international affairs, honing a vision for a more moderate religious party that could reach beyond the pious voting bloc to merchants and nationalists, according to Hüseyin Besli, a former aide who was a legislator in parliament until 2011. Maybe this was his change of tactics that, while not altering his fundamentally religious views, enabled him to address non-religious groups from the urban elites, which finally helped him to achieve power in the 2000s.[73]

The symbolism of Mr. Erdogan's jail term boosted his popularity with conservatives and liberals who were uneasy with the government's heavy-handed approach to religious politicians. He was inundated with fan mail—13,000 letters, according to Mr. Besli—and a stream of visitors bearing gifts of *baklava*, the sugary pastries. Once released, Mr. Erdogan and his partners Abdullah Gul, PM and then President, and Bulent Arinc, deputy prime minister, who founded the Justice and Development Party to encompass a broader spectrum of Turkey's center and right. They toured European capitals to convince policy makers that their more moderate vision sup-

---

[73] Ibid.

ported rather than shunned Turkey's EU membership bid. "Previously, Turkish Islamism was based on dividing the country between believers and nonbelievers, and there was a limit to how many votes they could win" says Ihsan Yilmaz, a columnist for the Turkish pro-government daily, *Zaman*. "Erdogan and other young leaders wanted to broaden the appeal." The move capped a turn to the center for Mr. Erdogan, who had said in speeches and interviews in the early 1990s that it wasn't possible to be both secular and Muslim. The pivot was sustained after Mr. Erdogan became prime minister in 2003. During his first term, he enacted sweeping reforms to democratize Turkey's secularist-dominated institutions and bolstered ties with Brussels and Washington. He championed human-rights reforms and the opening of European Union entry talks, brought powerful generals to heel and put the military-dominated National Security Council, which had broad control of state affairs, under civilian control. The breaking of the power of Turkey's military, which had toppled four governments in the second half of the 20th century, was perhaps Erdogan's most striking achievement. Hundreds of officers were jailed after coup trials. The prime minister's popularity was boosted by a remarkable decade of economic growth that has seen a near tripling of nominal incomes. The average Turk today earns $10,500 a year, up from $3,500 when Mr. Erdogan took power.[74]

"Many people were unhappy with the direction of the government, but the trade-off was clear: economic growth and a government that was socially conservative but didn't encroach too much on lifestyles," said Sinan Ulgen, a former Turkish diplomat with the Carnegie Endowment in Brussels. But while seeking election for a third time in 2011—which he ultimately won with his biggest margin yet—Mr. Erdogan gave a speech that many analysts say foreshadowed a more autocratic and Islamist style of governance.

---

[74] Ibid.

Erdogan felt strong and established enough to revert to his roots, and he did it in his blunt and coarse style, which in some regards, including his anti-Israeli attitude, is reminiscent of his patron and mentor, Necmettin Erbakan's uncivilized demeanor. Before tens of thousands of party loyalists in Ankara, Mr. Erdogan said that following a June 2012 election victory, he would transition into an "*Ustalik*," or "masterful," phase, which was very revelatory of his roots. "God willing, we will reconstruct Turkey. The apprenticeship started in 2002. In 2007, the foremanship began. Until when? Until 12th of June. After that date, the mastership will begin," Mr. Erdogan said, as the big crowd chanted "*buyuk usta*" or grand master. The masterful period has indeed seen political power increasingly centralized around Mr. Erdogan, who has final word on every issue. He has stifled dissent, using a broad coup investigation designed to subdue the military and to purge other enemies, including opposition journalists and Kurdish activists."That 'masterful' speech showed us that Erdogan was no longer fighting reactive battles, but would from now on take daring measures to redraw Turkey as its paramount ruler," says Ziya Meral, from the Foreign Policy Center, a London-based think tank. "The switch had been completed and a new system had superseded the old guard: The same Turkey but under new management."[75]

In a series of combative speeches, Mr. Erdogan has blamed unrest on "terrorist groups backed by foreign powers" and labeled demonstrators as "looters" and "bums." He told a large crowd of supporters: "They beat my girls wearing headscarves…they entered our mosques with their beer and their shoes."In a speech in Ankara aimed at those who have urged him to adopt a more conciliatory tone, the prime minister said: "Sorry, Teyyip Erdogan is not going to change". An opinion poll showed that 50% of respondents felt the government was becoming more authoritarian, with 54% saying

---

[75] Ibid.

that it was interfering with their lifestyles. According to the survey of 2,800 people, support for Mr. Erdogan's party has declined in the wake of the protests of Summer 2013, though it remains by far the most popular party. Some observers of Mr. Erdogan say that his charisma has been the key to his success, but could also be a roadblock that could frustrate reaching a resolution. "Erdogan is at his root a pragmatist and not unlike Bill Clinton—he would make you feel like you were the only person in the room," said Jenny White, a professor at Boston University who once shadowed Mr. Erdogan when he was Istanbul mayor. "Erdogan is a product of Turkish culture that is characterized by militant masculinity that can easily turn to violence. It's a loaded gun that can be manipulated and pointed, which makes it dangerous."[76]

Part of Erdogan's metamorphosis, both ways - towards pragmatism and back from it, including his anti-Israeli virulence and lies, matched his mentor's, but it turned out that the terrorist organization IHH, which staged the anti-Israeli flotilla in 2010, had acquired the *mavi Marmara* from the AKP-run municipality of Istanbul. IHH was an example of how NGO's are used by the Turkish foreign ministry to execute dirty missions without ostensibly sullying its hands openly. Indeed the IHH, wich originated in the *Milli Gorus,* was also used by the Turkish government to distribute aid to populations in Northern Iraq without seeming to have invaded that foreign land in order to thwart any Kurdish inroads into Anatolian territory.[77] If one adds to that Erdogan's attacks against the secular Turkish constitution while serving as Mayor of Istanbul (1994-8), describing it as a "huge lie" and declaring unequivocally that "Sovereignty belongs unconditionally and always to Allah", and that "one cannot be a Muslim and a secular",[78] one

---

[76] Ibid.

[77] Yaakov Lappin, http://web.archive.org/web/20100428140334/http://eng.ak-pati.org.tr/english/lifestory.html

[78] MEMRI, Special Dispatch no 1596, 23 May 2007.

understands the avenues to which he proposed to lead the Turkish people so as to permit himself to reign supreme as an executive President free from the supervision of Parliament.

The more serious problem with Turkey is that it has been peddling the "Turkish model" to be emulated by other Islamic countries emerging from the Spring . Egypt seemed to be the first to follow it, when the rule of the Brothers seemed assured (2012-3), and Erdogan visited them in Cairo, after they won the elections, and prevailed on them to emulate the same tactic which enabled the Islamic Party of Turkey to emerge from long years of civil government and conquer the necessary votes to win a landslide. The tactic consisted of building silently and patiently a pool of support in the countryside, and use those bases to assault the cities which were the strongholds of the intelligentsia and the bourgeoisie, and take them over. Later, Erdogan moved to dismiss the top military brass in order to avoid a repetition of the Ebakan ouster. The assumption that prevailed thereafter in the Spring circles and in the West was that the Turkish model married moderate Islam and democracy, both accompanied by the impressive economic success which moved Turkey forward. Egypt had begun to copy that model, prior to the crisis of the military coup of July 2013, for example as President Mursi removed the Heads of the military and Intelligence establishment and several senior military officers, to replace them with his appointees, in order to avert any possibility of the military command rising against him when he decided to neutralize military influence over government, as Erdogan had done. But the events of the Summer of 2013 showed that Egypt was not stable enough and Mursi not established enough to take that daring step, because one year after their appointment, the new military chiefs rose against him and sided with the opposition, despite the legality of his elected office.

In Morocco, where the elections of April 2012 have delivered a great victory to the Muslim parties, there was also talk of following that model. The founding of the Party of Justice and Development there, also a close imitation of successive Islamic Parties in Turkey, had been the first step in that course. But the name of those Islamic parties is the easy part, it remained to be seen whether the matters of religion and state, secularism and Islam, and personal piety and public service could be addressed in the new mood of revolution that had swept the Islamic world but spared other monarchies there. The AKP example had been considered to be the epitome of moderation, pragmatism, good governance and the convergence between Islam, democracy and modernity. But the question was whether that image was justified. For example, the Turkish model had been famously known for its peaceful and gradualist strategy, which respected the red lines of the established order, and professed the reduction of the number of the Islamic candidates it fielded in elections, while avoiding revolutionary rhetoric, as long as it was struggling for hegemony. Along these lines, when debate raged about the compatibility between Islam and democracy, the Islamic party sounded more democratic than all the rest, in order to avoid raising suspicions as to its designs. But after Erdogan came to almost absolute power, all those hopes and calculations collapsed.

Indeed, things changed radically when the Islamic Party gained power, won a majority which allowed it to take over the government machinery and to remove into retirement the old military brass which alone could threaten its rule. For example, Erdogan's and Gul's wives appear completely veiled in public, on campuses students are again permitted to sit in classes covered, journalists who bluntly criticize the rulers are arrested, the state media go into blunt and bigoted incitement against rivals and enemies, and in general, their style of Islam does not appear to be moderate, but rather following the outrageous wordings of Erbakan and Erdogan cited above. At the same time, democratic procedures are enforced as a choice tactic to win the trust of their constituencies, something which was taken in the Arab countries of the Spring as an example of "reinforcing democracy", which they might emulate to assure their followers of adopting the same means of instituting democracy in their countries. In this regard, Ghannouchi, the head of *al-Nahda* fundamentalists in Tunisia, praised the Turkish model for promoting human rights and for extending political freedoms to meet European standards, as an example to follow in erecting his own democratic state. Similarly, the Egyptian Freedom and Justice Party, the political arm of the Brotherhood, also consulted with the Turkish AKP before the Egyptian elections, in order to make their platform and campaign more palatable to their general electorate. They wished, as they promised, to assure the public that they did not intend to monopolize the political process. But, judging from their repeatedly broken pledges to field less than half the candidates in Egypt, for example, and then not to present a candidate to the presidency, it is evident that as they gained in self confidence, their expectations and ambitions increased.

The Turkish model can also have international repercussions. At first, when the AKP came to power, and knowing that the army was in favor of a good relationship with Israel, for example, it maintained on the surface the good relations between Ankara and Jerusalem. But after it removed the old guard and replaced it with its own people, it came out openly and totally against Israel and adopted a hostile attitude towards it. Tunisian Ghannouchi referred to that aspect in the shift of the AKP conduct, and presented it as part of the Turkish model worth emulating, because it precisely "strengthened Ankara's Islamic identity". This kind of all around praise for Turkey by the Islamic parties that have come to power (though temporarily) in the Spring countries, has indeed endeared it as the model to be followed, making even the *Salafi* Movement in Egypt, which came in second in Parliament (30%) to the Brothers (45%), turn to Turkey for guidance on the much damaged Egyptian tourist industry during the upheval. They suggested that since the Turks had successfully adopted "male beaches" that are segregated from "female beaches", but still attracted Arab and other foreign tourists, Egypt should act similarly. Morocco too, which has not suffered so decisively from the ripples of the Spring, but has experienced the rise of the Justice and Development Party in the last elections, has been inspired by the successes of the AKP in Turkey, which have been accompanied by all the amenities of democracy for now. What remains to be verified over time is whether, as the AKP rule is perpetuated, and Erdogan's personal rule affirmed, the government will not move to Islamize the country even further, first by soft measures of persuasion, then through social pressure to conform, and finally through means of coercion under *Shari'a* law. One thing is sure, when the West had recommended to other Arab countries to democratize following the Turkish model, that was in the days of the civil governments of Menderes, Demirel, Ozal, Ecevit and Ciller, when indeed Islam was moderate and arguably married well with democracy. But since December 2002, when the AKP came to power, the rule is no longer "moderate Islam", neither domestically not externally, as the embrace of that model by Muslim Brothers affiliates elsewhere well testifies.

Most outstanding in Erdogan's turn around is the current Turkish bashing of Jews and Israel since the AKP came to power in 2002, and more emphatically since the *Mavi Marmara* incident, which was initiated and orchestrated by Erdogan's government with a view to trigger a crisis, thus turning the previous years' virtual honeymoon alliance between the two countries into a hostility which threatens to degrade into open enmity. America's mediation to put an end to the rift between two of its main allies in the Middle East, turned sour like any other imposed settlements which are not independently accepted by the parties concerned. It is clear that Turkey was interested in that rift, in order to abandon its intimacy with Israel as a price for its new alliance with Iran and Syria. The *Marmara* was not the only ship in that convoy, but it was the only one which violently resisted the boarding by the Israeli Navy which enforced the legal blockade on Gaza, and threatened the lives of the Israeli soldiers, who had to defend themselves, and unfortunately caused the unintended death of 9 Turkish marauders who wanted to break the blockade. In view of the documented violence used by the Turks, they should have apologized to Israel, which they were in no mood of doing. America wrongly prevailed on Israel via its many levers of influence to apologize to Ankara instead, but despite the humiliation of Israel, the Turks kept raising their demands for a settlement. It is safe to assume that the more Erdogan is battered at home, by the civil strife and opposition criticism, the more he will be likely to accuse the "Jews" of his troubles. A string of events points in that direction:

- There is a tendency in Turkey, encouraged by the Islamic government, to demonize the Jews, thus triggering anti-Semitism. Erdogan, for example, raised, hours before the cease-fire between Israel and Hamas in Gaza on 21 November, 2012, the question of "dual loyalty" of Turkish Jews. The daily *Yeni Safak,* a supporter of Erdogan claimed in a front page story, under the headline "Murderers amongst Us" that there were "Turkish-speaking Israeli soldiers who had boarded the *Mavi Marmara* on May 30, 2010 and killed nine Turks[79]. That newspaper, like Erdogan himself, were eager to twist the truth and paint the picture as if having a dual citizenship equals treason in Turkey. When the readers' comments on the article warned of physical threats to Jewish citizens in Turkey, the spokeman of the Association of Turkish Jews in Israel condemned the news report. He announced that at the request of the Israeli Interior Ministry at the night of the *marmara* raid, he sent 8 volunteers to Ashdod Port to help in translation, as those detained Turks who did not rebel were going through

---

[79] *Yeni Safak,* 13 December, 2012.

passport control. (That had nothing to do with the boarding itself). Then, the Prosecutor's office in Istanbul that tried *in absentia* the Israeli soldiers who boarded the Turkish ship, asked the Turkish National Intelligence Office for a list of Turkish Jews who traveled to Israel two weeks before and after the incident. No democratic country maintains asurveillance on the travels of its citizens in this suspicious manner.

- A Turkish Jew attested to *al-Monitor* : "Whenever there is fighting between Israel and the Palestinians, the atmosphere in Turkey turns against us and people start acting as if we committed a crime". Another Jew sounded the same alarm bell:" The media are paintaing such an image that many won't even consider us human"[80].

- Since Israel's operation Cast Lead in Gaza (2008-9), the Israeli-Turkish relationship has suffered dramatically. This can be seen in the cancellation of joint military exercizes, the rise of pro-Palestinian television programming in Turkey and various diplomatic crises, including Prime Minister Erdogan's walkout in Davos and the flotilla incident. That policy was shaped by Foreign Minister Davutoglu, who had published in April 2001 his book, well before the rise to power of the AKP, where he had outlined his anti-Israel sentiments, declaring that a Jewish Israel is not suitable to the Middle East, and emphasizing differences between anti-Semitism and anti-Zionism. As the mastermind of neo-Ottomanism, he argued that Israeli-Turkish relations undermined the implementation of Turkish responsibilities derived from the Ottoman past. He accused the Armed Forces of adopting an Israeli-oriented for-

---

[80] Tlin Daliglu, "Turkish Intelligence Service Targets Jewish Population", *Al-Monitor* 19 December, 2012.

eign policy after the soft coup of 1997 when Erbakan was removed from politics and his Islamic party banned.[81]

• In February, 2009, after harsh and constant international criticism surrounding the Davos Summit incident of January 2009, in which Erdogan raised international outrage for walking out on Shimon Peres, Istanbul hosted the "Victory in Gaza" Summit where 200 Arab and European Sunni Sheikhs and clerics, including members of the Hamas which had been repeatedly declared an "International terrorist group" by the US, and they declared *Jihad* on Israel and support for the Hamas terrorists.

• In October, 2009, the Israeli Foreign Ministry protested against Turkey over the state-run TRT-1 TV Channel's program: "Separation: Palestine in Love and in War", that falsely and deliberately portrayed Israeli soldiers as intentionally murdering unarmed civilians in Gaza, in complete denial of the massive rocket attack by the Hamas on Israeli towns which had necessitated Israel's incursion in the first place in order to silence the rocket launchers. Two years later, when during the Syrian civil war a stray-rocket hit Turkish territory, Ankara threatened a war if that should be repeated. Namely, for Turkey it is not the shooting that matters and justifies response, but who shoots: by Arabs, it is always right, except if on Turkish territory; by Jews, it is always wrong, even if in self-defense.[82]

• According to a poll conducted in 2009 by Istanbul's Frekan Research, 42% of the Turks declared that they would not want

---

[81] *The Jerusalem Review*, 3 October, 2012.
[82] Ibid.

a Jewish neighbor. In 2012 (after the *marmara*) that percentage rose to 54%.

- The relations between the two countries suffered the most severe blow over the September 2011 UN Palmer Report, which stated that the blockade on Gaza, which was the excuse for the Turkish flotilla, was legal. As a thug mimicking his Prime Minister, Davotoglu rejected the UN Report, reiterating that the blockade was illegal and that his country's intervention was in order, and issued sanctions against Israel, stating that he would be forced to back down over his lenient policies. He forgot that the times of the Ottoman Middle Eastern bully were gone, and that Israel could stand by its position without submitting to threats.[83]

- A teachers union in Turkey initiated legal action over the distribution of a series of books for primary school pupils, describing Charles Darwin as a Jew, with a big nose, who kept the company of monkeys (as in the Qur'anic tradition) and other historical figures of anti-Semitism. The books were distributed to 1,000 children in Istanbul, though the authority which approved them denied any knowledge of their content. Another book on Albert Einstein described him as "filthy and slovenly". The book on Darwin said that the proponent of natural selection "had two poblems: first he was a Jew; second, he hated his prominent forehead, big nose and misshapen teeth… He threw nuts to monkeys at the zoo rather than go to school [a minor detail: Darwin was not Jewish…, but that is not the most terrible lie concocted to humiliate Jews in Turkey].[84]

---

[83] Ibid.

[84] Daniel Dombey and Funja Guler, "Turkish book on Darwin Sparks Outrage", 19 October, 2012 www.ft.com/cms/s/0/f27adba8-1a01-11e2-a179-00144feab-dc0.html#axzz2A3AovbTy

It was also reported that as a member of the banned Islamic Party in 1993, Recep Erdogan had made a speech where he said:

> Zionists, what are they afraid of? America does not like my leader [Erbakan at the time], the West does not like him either. There is nothing more meaningful than the declaration of one's enemy. Thus, he [Erbakan] said, the ones they hate, I must love…[his stated hatred for the Jews and their likening to 'bacteria', does not exactly corroborate this statement, which is, on the contrary evidence of the double talk of Islamic Party in Turkey and elsewhere].[85]

In fact, already in October, 2009, some AKP insiders told the British *Guardian* what had been in evidence for years, namely that the Turkey-Israel strategic alliance was over. When Erdogan was asked about Ahmadinejad, he replied: "There is no doubt he is our friend". That friendly approach was reciprocated by Tehran, when the Iranian President expressed his admiration for Erdogan, praising his decision to ban Israel from a planned NATO maneuver in protest of Operation Cast Lead.[86] Another way in which Erdogan encouraged anti-Semitism was his backing to radical Islamic papers like *Vakit* (which was banned in Germany due to its anti-Semitic content), and to anti-Israeli television programs, such as "the Valley of the Wolves" that were approved by the Turkish censor. Turkish journalists have confirmed that the editorial policy of their papers was dictated by government bodies, that journalists' phones and offices were wiretapped, that pressure was applied on the owners of

---

[85] "Erdogan's anti-American and Antisemitic rant in 1993, lifted from Israeli Channel 10 broadcast on 18 March, 2010.

[86] Robert Tait, "Iran is our Friend, says PM ERdogan", *the Guardian*, 26 October, 2009.

major media outlets to conform and that tight supervision was exercized on Internet sites[87]. Leaked US cables suggested that Erdogan was an Islamic fundamentalist who hated Israel. In 2009, James Jeffrey, the US Ambassador in Ankara, reported that his Israeli counterpart blamed Erdogan personally for the worsening relations with Israel. The Turks tried to convince the Israeli Envoy that Erdogan's public criticism of Israel was only for "domestic consumption" to placate his Islamic radicals, but at any rate, it showed his hostility towards Israel and it caused the irreparable damage that it caused.[88]

Erdogan's one track-mind of only blaming Israel on the one hand, and denying that any Muslim can do any wrong, on the other, was reflected in his scandalous denial of the Darfur massacre and his exoneration of Umar Bashir, the President of Sudan, who has been a fugitive from the Hague International Court. He said that he had visited Darfur and saw "no evidence of genocide" while hundreds of thousands were massacred by the Sudanese *Janjaweed*; and at the same time, without visiting Gaza, where most of the thousand Palestinian fatalities were sustained as a result of fighting, he saw "massacres and extermination". He also outrageously claimed that Bashir was innocent, the rationale being that "a Muslim can never commit genocide. That is not possible"[89], ignoring his own country's history with the genocide of Armenians during W W I, his own onslaught on hundreds of Kurdish villages in Anatolia, and the wide-ranging daily killings of civilians across the Islamic world : Syria, Libya, Yemen, Afghanistan, Iraq, Pakistan and Mali. Erdogan knew what was happening there, but lying without

---

[87] Barak Ravid, " Israel accuses Erdogan of inciting anti-Semitism, *Ha'aretz*, 26 January, 2010. That was before the Marmara incident of May, 2010, so it could not be the reason, just a pretext.

[88] James Bone, "Turkey Denies anti-Semitic stance in wake of leaked documents", *The Times, 30 November, 2010.*

[89] Maayana Miskin, "Erdogan: Israel worse than Sudan, Muslims do not cause Genocide", 8 November, 2009
www.israelnationalnews.com/news/news.aspx/134297#.ULQrSGdryCk

blinking in order to protect the reputation of Muslims is considered in his culture more favorably than the truth.

Another blatant lie from the mouth of Erdogan, was reported in the Saudi *al-Watan* in March, 2010 as he was criticizing Israel's national heritage and saying that the Cave of the Patriarchs in Hebron and Rachel's Tomb near Bethlehem "were not and never will be Jewish sites, but Islamic sites"[90]. That gratuitous statement occurred several months before the Flotilla incident of May 2010, so that could not have been caused by any Israeli "provocation". It was reported that while in prison for his anti-religious incitement, he read history; but he apparently did not read or internalize enough the history he would continue to ignore all his life. Had he read it, he would have learned that Jews had lived for a millennium in the Holy Land and sanctified its holy sites some two millennia before his Turkic forefathers had come as nomadic conquerors from Central Asia and taken over the Anatolian plateau in the late Middle Ages, obliterating the Christian Byzantine Empire that had existed for a millennium before them, and turning its churches into mosques. He also lied blatantly when in an interview in June 2010, this time after the *Marmara* incident, as he was furiously upset about Israel, denying the 8,000 rockets that had been showered on Israel by the Hamas and caused the Israeli incursion into their territory in the first place.[91] Little did he know then that two years later, during the Syrian civil war, he would threaten a war with Syria just because one stray bomb fell in his territory. In November, 2012, Erdogan described Israel as a "terrorist state" when it retaliated against Gaza again for its relentless and unprovoked bombing of Israeli cities and villages which spread terror among Israeli civilians. His excuse was simple: "Those who associate Islam with terrorism close their eyes in the face of mass killing of Muslims, turn

---

[90] "Rachel's Tomb was never Jewish", *Jerusalem Post, 7 March, 2010.*
[91] Charlie Rose, "Turkish PM Erdogan: Hamas Rockets is a hoax", 28 June, 2010 www.youtube.com/watch?v=Ptwir8pCnBU

their head from the massacre of children in Gaza", as he told a conference of the Eurasian Islamic Council in Istanbul. "For this reason, I say that Israel is a terrorist state, and its acts are terrorist acts", he added, while accusing Israel of "ethnic cleansing in Gaza".[92]

This anti-Israeli and anti-Semitic stand by Erdogan and his party largely reverberates through the Milli Gorus movement, created by Erbakan in Turkey way back and disseminated throughout the Turkish diaspora in Europe, notably in Germany where three million of them have taken root and established their *Milli Gazette* where they spread an anti-Western and anti-Semitic message, and urge the Islamization of society and the overthrow of the secular trappings of the Turkish regime. They attribute sovereignty to Allah alone and predict the establishment of a new Islamic world order where the hatred against Jews, Erbakan-style, is a central piece. The combination of his Islamic hatred, together with the Nazi-like obsession with Jews, which Turks in Germany may have picked up locally from Neo-Nazis and other extremists of their kind, have turned them into the hot spot of the Muslim Brothers in Europe. According to German scholar Johannes Kandel, the anti-Semitic literature distributed by the Milli Gorus in Europe includes Henry Ford's *The International Jew,* and the infamous *Protocols of the Elders of Zion,* which are sold in the mosques of the movement throughout Germany and Europe. That is the kind of books that Erdogan must have grown up upon in his youth, and has had great difficulties to part with in his adulthood and after his ascent to power. He became involved very early with the Muslim Brothers, maybe appreciating their capacity to endure, and ended up wrecking his relations with Sisi's Egypt by reason of his affiliation with them.

---

[92] *Hurriet Daily News,* 20 November, 2012.

CHAPTER FIVE

The Fiasco in Central Asia

The resurgence of the Muslim nations in Central Asia and the Caucasus following the dismantling of the Soviet Union naturally caused the question to be raised of the future course that these emerging states were to follow. In other words, one wondered whether their long integration into the Russian and then into the Soviet Communist system has lent them a European (though authoritarian) bend or rather, as soon as the yoke of their alien rulers was shaken off, they were likely to revert to their Islamic traditions, from which they had been alienated for decades. Judging from the example of other Islamic societies which had undergone "revolutions" of all sorts, like in the Arab world and in Afghanistan, or a process of modernization under the European aegis, like Algeria, Tunisia and Sudan, the newly emerging Central Asian and Caucasian nations might have been suspected of trekking their way back to Islam. The new states of Central Asia and the Caucasus were indeed looking for a model to follow. On the one hand, they looked up to pre-Erdogan Turkey which ethnically, linguistically and culturally was close to them, maybe with the exception of the Tajiks who are Iranians, to provide an example of both a secular-minded country in the tradition of Kemal Ataturk, developing in close collaboration with the West; but on the other hand the fiery model of Islamic revolution in nearby Iran, which proceeded in spite of the West, carried a tremendous appeal to radical Muslims. What track would they choose?

The new horizons opened to those countries were conditioned not only by the existence in their immediate vicinity of fundamentalist Iran but also by the recent victory of the *Mujahidin* in nearby Afghanistan which had also just emerged from a long struggle with, and a virulent challenge to, the Soviet ideological and military machine. Afghanistan had common borders with some of these new republics and it maintained strong informal links with certain Muslim elements in them during all those years of conflict with Moscow. The question was whether the common experience of the Afghans and the other Central Asian nations, in addition to their religious and ethnic attachments, would permit the spillover of the new mood in Kabul into its adjoining neighbors? Iran bordered with Azerbaijan, and Ashkhabad, the capital of Turkemenistan, is only 40 kms away from the Iranian border. Afghanistan also bordered with pivotal Uzbekistan and problematic Tajikistan. Because Afghanistan also borders on Iran, it provides the only territorial continuum between various contenders in the Middle East for access into the landmass of Central Asia. Iran also borders on the Caspian Sea, which gives it a unique position of naval access to Azerbaijan, and also a sea route to Turkemenistan and Kazakhstan further to the north. The much invoked Pan-Turkic Alliance centered on Turkey may therefore be easily balanced, by the Caspian Alliance boosted by Iran, or a radical alliance bringing together Iran and Afghanistan in immediate territorial proximity with the rest of Central Asia. The question stood: Who will prevail.

Not all countries of Central Asia carry the same weight. Kazakhstan, the largest of them in territory, had a population of some 17 million, a sizeable portion of whom (perhaps 40% were neither Kazakh nor Muslim, but original European settlers, Russian or otherwise, who have made an impact on the cultural and economic life of the country over the previous decades. The Kazakh constituted no more than another 40% of the population while the rest were Muslim non-Kazakh minorities. Kazakhstan was also the only place in Central Asia sheltering an arsenal of nuclear weapons and space program facilities which increased its strategic value. Oil discoveries also made it attractive to various eager Western investors. Uzbekistan, the most populated (some 20 million) is also by far the most anchored in Islamic history and symbolism. Its great Islamic centers of Bukhara, Tashkent and Samarkand have no rival in any other place in Central Asia. Its polulation is over 70% Uzbek, which lends ethnic near-homogeneity to it in the long run. It used to be the major cotton producer of the Soviet Union, but due to severe land and water pollution, it suffered from long years of irrational exploitation of those resources, and was crying for a reordering of its priorities.

Kyrgyzstan, Tajikistan and Turkemenistan were poor, and their populations did not exceed four or five million each. However, while the Tajiks were Iranian ethnically and linguistically, the others were Turkic. In all three the indigenous population constituted more than half the total, which contributed to their ethnic near-uniformity and stability, in spite of the far from negligible minorities in their midst. Azerbaijan was quite another problem: It was Turkic like most of the rest, but its population was Shi'ite, unlike all the rest, especially that exactly then the deep Shi'ite-Sunnite rift began to yawn in the entire Middle East. It had a population of some 8 million and a substantial production of oil, but it was plagued by an ethno-religious strife and controversy, an Armenian enclave within Azeri territory, countered by the Azeri enclave of Nakhichevan in Armenian territory. What is more, since most Azeris live on both sides of the Iranian border, they have always raised the suspicion and threat to Iran's stability, conjuring up a "greater Azerbaijan" notion that can only be unsettling for

Teheran.[93] In this maze of ehthnic, religious, linguistic, factional, communal and economic diversity, strife is almost inevitable. In their orientation toward the Middle East the new states had to determine what elements were to shape their fate, for if ethnicity and language prevailed, then Turkey would lead the competition, but if religious radicalism gained primacy, then Iran might be better positioned; and if economic development and free enterprise cut through all these leanings then perhaps large money holders, such as Saudi Arabia or Iran and the Gulf States might play the preponderant role.

The stakes were high and to no small measure defined by the way the Soviet Union had been gradually dismantled in three steps like the layers of an onion, where the outermost layer peeled off first, namely the countries of Eastern Europe (the Warsaw Pact) and Afghanistan and Mongolia, which did not belong in the Soviet Union and were "only" practically part of its political and military empire. Then the Union of the 15 republics (USSR) fell apart, with its constituting "republics" becoming associated in the loose and transitional confederation of the CIS. Then the turn of the innermost Russian Federation itself came, with Tatars, Chechens, Ingosh and others, Muslims and non-Muslims, seeking to self-determine themselves in order to survive the emerging political chaos. Confronted with these new political developments, the Muslim republics of Central Asia had been tormented by existential problems of self-definition, orientation and alignment in search of a course to charter. The Russian north being alien in terms of culture, religion, language and holding no promise in terms of economic development and political stability, these new republics, reluctant to embrace the unenviable Communist model of China to the east, at

---

[93] For the basic data, see: "Report from Turkestan", *New Yorker*", 6 April, 1992; "La Grande Turquie", *Valeurs Actuelles*, 27 January, 1992;Martha Olcott,"Central Asia's Catapult to Independence",*Foreign Affairs*, November, 1992; "Lessons from Central Asia", *US Institute for Peace Journal*, June 1992

a time when the post Mao revolution was still at its prime, could only head south or west, which they did.

The expectation that other Muslims in the Russian Federation might rise as a result of the Slavic culture's xenophobia, only added impetus to the Middle Eastern orientation that these new states were attempting to forge. Instinctively, they were preparing themselves, as it were, as a base of Muslim Central Asian resilience to stave off the potential threat of their northern neighbor, and to succor their fellow Muslims who had remained there after the crumbling of the Soviet Union. In other words, they were reconstituting their eroded onion in a reversed direction: around the nucleus of the core of Islam in the Middle East, they were forming a second layer of their own, and envisaging to crystallize a third stratum from whatever Muslim minority might fall off the Russian Federation, like the turbulent Chechens who were not only brewing in rebellion but had also sent their tentacles to other areas of Muslim conflict, such as the Bosnia War (1992-5), and in the future also Iraq and Syria. As to the course to be followed, the choices were many as some of these options looked attractive due to their association with the West, while others were attracted by the Turkish model (the Kyrgyz President called Turkey the region's Morning Star).[94] But some Muslim elements in those countries would rather follow in Iran's footsteps. They looked at growing democracies, like Turkey and Israel, but they were better able to understand the authoritarian regimes of the rest of the Middle East, which were much closer, structurally and functionally, to what they had been accustomed over the years of the centralized Communist system. Rich countries, like Saudi Arabia, Iran, and Iraq seemed the best objects of courtship in order to obtain the funds they needed desperately, but the *savoir faire* of the resourceless Turkey and Israel

---

[94] " Central Asia: The Silk Road Catches Fire", *The Economist*, 26 December 1992- 8 January 1993' p. 80. See also *Newsweek*, 3 February, 1992, p.20

loomed as perhaps more promising in the longhaul. Isolated Iraq or Iran may have seemed as good examples of lonely survivers against all odds, but the conduits to Europe and the US that Turkey and moderate Arab countries (and for that matter Israel) could provide may have seemed more attractive to the new nations of Central Asia.

For all those reasons, one could observe those Muslim republics hesitating and meandering, sometimes pursuing what seemed to us as contradictory courses. In fact, they explored the reality first, then responded by trial and error to combinations of alternatives which seemed to them the most promising at a particular moment. The choices offered to them revolved around three sets of rivalries which had evolved simultaneously in the Middle East vis-à-vis Central Asia:

1. The competition between Turkey and Iran, which was by far the most potent and important, and also expressed the two poles of modernity-cum-Islam, on the one hand and an Islamic revolution on the other; naturally, Israel, with the encouragement of her allies and partners, Turkey and the US, weighed in on Ankara's side, believing in pre-Erdogan Turkey that the latter's successes would be her own too.

2. The rivalry between Iran and the Arabs, where the US also supported her moderate Arab allies, in an attempt to keep Central Asia from radicalizing; and, to a much lesser extent,

3. The contest between the Arabs and Israel, which consisted in the main in the Arabs trying to block and undo whatever Israel succeeded to achieve in her bilateral relations with those countries.

Arab countries, which have emerged from the Gulf War of 1991 as America's allies, found themselves threatened on the morrow of the war by radical Islam which posed an imminent danger to their regimes. For those countries, like Saudi Arabia, the Gulf States, Syria, Egypt and North African states (where not incidentally the Arab Spring was to erupt a decade later), it had become desperately imperative and urgent to arrest the sweep of Islam lest their own regimes might be submerged under its tide. For after the success of Islam in the Sudan and its near success in Jordan and Algeria, they knew that they were next in line, unless they did something to stem it. An Islamic takeover in Central Asia, under Iran's helm, would directly contribute to the contagious spread of fundamentalism into their own countries. This was all the more feared in light (or obscurity) of the Muslim *Mujahideen* takeover in Afghanistan, where pro-Iranian factions were strong contenders for power, and Tajik Shah Mas'ud was hailed in neighboring Tajikistan as a hero[95].

Saudi Arabia, using its huge resources and religious influence, has heavily invested in mosques, copies of the Qur'an, dormitories for Muslim visitors in Samarkand, a center of Islamic studies in Tashkent, religious teachers in Dushanbe and even word processors in Arabic for Tajikistan. The Islamic Bank based in Saudi Arabia has also pledged financial assistance to Tajik religious students. According to one report, while in 1989 there were merely 18 mosques in all Tajikistan, some 2,000 more have sprouted since. Mosque building was pursued with great momentum in other republics as well. Saudi Arabia, which had supported for years Afghan *Mujahideen* (when they fought against the Soviets), like Gulbuddine Hikmatyar, found itself trying to wrest influence from pro-Iranian elements in these republics, perhaps defeating itself in the process. For the Saudis, unlike the Turks, were not providing a secular and modern alternative of Muslim radicalism to Islamic rule, but an anti-Iranian brand of Muslim fundamentalism which might ultimately backfire

---

[95] FBIS-SOV-92-OSS; FBIS-SOV-92-062.

on them[96].Finding themselves on opposite sides a decade later, with Saudi Arabia on the Western side and in deep rift with Erdogan's rule, while Ankara had shifted to side with Iran, all those fears and evaluations have evaporated like morning dew drops in the desert sun. Other Arab regimes, such as Egypt and Syria, were trying the secular/economic track in this regard, following in the Turkish footsteps, before they ironically quit due to Cairo's new alignment with the Saudis and against the Turks, and to Syria sinking in her deep civil war troubles. In March, 1992 Syria's foreign minister visited these republics and signed cultural and economic accords with them and even offered to mediate in the Nagorno Karabakh crisis, hailing the view that his country "has always stood for a peaceful settlement of all conflicts " (don't we know?) In early 1992 the Egyptians mounted a major trade exhibit in Baku, but the emphasis of the Arab countries remained in the cultural and religious domains[97]. Muhammed Sadiq, the Chief Mufti of Tashkent, had been educated in Libya, while in the border region of Ferghana which is inhabited by Tajiks, Uzbeks and Kyrgyz, the local mullah was said to be Wahhabi- trained and Saudi-paid, which is supposed to lend a conservative Islamic flavor to local Islam. In the Valley of Ferghana, women were observed wearing the veil more than anywhere in the Islamic republics.[98]

As to Azerbaijan, President Aliyev visited Turkey in March 1992, to counter the crowds who had appealed to join Iran earlier that year. In early 1992 the Egyptians mounted a major trade exhibit in Baku, hoping to draw that rich country in oil to the Western orbit. Judging from the wealth and warmth of the relations that developed between Jerusalem and Baku since then, it seems that this has been the most stunning success that Israel has marked in her evolving link with Central Asia and the Caucasus, and this needs to be

---

[96] *Newsweek*, 3 February, 1992.

[97] Ibid.

[98] *New Yorker, op. cit.*

acconted for. Indeed, surprisingly enough, all the newly emerging Muslim republics of Central Asia and the Caucasus established diplomatic relations with Israel, though for lack of funds some of them did not open their embassies immediately. It was surprising because apart from Turkey and Egypt, the rest of the Islamic world continued to boycott Israel and to alienate itself from it. However, when one considers the potential appeal of Israel to these new nations, one is struck by the prospects, aside from the fact that these nations had been so secularized under Communism that Islam had been noticeably sidelined there in domestic politics. In effect, any visitor to Baku the morrow of the "Islamic" takeover of the country, one was stunned when a bottle of vodka was served to one's table in any café house in the city, as a matter of course. Partly, this surprising *rapprochement* is certainly due personally to President Aliyev, whose authoritarian regime permitted him to make the law and to enforce it, after he had fallen for the Israeli model, with a staunch American support. Already in the 2000s Israel had offered assistance in school curricula of Azerbaijan with a view of teaching (inculcating, some would say) a moderate and tolerant interpretation of Islam in the local school system, away from the radicalism that some Shi'ite scholars were trying to preach. The close relationship between the two countries has already produced oil deals from Azerbaijan to Israel, and a reverse track of technology and military hardware from Israel to Baku. Having been deprived of the Turkish airspace for military training, there are reports that Israel is permitted to use Azerbaijan's for that purpose. There were even never-confirmed reports about Israel possibly scheming to use some of its air "base"s in Azerbaijan for its eventual air strike against Iran, if the latter did not desist in time from developing its coveted nuclear arms. Baku and Alyev must be acting out of a straight jacket, realizing that they border on their formidable Iranian neighbor, who cannot accept passively Israeli meddling in the vicinity of its territory, in a country though Turkic-speaking follows the Shi'ite creed, and at a time when a mortal enmity exists between the two factions of Islam. When these relations started under the pre-Erdogan's governments of Turkey, they were acceptable to Israel's allies in Ankara, such as Ozal, Demirel, Ecevit and Ciller, but since Erdogan, he must be furious at what his country had allowed to happen between Israel and Azerbaijan. At any rate, Baku stands as a model for Central Asia of how far relations with Israel can get them, for the following reasons:

1. Most of the emerging new of states are small in population and in size, and they must be attracted by the model of a small but relatively successful state in the political,diplomatic, economic, industrial, technological, agricultural, scientific and military domains.

2. The stability of Israel's regime and its democratic nature must offer some hope to these new nations that by adopting certain socio-political means; by adapting to the technological and scientific environment of the modern world, and by internalizing certain values of modernity and progress, even a small and resourceless country like Israel can make it into the 21st century.

3. Israel is considered by third world countries, rightly or wrongly, as a sure conduit to the US and the West in general. Emerging nations (except if they are Muslim), who seek development and foreign investment, have usually established diplomatic relations with Israel as soon as they shed their doctrinaire third world ideology and adopted pragmatic policies. There was no reason to exclude the Central Asian nations from this rule.

4. Israel has a tremendous knowhow to share in the fields of water and land conservation, farming technology and devel-

opment of arid areas, and many of those countries have already benefited from that expertise, except for the Arab countries which prefer to cultivate their hatred and boycott of Israel over needing her help in developing their dwindling agricultural resources. Devastated Uzbekistan and Kazakhstan, following the many years of the monoculture which polluted their land and water, would have been of much need of Israel's prowess in these fields. So would be the poor nations of Kysgyzstan, Turkemenistan and Tajikistan, which might adopt, and some have already done so, some of Israel's advanced technologies.

5. In Kazakhstan vast Israeli investments in farming have already born fruit, as do some high-tech enterprises where Israel excels.

It turns out that the question of Islam apart, when not interfering with rational and practical measures of development for the benefit of the masses, no country can provide a sufficiently strong incentive in the practice of pragmatic policies in Central Asia and the Caucasus to hamper the evolving relationship between them and Israel. By contrast the Arab states which are attempting to foil Israel's rapprochement to these new Islamic entities, provide no positive alternative to succor Central Asian plights. Of course, Saudi Arabia and other rich Arabs could provide funds and Imams to these countries, but most of these contributions merely underline the common heritage of the Muslims on both sides that are hardly of significance as far as economic development is concerned. Nonetheless, many of the regimes in these republics are wary not to rouse local and outside Muslim tempers against their sympathetic approach to Israel, and they adopt a rather low profile in this regard. With the Arabs, these republics engage in lip-service statements about their common patrimony. During the (pre –civil war) visit of the Syrian Foreign Minister to Tajikistan [99], in 1992, his hosts stated their support to "Syria's struggle to regain all occupied Arab territories and to implement all UN resolutions". But beyond this kind of generalities, it is doubtful whether the Tajiks or other Central Asians are eager to embroil themselves with Middle Eastern politics that they ill comprehend. But it remains possible that if any of those countries should succumb to Islamic radicalism of one sort or another, the policies might change overnight, like in Iran, towards anti-Israeli virulence.

With the ascendance of Erdogan to the Turkish helm since 2002, all those ground rules, policies and calculations had to be revised. For Erdogan has set new policies that have challenged all the existing assumptions, and in so doing his country has practically ceased serving a model to Central Asia, and his Pan-Turkic ambitions may have irretrievably sunken into oblivion since those republics have come of age, acting more each to its interest and watching the growing power of Vladimirr Putin to the north, with his neo-imperialistic designs taking shape in the Ukraine and Crimea and in the Middle East (especially Syria). For Erdogan has changed the map of Turkey and of world politics in more ways than one:

1. He altered Turkish society by Islamizing it, returned to the "Islamic dress" for women and legalized it in the public square, seeking to be an example to be emulated by other lands of Islam. He also shifted the center of gravity of his political base from the cities to the countryside, imposed an authoritarian regime under his Presidential aegis and debased all the potential opposition to his rule (Fethullah Gulen, polititicians, journalists, academics, the military, the Kurds and government officials).

---

[99] *Haaretz*, 16 June, 1992; 16 January, 1992; and 13 April, 1992.

2. Having been shunned by the EU and gone into vocal rifts with the Trump Administration and with NATO, he changed his orientation to his new tri-partite alliance with Russia and Iran, ostensibly on the question of Syria but in practice on all arising issues between them. In one stroke then, he eliminated both the Turkish and the Iranian models from the purview of the Central Asians, while associating with the redoubtable Putin whose imperialistic designs, they fear, might be directed against them next.

3. The old and reliable ally- Israel, whose promotion had been encouraged in Central Asia by the civil governments of Ozal, Demirel and their civil successors, has now become anathema for Erdogan. While for him it was political to reverse his politics overnight, and to ally with other powers which similarly had no compunctions about abandoning allies and partners, for the Central Asian states which have cultivated over the years a useful and beneficial relationship with Jerusalem, it will not be easy or useful to reverse themselves.

4. Democratic Turkey having died with Erdogan, and due to his association with other authoritarian regimes like Russia and Iran in support of his style of rule, it is likely that the more he shifts toward them, the more the Central Asian governments will hold on to their present governments which in effect constitute a continuity to the defunct Communist rule. Since the coveted Turkish model of democracy with moderate Islam has been buried by Erdogan, and the Central Asians no longer have a model to emulate, it is likely that they will have to preserve what they have rather than embark on the abortive Turkish model. Paradoxically, only as long as the present regimes can impose their authoritarian rule, can they also ensure the existing balance between ethnic and

Islamic identity in their countries, namely between the Turkish and Iranian models, the Arabs and Israel, and a pragmatic course of development. For if any of them should go Islamic, the choices could embrace Erdogan's model of Islam and modernity with an anti-Western and anti-Israeli bias.

5. Unlike great Western powers which usually condition their aid to third world nations on respect for human rights, Israel is so small and insignificant internationally, and itself often the object of such accusations by Arabs and other abusers of human rights, that the assistance it tends to others can never hinge on any conditions. Israel is happy to help and do business with any country and all regimes, so it is never likely to pose conditions or to put on probation the countries it deals with.

6. Erdogan's choice to quarrel with moderate Arab countries, like Egypt, the Gulf States and Saudi Arabia, with which Israel maintains good contacts under the table, and to associate with the most fervent supporters of the Muslim Brothers, like Qatar and Hamas, is channeling him to a course which can only alienate him further from the Central Asian rulers who fear the same radicalism in their countries.

When Ankara named 2012 as a Year of Chinese Culture in Turkey, versus the Year of Turkish Culture in China[100], that was a sign of the expansive cultural ambitions of Erdogan's Pan-Turkism into the Uyghur-Turkic region Xinjiang in northwestern China, at least in terms of influence, in view of the growing distance that the other Central Asian nations have taken from his brand of Islamic

---

[100] Yitzhak Shihor, "Turkey and China in the Post Cold War World :Great Expectations," in: Bruce Gilley and Andrew O'Neil (Eds.), *Middle Powers and the Rise of China* (Georgetown University Press, 2014), pp. 192-212.

Turkism. Ankara's offer of a substitute homeland, shelter and base of operation to a number of Uyghur leaders on the eve of Xingjiang's "liberation" by China in 1949, and Turkey's asylum to Uyghur nationalism ever since until the 1990s, had gone hand in hand with the pre-Erdogan Turkish governments which had cultivated the link to Central Asian countries. That state of affairs had afflicted Cold War-inflicted China with the paranoia that Washington had been concocting with Turkey: about the Middle East which sheltered and schemed subversion inside China by its "fifth column" Uyghurs. It was Erdogan's far-reaching reforms in Turkey which attracted China's attention, although Beijing was less than enthusiastic about his Islamization program. When Vice President Xi Jinping visited Turkey in 2012 and identified it as an important emerging market, which strove to grow into one of the top world economies by 2023, Erdogan represented for him a model for Middle Eastern and Central Asian countries, precisely at a time when he had effected the reforms which pleased China but alienated Central Asia from that model. After all, it was the authoritarian style of rule adopted by Erdogan, which could not be exactly coveted by any democratic-minded regime, which appealed to the Chinese rulers. Erdogan's rejection of Ataturk's heritage, including a renunciation of Turkish custody on Central Asian Muslims, which reflects Turkey's growing regional and global activism, have been providing the engine of the new Turkish foreign policy in spite of the residual sympathy that the Turks evince toward the Uyghurs in particular and Central Asian Muslims in general.

In 2009, President Abdallah Gul visited China, centering on Urumqi, the capital of the restive Xinjiang region, and that was a great Chinese concession despite Beijing's insistent rejections of the Turkish plea to establish a consulate in place. Maybe an indication of the resentment and unrest that visit raised were the violent riots that broke out there within a week since Gul's departure, which left many dead in their wake. Uncontrollable Erdogan burst in fury as is his wont (not only against Israel which he accuses daily with committing genocide against the Palestinians, making one to wonder how many times can any people survive genocide and still undergo the next)), calling those events "looking like genocide", followed by calls to bycott Chinese goods. Thus, despite the fact that successive Turkish governments had offered shelter and aid to transnational Uyghur organizations worldwide, and promoted their vision of "independence for Turkestan", while China itself took cognizance of the problem only after the Central Asian nations became independent, Turkish authorities arrested in 1999 Uyghur leaders who were involved in violence, leading to a period of collaboration with China on security matters, where Turkey agreed to take measures against anti-Chinese activism in her territory. Shichor locates the shift towards the "eastern orientation" in Turkey's foreign policy in 2012 when Erdogan suggested in jest that Turkey ought to abandon EU efforts if Russia and China allowed it to join their organization for development and security in Central Asia, arguing a year later that the organization was more powerful, better and "we have common values with them… in terms of populations and markets. The Organization significantly surpasses the EU in every way", he said. And so, that organization became a partner to Ankara for dialogue in 2013, a first NATO member to negotiate with SCO (Shanghai Cooperation Organization)[101].

While Ankara had been, before Erdogan, the partner of Israel for the choice of the Turkish model by Central Asia, it became literally its most virulent rival, if one remembers that it was in the context of the Turkish boycott of Israel in 2010 from participating in the traditional Anatolian military Eagle Exercizes, that it invited instead the Chinese military. The fact that the US did not participate in the maneuver, for the first time in protest of Israel's exclusion, was a clear signal to all that Ankara had taken its distance from its staunch

---

[101] Ibid.

Western allies and thrown in her lot with the Russian and Chinese option, a follow up on the 2003 Turkish refusal to allow the Americans to operate from its territory, which would have permitted America to lead the incursion into Iraq on two fronts simultaneously, thereby increasing its speed and decreasing its own losses. The US was thus compelled to ferry its troops around the Suez Canal and channel them for combat through the already congested front of Kuwait. With allies that that, who needed an enemy? Indeed, as soon as the Chinese troops left Turkey, the Chinese Prime Minister rushed to Ankara, and a month later Chinese and Turkish special forces were exercizing together in Turkey counter-terrorism operations, creating the first precedent of Chinese troops operating inside a NATO member-state[102].To the West and to Central Asia the message was loud and clear: Turkey was not in anybody's pocket and its independent conduct was guaranteed to continue; and anti-terrorist exercizes also included potential anti-Uyghur action if and when those rebellious groups continued to threaten Chinese domestic security. No clearer sign was needed to signal Turkey's change of orientation and its further alienation from Central Asia and from Israel on account of its reorientation.

---

[102] Ibid. See also Y.Shichor, "Ethno-Diplomacy: The Uyghur Hitch in Sino-Turkish Relations", *Policy Studies 53,* The East-West Center, 2009, Singapore; and Y. Shichor, "Turkey Trot: Military Cooperation Between Beijing and Ankara", *China Brief,* Vol IX, Issue 8, April 16, 2009, pp. 4-7

CHAPTER SIX

The Mavi Marmara Watershed

The *Mavi Marmara* was an old ship purchased in 2010 by the IHH, a Turkish NGO active as a façade of a charity organization in many countries. It is endorsed by international figures that include South African Archbishop Desmond Tutu and Nobel Peace Prize laureate Mairead Corrigan Maguire, both adversaries of Jews, Zionism and Israel. However, in Europe, it is viewed as a terrorist organization and designated as such by the US due to its links with the Hamas group. Israel has accused the goup of smuggling weapons to terrorist groups and maintaining links with al-Qa'ida. The ship took part in a flotilla operated by activist groups from 37 different countries with the intention of directly confronting the Israeli blockade over Gaza which had been approved by the UN as legitimate. On May 30, 2010, while in international waters and en route to Gaza, Israeli Naval Forces communicated that a naval blockade over the Gaza area was in force and ordered the ships to follow them to Ashdod Port or to be boarded. The ships declined and were boarded in international waters. While reports from journalists on the ship and from the UN report on the incident concluded that the Israeli military opened fire with live rounds before boarding the ship, video evidence demonstrated that fire was opened only after the landing Israeli soldiers were attacked with iron bars and one of them was ejected by the *Marmara* activists from an upper deck to the deck below. In self defense, the Israeli squad killed 9 of the activist passengers who defied the blockade and violently attacked the boarding Israelis. Israel accounted for 10 of its soldiers being injured, one seriously, in stark denial of the ship's activists who insisted that they were sailing to Gaza with "peacedul" intentions. The Israeli government appointed a former Justice, Jacob Turkel, to head a Commission which found both the blockade and the force used by the Israeli soldiers to be legal and proportionate. A Polish authority on admiralty law, Professor Andrzej Makowski of the Polish Naval Academy in Gdynia, also upheld this view in an extensive article in the *Israel Journal of Foreign Affairs* in May 2013.

It was found indeed that The *Mavi Marmara* was a passenger ship and did not carry any humanitarian aid, though other ships (four of the six in the convoy) did carry aid supplies that were unloaded in Ashdod and duly transhipped to Gaza. The Israeli government decided to release the three ships of the Gaza Freedom flotilla, two of which had been moored at the Port of Haifa and the third at the Port of Ashdod since their interception. Three Turkish tugboats were dispatched to bring the ships back to Turkey. As a follow-up to that grievous incident, a coalition of 22 NGOs announced on May 9, 2011, that a second "Freedom Flotilla II" was planned for the third week of June 2011. The IHH said that after the damage caused the previous year to the *Mavi Marmara* ship, it was not in a position to sail again, and nothing came out of that. The incident, which was planned by Turkey to provide an excuse for ravaging its relations with Israel, and at the same time for displaying to the Islamic world its staunch support for Gaza, was in fact a continuation of the same policy line that Ankara had pursued during the first Gaza War (*Cast Lead*, 2008-9), and was exceeded in importance by the political and diplomatic reverberations that ensued. The Turkish Flotilla, which showed much the same pattern of distorting the truth as in the Gaza War, exposed PM Erdogan's determination to make his fraudulent version of events prevail as long as it contributed to the blackening of Israel's face in the world. In both cases he blasted Israel in an aggressive and libelous ways, accusing it of "killing civilians and lying to the media" of the world, at the same time that he was inciting his mobs against his supposedly "strategic ally" and emitting lies and vulgarities worthy of a market place mobster. Once again, as part of the scheme to weaken Israel, lambast it, demonize and delegitimize it, asymmetrical war tactics and lawfare were adopted, and they worked perfectly for those who had planned the provocation to the detriment of Israel, who could not suspect such schemes coming from its "strategic ally", and therefore was not prepared for this latest manifestation of blood libel. However, like in the Gaza War, the truth emerged eventually, but only after the blood libel attached to Israel for its "wanton killing of peace activists on board an innocent civilian ship in international waters" stuck, Israel was condemned internationally, and its relations with Turkey were irreparably damaged. It is now clear that due to its frustration with the Western and NATO alliance, and its shift to the Iranian, Syrian and Hamas camp, as a result of the Islamic policy that his Muslim Party chose to pursue, that this shift in policy was bound to unfold sooner or later. But if he could wade the turbulent era of the change while also attacking Israel, weakening it and disengaging from it, so much the better. Again, the corrupt, distorted and biased UN machinery was used (or abused) to attain the desired effects. A *National Post* editorial revealed this truth with no frills attached:

A report by three UN-appointed human rights experts said that "Israeli forces violated international law when they raided a Gaza-bound aid flotilla killing 9 activists…." With these words did a Toronto newspaper lead off its report on the international community's latest ritual excoriation of Israel…Only later in the article does one learn that these "experts" had been commissioned by the UN Human Rights Council (HRC), a sham organization that is dominated by rogue dictatorships…[and was abandoned by the US in 2018, as a result]

Echoing the debunked propaganda that circulated in the days immediately following the flotilla confrontation, the HRC report presents a black-and-white narrative of marauding Israeli soldiers willfully slaughtering helpless do-gooders. Indeed, the report authors go so far as to denounce Israel's larger campaign to prevent weapons and terrorists from being smuggled into Gaza – even though Gaza's Hamas leaders consider themselves in a state of war against Israel, are holding an Israeli hostage, and repeatedly have used Gaza as a staging ground for rocket attacks against Israel [in spite of the DOP of 1993 which forbade all that]. The HRC could have saved time by dropping the pretense of objectivity and simply asking Hamas to write the report itself [as it almost did for Goldstone which followed the Gaza war]. Fortunately, the report to HRC attracted little attention… because the Council's effort to investigate the flotilla's incident has been superseded by a more credible inquiry launched by Secretary General Ban Ki-moon [the best proof that he himself did not think much of the HRC investigation]. But there is no need to wait for this report, led by former PM Palmer of New Zealand, who will enjoy the collaboration of Israel itself, which properly boycotted the HRC effort [following the Goldstone experience], to know the truth about the flotilla episode.

The Israeli government has released numerous eyewitnesses, film clips showing its commandoes being mobbed and brutalized by flotilla activists who, as we know, from studying their own words, were seeking "martyrdom"… Turkish reporter Sefik Dinc, who was sympathetic to the flotilla militants also pointed to the responsibility of the

Turkish government and the sponsoring Islamic group (IHH) for the crisis. His text and pictures show the Jihadists [those peaceful humanitarians] taking out iron bars and clubs, preparing for battle, beating Israeli soldiers, and trying to throw one of them into the sea. Mr Dinc also reports that Israeli soldiers opened fire only when trying to rescue soldiers taken hostage. His account corresponds in almost every detail with that given by Israel [and exposes Erdogan, not the Israelis, as the effronted liar]. An expert intelligence analysis of Dinc's writings concluded that the IHH operatives and their supporters fired live ammunition as soon as the first soldiers descended from the helicopter. One IDF soldier suffered a knee injury from a non IDF weapon as soon as he came on board the ship… IHH operatives used three weapons taken from the Israelis against other IDF soldiers. It appears that two of them were thrown into the sea, as were one or two non-IDF guns, at least one of which was used to fire on the commandoes descending from the helicopter… All in all, nine activists died on board the flotilla- not as victims of Israeli aggression, [as the Turkish government keeps repeating, and demanding reparations to their families] but as casualties of what we now know to be a violent "martyrdom" operation orchestrated by Israel's enemies[103]

For months this flotilla, around the flag ship *Marmara,* had been prepared in Turkey to break the blockade of weapons to Gaza, by the militant Islamic movement IHH, whose operatives were indoctrinated for Jihad and trained for confrontation with the Israelis. They used truly peaceful and naïve western humanitarians, who

---

[103] *National Post,* 27 September, 2010.

truly wanted to deliver food and medicine to Gaza, knowing that the goods could go to their destination if the cargo were checked first by Israelis. But the IHH on board the ships wished to break the blockade more than it wanted to deliver humanitarian aid. Therefore when prevented to go to Gaza, and having refused to anchor in the Israeli port of Ashdod and let the control of the cargo take place, the *Marmara,* the only one of the ships which refused to heed the order to turn back, was boarded from the air by Israeli commandoes, who were immediately assaulted with iron bars and some of them taken hostage and others thrown into the sea. The Israeli commandoes intervened to rescue their colleagues, resulting in the unfortunate death of 9 IHH operatives and the abortion of the whole "humanitarian" operation. Israel later transported the aid products to Gaza and the recalcitrant militants were repatriated.

But, once again, the blood libel was diffused, misinformation and defamation of Israel gained the headlines, and the unnecessary death of 9 people (some of them had said they were eager to commit martyrdom) afforded the Turks and their allies the opportunity to smear Israel once again. Claire Berlinski, in the September (2010) issue of *Standpoint* described how the overwhelming majority of Turks had no idea what really happened earlier that year (2010) aboard the Turkish *Mavi Marmara* vessel, where an Israeli boarding party enforcing the blockade of Gaza was ambushed in a premeditated attack with knives and iron bars. She canvassed Istanbul, where she lives with a Turkish documentary filmmaker, and interviewed a number of local people about that now-notorious incident. None knew the Israelis acted in self-defense when they shot their attackers. The men and women to whom she spoke were astonished when she told them that Israeli officials had invited the ship to disembark at Ashdod and deliver the aid overland. But they were not disbelieving and importantly, when she old them this, it changed their view. Many spontaneously said that they knew they could not trust what they heard in the news, that the situation confused them and that something about the story just didn't sound right. Unfortunately, few Turks will ever know what really happened that night. The Turkish media reported a grossly distorted version of the events, describing the real attackers as "activists" and the Israelis who fought back as "murderers". Most Turks can't read or speak foreign languages and were therefore unable to learn the truth from newspapers abroad. If that is the way Erdogan and his gang of thugs planned to make themselves, their democracy and their freedoms credible to Europe and the rest of the world, they were deluding themselves.

Erdogan's government will have been used to this sort of cheap propaganda. They had already produced a film where big lies are the main theme. *Kurtlar Vadisi Filistin*, or *Valley of the Wolves: Palestine*, was the sequel to the notorious *Valley of the Wolves: Iraq*, which was released in 2006. The first instalment portrayed American soldiers massacring civilians at an Iraqi wedding party and harvesting the internal organs of prisoners to sell to Israelis. The trailer for the second installment began with an obviously false portrayal of the *Mavi Marmara* incident, and a later scene showed Israeli soldiers shooting more than a dozen handcuffed prisoners in the back. The film's main character is a Turkish special agent who sets out to avenge those killed on the boat by assassinating the Israeli commander in charge at the time, who is cartoonishly outfitted with an eye patch. Our hero acts purportedly for the rights of the oppressed. "It's too bad the story is based on a lie", said Michael Totten, who reviewed the television series. The first film in this libelous series was the most expensive ever produced in the country, and the second was slated to cost even more and to be a big hit. Hopefully, the Turkish documentary filmmaker that Claire Berlinski was working with could push back a little, at least.[104] In any case, this was a

---

[104] Michael J. Totten, *Blood Libel: The Sequel, Commentary blog, 11 November 2010.*

blood libel live on TV, backed by the Turkish government which got deeper and deeper involved to its neck in the lie of defending it. It could not have survived a 15 minute logical debate. Some writers saw in this mode of behavior an emerging pattern in the lawfare against Israel. Trevor Norwitz saw in this emerging pattern an abuse of the instruments of international law to delegitimize and demonize Israel. Referring to the report for the Human Rights Council on the Flotilla, which he suggested to dub the "Guerilla Flotilla" or the "Intifadah Flotilla", he offered some thoughts which cut the HRC into shreds, and would probably cater not much favor with either that institution or with anything connected to the UN:

> The Flotilla Report is the "son of Goldstone", cut from the same cloth, it is a political manifesto masquerading as a fact finding report,... and like all the other anti-Israeli detritus that has come of the UN over the years... It is not susprising that the Flotilla Report looks, feels and smells like the Goldstone report... Hamas leader, Khaled Mash'al, specifically called for the HRC to commission "another Goldstone Report", because Goldstone excoriated Israel and exonerated Hamas... Needless to say, Hamas—along with Hizbullah, al-Qa'ida, Iran and all those other champions of human rights around the world, are simply thrilled with the results of this mission as well. They could not have written it better themselves...The creation of this document, however preposterous, is a perfect example of Lawfare in action: a massive public relations coup ("UN flotilla" gets you 3 million Google hits in one tenth of one second), and a precedent not only against Israel but also against the US and other countries if they try to tackle asymmetrical threats in the future...

> The most important thing to understand about the

flotilla is that it is a political document hinging on the Commissoners' subjective determination of proportionality. Its essential finding is that, since the Israeli sea blockade of Gaza was itself disproportional, namely that it inflicts a disproportionate damage on the civilian population in Gaza in relation to the military advantage sought by Israel, - it was illegal *per se,* so the boarding of the ships was illegal, justifying virtually everything the militants on the ships did to "protect" themselves and their ships, and negating the legitimacy of almost everything the Israelis did [or would do in the future in self-defense]… The whole report then derives from this interpretation and renders Israel's actions illegitimate. But there is no discussion of Israel's reasons for the blockade [the smuggling of prohibited weapons], which would have had an impact of the proportionality argument… The report also gave more weight to the eyewitnesses on the ships who made their hostile reports of Israel to the commission and dismissed the TV clips which showed the physical attacks by the militants on Israeli soldiers, because they did not accord with the eyewitnesses.

So here, like in the Goldstone Report, the two missions refused to investigate the critical facts [and the causes and effects thereof]. Goldstone refused to look at anything but the "evidence" presented by the Palestinians, and made no effort to locate their weapons in schools, hospitals and private apartments [as the Flotilla report disregarded the clips which did not accord with the eyewitnesses' fantasies]. Both reports demonstrate shocking double standards… Today, what is really under attack is the most fundamental value in Western culture – truth. And it is ironic in the extreme that it is the law, which was created and designed to be the servant and protector of the truth, that is the enemy's weapon of choice to undermine the truth… When the so-called human rights organs of the UN are so obsessed with demonizing one country that they make a mockery of the very idea of human rights, and allow real violators to get away with murder and genocide, something is terribly wrong…[105]

Israel and Jews have many enemies, for better or for worse, and even more than that, they have a long trail of people who do not like them, or dislike and despise them in various degrees of intensity. It would be very difficult, nay impossible, to try to analyze in rational scientific terms the irrational phenomenon of Judeophobia, which translates into a virulent anti-Israeli sentiment. However, one must single out Palestinian hostility to the Jews and Israel because, unlike all others who may have their own reasons for their virulence, the Palestinians stand to delegitimize Israel with a view to seeing it vanish and replacing it. Thus, not unlike their Arab and Muslim brethren, they in many ways support their own grievances against Jews and Israel due to their common cultural and historical experiences with the Jews and involvement in the modern Middle Eastern conflict. However, since the Palestinians have the highest stake in their attitudes towards the Jews and Israel, they hold in their hands, to please their whims, the controls of all the conduits to the various modalities of struggle against Israel, according to the fortunes of the conflict and to their vacillating assessment of the chances of attaining a settlement with it. Hence the extraordinary sensitivity of the Israelis towards the measures that the Palestinians might adopt next in their struggle against Israel, which find automatic support in the Arab and Muslim world, including Erdogan's

---

[105] Remarks by Trevor Norwitz, delivered to the Lawfare Project Conference, October 5, 2010.

Turkey, and are constantly imbued with an obsession to undermine Israel's existence, via lawfare, BDS, asymmetrical war, terrorism, "negotiations", propaganda and libel.

In a rarely insightful autopsy of the *Mavi Marmara* incident, Israeli scholar David Kushner[106] offered some remarkable clarifications. He thought that it was Operation Cast Lead (1998-9) which brought the deterioration in the Turkish-Israeli relations to a head just before, and as an immediare trigger to the Gaza Flotilla, which for the first time ever produced a confrontation between the two countries violently in the open seas. It was all the result of Edogan's ambition to place his foreign policy "within a comprehensive ideological framework". He attributes the shift under the AKP rule mostly to domestic issues, notably the inability of the preceding civil governments to plan and run the deep reforms necessary to pull Turkey out of its lethargy and its governmental corruption. In its first mission, AKP proved a great success in promoting the country into the G-20 of the large economies worldwide, but in matters of corruption, that is Erdogan's nepotism and corruption scandals, his promises were not fulfilled. Nonetheless, his peddling of the revival of Islam that he has been marketing widely and successfully, which ensured his hold on successive governments in the country for 15 years in a row (by 2018), together with his democratic game that he maintained through elections and referendums throughout, have guaranteed so far both his popularity domestically, based on his powerbase in rural Turkey, and externally on the visibility of his democratic demeanor, his anti-democratic authoritarian style of government, which won him the title of Sultan, notwithstanding. Erdogan has also capitalized on the widespread disenchantment of the Turks with the West, which they regard as having been less than respectuous towards their stature and their Western proclivities,

---

[106] David Kushner, "Before and Beyond the "freedom Flotilla": Understanding Turkish-Israeli Relations", *The Israeli Journal of Foreign Affairs*, Vol. 4, No. 3, 2010, pp. 21-30.

which have impelled them to seek glory elsewhere, either among their ethnic (Turks of Central Asia) or religious kin (Muslims of other lands).

The result of all this has been Turkey's willingness to adopt positions and policies not altogether acceptable to the US and Europe which have been seen as "betraying her". The most obvious example is that of Iran and Syria, which were considered previously as threatening its security, suddenly becaming close allies; and Russia, against which Turkey had joined NATO and the Baghdad Pact (1955), and had constituted a major component of the "Northern Tier" that was concocted under the Eisenhower-Dulles administration in the 1950s, has unexpectedly become a partner of the tripartite forum Putin-Erdogan-Rohani (and one might also add the new partnership with Beijing) In consequence, Turkey has refused to join the Western regime of sanctions against Iran and as a side-effect has also widened its support to Hamas, in spite of its designation as a terrorist organization by the West. Thus, although Turkey claimed officially that it had no part in the Gaza flotilla Affair, which was all allegedly the initiative and execution of a private charitable organization (IHH), it is evident that without Erdogan's approval no such a dangerous venture which risked an open military confrontation with Israel could have set out of Istanbul. Israel could therefore see that incident as anything but a challenge to its direct security interests and as a plain and intentional Turkish provocation. In consequnce, the debacle of that operation could not have been seen by Turkey as anything but a humiliating failure to its attempt to test Israel's determination in that clash of wills, and an infringement by Israel on the honor and sovereignty of Ankara.

Going into the nitty-gritty of that unfortunate encounter, would reveal the depth and amplitude of the hurt, offense and insult that all Turks have felt and which the Erdogan government have seen as impossible to disregard or swallow without proper retribution. Thus, despite the fact that it was all engineered, managed and aimed by the Turks to hurt Israel, the tide had turned against them and they have become its first victims. A remedy had to be produced to redeem the wounded pride of the nation. For the sight of the Turkish vessel, decorated with a huge Turkish flag, being seized by Israeli troops, and the reported killing of nine Turks, were unbearable for the Turkish public, and abhorrent to their government. The demonstrations launched in Turkey against those events were grounded on both nationalist and religious feelings, and the fierce condemnation of Israel and its conduct was furious and encompassed large strata of the population, AKP and opposition alike. On that occasion, the Turkish government continued to manufacture horror stories against Israel, citing its alleged acts against the Palestinians, which had already been used to stain Israel's previously positive image in public eyes, and had even characterized them as "worse than what was happening in Darfur by the murderous *janjaweeds*", thereby "endangering security in the region". So much so that relatively moderate Abdallah Gul predicted that the Turkish-Israeli relations had gone beyond repair and rehabilitation. The Turks therefore recalled their Ambassador to Israel and advanced a list of outrageous demands of Ankara for "reparations" from Israel, that the latter foolishly accepted under American pressure. But like the famous Jewish story where a Jew in Poland, who was threatened by his Gentile landlord that unless he ate a pound of rotten fish, he would be evicted from his land, he ended up both suffering the stench and revulsion of eating, and then of being deported from the land; or the criticism by Winston Churchill of Neville Chamberlain his predecessor, that in order to save peace in Europe he gave up Britain's honor, but ended up losing both; so did Israel forfeit both by submitting to Erdogan's threats and to Obama's urgings.

Two years after the Gaza operation, which had provided the occasion to both Erdogan to calumniate Israel, and to the infamous Goldstone Report which put the blame on Israel, details started to emerge in the open which debunked both accusations and caused data to be reversed, but never officially mended. For example, exactly as Goldstone himself had reneged on his own report, the author of the Report to Human Rights Council on the flotilla rejected it as a distortion of the reality, thus contributing himself to debunking the pretext on which the flotilla event had been founded in the first place. For the accusation had been floated which blamed Israel for killing 2000 innocent Palestinian civilians, including children, during the Gaza operation, to counter the Israeli claim that the victims included 700 Hamas terrorists, but it was reversed after the full blame was put on Israel and the Goldstone Report was set in stone and became irreversible. Those false claims were so baseless as to annul in retrospect both Turkish calumniations against Israel and the resulting Goldstone Report which was to be rejected by its own author later, together with the pretexts that justified the flotilla operation *a priori*. Two years after the operation, Hamas admitted that 600-700 of its men had been killed in the battle, nearly the 709 reported by Israel from the outset but never accepted by its calumniators and their believers. In an interview with the London-based *Al-Hayat*, Hamas Interior Minister, Fathi Hamad, detailed the heavy price his group had paid during the war:

> They say that it was the people who were harmed in the last war. Are we not part of the people and the nation? On the first day of the war, Israel attacked he police command and killed 250 martyrs from Hamas and other factions. This was in addition to 200-300 members of al-Qassam Brigade [Hamas' military wing] and 150 security personnel. The rest of the fatalities were from among the civilian population.

Hamad also accused Israel of concealing the precise number of

IDF troops during the operation[107]. He must have been convinced that if Hamas concealed his fatalities, Israel must have done the same. Nonetheless, Goldstone must have come to the conclusion that while Israel was credible in the statement of its casualties so that it could be blamed for its "disproportionate" use of force, causing 100 times more the number of casualities than it sustained, the Hamas was less than credible in its body count. And so, the Hamas-Goldstone thesis was sustained that Israel engaged in "wanton massacre" of civilians, while the truth and facts once again fell victim. At any rate, the brilliance with which the Hamas, with vehement Turkish support, led the asymmetrical war and tarnished Israel's reputation with that blood libel, brings to mind what Abba Eban had said of the 1967 War:"That was the first war in history which has ended with the victors [Israel] suing for peace and the vanquished [the Arabs] calling for unconditional surrender". In truth, the disproportion in the number of casualties emanated from totally different and unmentioned reasons:

1. The Israelis used a trained and well equipped army which went to the battle in a full defense gear, and built shelters and missile defense to protect its citizens, which necessarily reduced their casualties, while the Hamas did not allocate any budget for defense, calculating that the more civilian casualties they sustained, the more would Israel be blamed;

2. More Germans were killed in Dresden under British bombing than Britons in Coventry and London under German bombs. Yet, that did not mean that the British were more to blame than the aggressor Nazis. Similarly, prior to the Gaza War, thousands of Hamas bombs and rockets fell in Israeli

---

[107] http://www.haaretz.com/news/diplomacy-defense/hamas-admits-600-700-of-its-men-were-killed-in-cast-lead-1.323776 9 November 2010.

territory, but civilians were protected and the Israeli counter-fire more effective and precise;

3. The Hamas bombed Israel haphazardly, aiming at hurting as many Israelis as possible, but Israel targeted specific military and strategic positions, aiming at reducing the damage and fatalities of the Palestinians. For otherwise, the devastation that could have been visited on them had Israel used even a fraction of its power, could have caused much greater ruin and death;

4. The Palestinians had used civilians on purpose as human shields to man the bombed positions, and to position heavy and forbidden weapon in immune facilities such as hospitals, schools, mosques and UN installations, assuming that Israel would refrain from hurting them, and if it did it could be blamed by the world.

5. Under the Oslo Accords (1993) the Palestinians were not supposed to possess, let alone fire, bombs and rockets in and from Gaza. But once they were smuggled in and used against Israel, it was necessary to eliminate them, and in so doing some people (some innocent, some less) unfortunately paid with their lives.

CHAPTER SEVEN

Throwing in His Lot with the Muslim Brothers and Qatar

We have seen how the poisonous anti-Semitic virulence of the Milli Gorus and Necmettin Erbakan was bequeathed to Erdogan and his Islamic Party and lay at the base of their anti-Israeli policy. Therefore, Erdogan's embrace of the Muslim Brothers and of their financial sponsor- Qatar, should be considered as the natural outcome of this course. For a while, during the brief term of Muslim Brother Muhammad Mursi as the elected President of Egypt (2012-3), Erdogan became one of his fervent supporters, in the hope that a new era under the aegis of Muslim Brothers in the Arab and Islamic worlds was dawning, in which his role as the champion of the Islamic cause would be preponderant. But as soon as the coup of Sisi in Cairo dismissed the elected president, seized power and outlawed the Muslim Brothers as a political movement, the relations between Turkey and the Arab countries which had feared that such an Islamic upheaval might topple their regimes, principally Egypt, Saudi Arabia, the Gulf states, the Republics of Central Asia and the monarchies of Morocco and Jordan, cooled off their attitude towards Ankara. The one exception remained Qatar, where the new and fiery Sheikh, in his attempt to buy an insurance policy that would guarantee the continutation of his absolute rule, elected to sponsor the Brothers rather than boycott them, putting trust in their promise to torment and criticize other regimes in the Arab and Islamic world, except Qatar rulers, for not toeing the Brothers' line, and he enjoyed the guidance of Turkey and the collaboration with Iran in that endeavor. Three potent tools are wielded by the young Sheikh of Qatar which accord him considerable power in his quest to turn his tiny and otherwise insignificant monarchy into a powerful actor in the international Arab and Islamic scenes:

1. A fabulous wealth emanating from the inexhaustible gas reserves which Doha exports in the billions, enable it to invest in other slacking economies such as Turkey, and to pose as the benefactor of Arab and Islamic causes like housing projects for the Palestinians and emerging humanitarian projects which lend the Qatari ruler an aura of generosity;

2. The powerful *al-Jazeera* broadcasting network, which operates from Doha and disseminates in Arabic and English worldwide the messages of that tiny emirate and its support for Muslim Brother causes; and

3. Yussuf al-Qaradawi, the most formidable theologian, ideologue and preacher of the contemporary Sunnite world, lives and operates in and from Doha, and uses the *Jazeera* channels to disseminate Islamic venom, which is enthusiastically listened to and religiously heeded by the entire Sunni-Islamic world. For example, he recently addressed the overwhelming issue of Muslim migration to Europe, and his speech on the topic was broadcast live and in recording in public places throughtout Europe, where he shamelessly urged Muslims to migrate to the West as a fulfilment of their Islamic duty, and argued that Islamic conquest and expansion do not have necessarily to be accomplished by the sword but can be performed "peacefully" via migration. Hearing him thus preaching, can only urge more Muslim millions to head to

Europe and impose on the Europeans a wave of new settlers that would accelerate the "Strange Death of Europe", to borrow the headline of Douglas Murray's title page[108],though his brilliant and scary analysis of Muslim immigration would have better deserved the "Tragic suicide of Europe" title.

Erdogan, as well as his mentor Erbakan, did not reveal a new trend in Islam, nor were they ignorant of the Islamic teachings which for eight decades the Kemalist leadership of Ataturk and his successors had attempted to diminish and sideline. Their trove of knowledge that AKP now activates, in addition to the classic sources of Islam since the time of the Prophet, and the Sunnah that the Turks have jealously adopted upon their migration to Anatolia, is nourished by two main sources: the state Islam that governed the half millennium of the Ottoman Empire, and following its demise in the wake of W W I- the rise of the Muslim Brothers in Egypt who have been attempting, with considerable success, to return Islam, as the state religion, to its glorious past. One could follow step by step the fortunes of the Ottoman Turks as they gnawed from the Byzantine Empire over centuries before they eliminated it, as part of the hailed "Islamic tolerance". Early modern Islamic conquests were marked by the simultaneous expansion of the Ottoman Empire in the Middle East, Central Asia and the Balkans, and of the Moghul Empire, in the Indian Sub-continent. We are talking of two Muslim Empires, ruled by powerful and lasting dynasties, dedicated to the spread of Islam and to the glory of their faith, which had been recognized on both fronts as a universal creed vying for world dominion, and had a considerable record of success to show. But there were also differences, let alone areas of competition between the two Muslim giants, which maybe had prevented them

---

[108] Douglas Murray, *The Strange Death of Europe: Immigration, Identity, Islam,* Bloomsbury, London, 2017.

from integrating, uniting and acting as a world caliphate, a status that the Ottoman rule asserted openly, while the Moghuls perhaps discreetly dreamt about it, while never really trying to implement it. In fact, the Ottomans had started to nibble at the southeastern part of the European continent, beginning with the takeover of the "impregnable fortress" of Constantinople, precisely as Islam was being expelled from its southwestern Iberian Peninsula, while the Moghuls remained confined to their Indian turf. This had generated a bifurcation in the consequences: while the Ottomans were and remained the nemesis of Christian Europe, which they tried to subjugate up to the gates of Vienna, the Moghul Muslims cultivated some sort of hyphenated Hindu-Muslim hybrid identity, which acquired its own characterisrics[109].

The Ottoman Empire, which came to encompass one of the largest territories ever under one rule, was as a matter of fact the result of the disintegration of the first Turkic state of the Seljuks under the Mongol conquest. The latter had increased Persian influence in their territories, including in Asia Minor, and in an attempt to please their Muslim audiences, competed with each other in their manifestation of their devotion to Islam, by building new mosques and *madrasa*s, and manifesting other expressions of their newly adopted victorious faith. The zealous ambience they created, certainly helped to crystallize the Muslim population around religious war (Jihad) against the dwindling Byzantine-Christian rule in Constantinople. Thus, while until 1277 they left the actual government in the hands of the Seljuks, they also ultimately caused its demise, when they took over direct rule in Asia Minor at first, and then, with the waning of the Mongol Ilkhanid rule, local provincial governors became virtually independent, and in the border areas of Anatolia bordering with Byzantium, groups of Turkeman fighters

---

[109] See Marshall Hodgson, *The Venture of Islam,* Vol III, Univ of Chicago Press, 1974, pp. 59ff.

arose, the two most important of them were the Karamanids in the south, and the Ottomans on the Black Sea. These were Turkic tribes which had been pushed westwards from Central Asia due to the Mongolian conquests in the 13th Century. Those newcomers to the Middle East had been Islamized for a while, and had served the Seljuk Rum principalty, which forwarded them to its western frontiers, to confront the Byzantines as *ghazi*s (raiders), in the Holy War that was to bring them to the conquest of the entire Anatolian Plateau and to the establishment of the Ottoman Dynasty.[110] From those local rulers grew Osman Bey (1259-1326) who founded a sultanate in Northwestern Anatolia, which united other local Muslim warlords, like himself, into a greater Muslim state in 1299, headed by his Ottoman Dynasty, which was to last more than 6 centuries (5 centuries encompassing the Empire) under 36 hereditary sultans until 1922.

The subsequent two centuries were the story of aggressive Jihad (or *ghazu* in local parlance), which meant a continuous battle of gnawing at the Byzanzines' lands, Islamizing the conquered territories, and relentlessly driving to put an end to Christian rule in the land; and when achieved, to push on into Europe. The big prize fell into the hands of the 7th Sultan, Mehmet II (1451-1481), who conquered Constantinople (1453), rebaptized it Istanbul, and turned its most prominent churches into mosques, the symbol of Muslim predominance. That won him the prestigious title of *al-Fatih* (literally the Opener, who opened new lands to Islam by Jihad), more readily translated as "The Conqueror", as in those days the conqueror was not viewed as an abject aggressor, but rather as a blessed facilitator of Muslim expansion, in implementation of the Will of Allah, hence the name of his realm:" *al-Dawla al-'Aliya*" (the Sublime Dynasty, later known in Europe as the Sublime Porte).

---

[110] Claude Cahen, *Islam* (Hebrew Translation), Dvir, Tel-Aviv, 1995, pp.405-7; and Haggai Erlich, *Introduction to the Modern History of the Middle East, Vol I (Hebrew)*, Open University, Tel-Aviv, 1987, pp.26ff.

The conquest unfolded under the imperatives of Jihad, to which thousands of Turks flocked to fulfill their Qur'anic obligation, under the illustrious Sultans who led them, from Orkhan (1326-1360) to Mehmet II. But even after the conquest and the establishement of the Ottoman organization of the Empire, the regime pursued a "peaceful" Jihad by either enticing the subjugated Christians to Islamize, which they did in masses, and by transferring thousands of Muslims to the conquered areas that were still inhabited by Christians in Anatolia and in the Balkans, so as to help spread the faith of the Masters[111]. They particularly specialized in the imposition of the *Devshirme* (literally "collection"), which meant to round up young Christian boys in the occupied areas, and send them to Istanbul as "the Sultan's slaves", where they were converted to Islam, and educated to serve in the military and the administration of the Sultan, mostly as part of the Janissary Corps, which became the most devoted and zealous administrative and military arm of the Sultan. In the long run, some of the Slavic families, as well as originally Serbian and Croatian families of the abducted children, were forced or lured to also Islamize, and so the Muslim parts of the Balkans came into being.

In this and other contexts, there developed a mixture of (or a balance between) institutionalized military power, in the shape of regular armies of mercenaries, which the rulers recruited to attain their goals, and the constant input of hordes of volunteers, who acted on their own to fulfill their personal ambition of zealous devotion, or of simply youthful adventurism. This explanation was

---

[111] See Ivo Andric's *The Bridge on the Drina*, Dereta, Beograd, 2011, where this Nobel Prize winning novel recounted in a day to day detail the forced "coexistence" of the ancient occupied Christians, who were constantly lured to convert so as to gain a higher social and political status in their subjugated lands. Muslim Bosnia and its torments of the 20th Century (see R. Israeli and A. Benabou, *The Bosnia War (1992-5)*, Strategic Books, Tx, 201

elaborated upon in Jean-Paul Charnay's *L'Islam et la Guerre*[112]. Brockelman before him had pointed out[113] that while local Turkic warlords had each used their private armies in their internal bickering, in which external allies were occasionally invited to take one side or the other, in the frontier lands the old *ghazi* (or Jihadi) ideals were revived from time to time, headed by religious leaders, resuscitating the idea of Jihad against the Byzantines. To be a *Ghazi* was a virtuous title, as Orkhan, the second sultan of the Ottomans, inscribed in his mosque at Bursa in 1334: "sultan, the son of the Sultan of the *ghazi*s...hero of the world", the way his father, Osman (the founder of the Dynasty) had had his sword girded around him by his father in law Sheikh Edebali, as *ghazi*, and as later Ottoman sultans in Istanbul were girded round with the sword of Osman, by the imam of the Mosque of Ayyub on the Golden Horn, and so invested with their rank. For, indeed, after Osman had resumed the war against Byzantium, "*ghazi* volunteers poured in to him from all parts of Anatolia and from the most variegated Turkish tribes"[114]. Down into the 1930s two King Ghazi' s reigned in Arabia and in Iraq, a token of the lingering symbolic power of that term, which in modern parlance has been replaced by *Jihadis* or fighters for Islam (the Path of Allah).

At any rate, when we get to the end of the Ottoman Empire, and the diminishing role of Jihad in international Islamic affairs, the issue of Jihadi fighters will acquire a totally different face. According to the analysis offered by E. Rogan[115], it was under pressure from its ally Germany, that the Ottoman Empire declared a *jihad* shortly after entering the First World War. The move was intended to incite

---

[112] J.P. Charnay, *L'Islam et la Guerre*, Fayard, Paris, 1986, especially Chap 3 "Le Combattant MUsulman entre la Puissance et la Vertu" pp.223- 296.

[113] Carl Brockelmann, *History of the Islamic Peoples*, Capricorn NY, 1960. Pp 259 ff

[114] Ibid, p. 260.

[115] E. Rogan., "Rival jihads: Islam and the Great War in the Middle East, 1914–1918". *Journal of the British Academy*, 4, pp.1-20.

Muslims in the British, French and Russian empires to rebellion. Dismissed at the time and since, as a 'jihad made in Germany', the Ottoman attempt to turn the Great War into a holy war failed to provoke mass revolt in any part of the Muslim world. Nonetheless, as German Orientalists predicted, the threat of this rebellion (particularly in British India) was enough to force Britain and its allies to divert scarce resources away from the Western Front to the Ottoman front. Britain's deepening engagement in the Middle Eastern conflict, across the four years of World War I, can be attributed significantly to its resolve to combat the threat of *jihad*. However, though frequently dismissed as a 'jihad made in Germany', many overtly secular Young Turks in the waning Ottoman Empire, also believed that religious fanaticism could be deployed against the Entente. Enver Pasha, the Minister of War, had utilized the power of Islam when fighting in Libya in 1911. Before setting out to Libya, he called for a guerrilla war against the Italians. Once on the ground, he increasingly viewed the conflict in terms of a *jihad*. In his letters, Enver described the Libyan volunteers as 'fanatical Muslims who see death before the enemy as a gift from God'[116].

Rogan pursues the story: As the Germans began to take Muslim prisoners on the Western Front—800 by the end of 1914—they created a special facility called the 'Crescent Moon Camp' (*Halbmondlager*) at Wünsdorf-Zossen, near Berlin. One veteran's experiences demonstrate how effective the camp was in recruiting Muslim soldiers. Ahmed bin Hussein was a farmer from far away Marrakech, one of a group of eight Moroccan soldiers who had been inducted into the French troops, and surrendered to German forces in Belgium… A parade of Muslim activists passed through the Zossen camp to promote *jihad* propaganda. The Tunisian Salih al-Sharif was a frequent visitor, along with other North African activists. These guest speakers reinforced the Ottoman *fatwas* that

---

[116] Ibid. pp. 4 ff.

urged Muslims to volunteer for war, explaining why fighting with
the Allies was an act against religion and joining the *jihad* a religious duty. Hundreds of POWs volunteered for the Ottoman
army—among them the Moroccan farmer, Ahmed bin Hussein. As
he later recounted, after spending six months in the Zossen camp,
a German soldier arrived, accompanied by an Ottoman officer.
'Whoever wants to go to Istanbul', they instructed, 'raise [your]
hand'. Twelve Moroccan and Algerian soldiers volunteered on the
spot. 'Others were afraid', Ahmed bin Hussein added. They were
given civilian clothes and passports and sent on to Istanbul to join
the Ottoman war effort. It is impossible to say how many Muslim
POWs volunteered for Ottoman service in this way. American consular officials reported that as many as 3,000 North African former
prisoners had been posted to Baghdad with Ottoman forces to serve
on the Persian and Mesopotamian fronts. The Moroccan farmer,
Ahmed bin Hussein, was in a unit dispatched to al-ʿUla in the
Hijaz, where he fought with Ottoman forces against the British-
supported Arab Revolt led by Sharif Husayn of Mecca and his
sons[117].

Another observer of the international and Muslim scenes noticed
a series of events just prior to World War I, which indicated a gradual awakening of the Near East to a sense of its somewhat humiliating position,and

> I fear that a terrible day of reckoning will come. The
> Tripolitan campaign [by Italy] is looked upon like a holy
> war, and Mohammedan soldiers, regular and irregular,
> are gradually coming in from all parts of the Moham-
> medan world. The Mohammedans of Egypt and India
> are beginning to talk of home rule. English officials are
> being murdered by fanatical Mussulmans; Russia and

---

[117] Ibid

England are dividing Persia, offering another object lesson to the Mohammedan world[118].

This is not very different from the *Jihad* that al-Qa'ida abd ISIS are waging today against the West, and by Hamas and Hizbullah against Israel, with the support of Erdogan, probably from the same tradition of *Jihad* that he cherishes as long as it is not directed against him or his rule. It goes on with the same flow of volunteers, regulars and irregulars, as before, and continues to converge on the Muslim battlegrounds today as it did centuries ago. Well known is also the Armenian tragedy where *Jihad* became a tool for genocide. Rubenstein claims[119], that the crimes perpetrated against the Armenians, were regarded by the Turks as legitimate defensive methods of dealing with *dhimmis,* who had violated the conditions of their dhimmitude and, hence, were outlaws for whom everything – including life, property, freedom and family – was forfeit. The persistent Turkish genocide denial has been due, at least in part, to the Turkish belief that they did no wrong in exterminating the Armenians, a belief that rests ultimately on the traditions of *jihad* and the *dhimma.* The course of events was such that on November 14, 1914, the Ottoman Empire declared war on the Entente powers (Britain, France, Russia and allies), one day after the Ottoman Sultan, in his capacity as Caliph, issued an appeal for *jihad.* The next day, Mustafa Hayri Bey, the *Sheikh-ul-Islam* and chief Sunni religious authority in the Ottoman world, issued a formal (and inflammatory) declaration of *jihad* "against infidels and enemies of Islam." *Jihad* pamphlets in Arabic were also distributed in mosques throughout the Muslim world, that offered a detailed plan of operations for the assassination and extermination of all non-believers,

---

[118] David Werner Amram, "The Jews of Fez and Politics in Morocco", *The Jewish Exponent, No 1308, 3 May, 1912, pp.1-2.*

[119] Rubenstein, Richard L. *Jihad and genocide.* Vol. 1. Rowman & Littlefield, Lanham 2010.

except those of German nationality, the Empire's wartime ally. Killing squads and their leaders were motivated by both the ideology of *jihad* and pan-Turkism, that was influenced by European nationalism. While the practical influence of *jihad* on the masses may have been limited, it certainly later facilitated the government's program of genocide against the Armenians. After all, the Ottoman Empire was governed as a theocratic state, at the apex of which stood the Sultan, both as the supreme head of state and, for Sunni Muslims, as the Caliph who, as such, was the successor to the Prophet and the supreme protector of Islam, who had the authority to declare the communal *Jihad* that he led. One would be almost tempted to see Erdogan in this role today, if it were not so anachronistic.

Another interesting angle of this joint venture of German imperialism at that time and Islamic *Jihad*, was offered by Rachel Mag-Shamhráin[120], who emphasized that one peculiar manifestation of Germany's growing imperialist intentions toward the Orient, was the Ottoman Empire's declaration of *jihad* on the Entente powers in November 1914. A note written by the Kaiser in late July of that year, makes it quite clear that this idea of an anti-British *jihad* was German rather than Turkish in origin. Thus, perhaps unsurprisingly, in the proclamation of *jihad* by the *Sheikh-ul-Islam*, the supreme authority on religious affairs in the realm, the enemies identified were not infidels in general, as one would expect, but the enemies are identified in the following terms:

> Oh, Moslems! Ye who are smitten with happiness, and are on the verge of sacrificing your life and your good for the cause of right, and of braving perils, gather now around the Imperial throne, obey the commands of the Almighty, who, in the Qur'an, promises us bliss in this

---

[120] MagShamhráin, Rachel . "Displacing Orientalism: Ottoman jihad, German imperialism, and the Armenian genocide." *Encounters with Islam in German Literature and Culture* (2009).

and in the next world; embrace ye the foot of the Caliph's throne and know ye that the state is at war with Russia, England, France, and their Allies, and that these are the enemies of Islam. The Chief of the believers, the Caliph, invites you all, as Moslems, to join in the Holy War[121]

The *New York Times*[122] (7 July 1918) held that a *jihad* of this kind was impossible, for this claim was based on the rationale that the average Muslims would not understand why they should embark on a holy war against Christians where Christian nations, such as Germany and Austria, were to serve as their allies. However, the idea of 230,000,000 Muslims worldwide, rising in unity and triggering the most historically terrible riot of destruction and massacre across the globe, was not initially considered to be a completely unlikely prospect. This is because the strange alliance between Turkey and Germany made such possibilities seem plausible. Thus the world was briefly shocked at the possibility of what could occur if the Muslims actually conceded and met the expectations of the Kaiser and the Caliph, by responding appropriately according to the tenets of Islamic faith. Another tool of Muslim recruitment worldwide for *Jihad* was the annual pilgrimage to Mecca (*haj*), one of the five *arkan* of the Faith, where the convergence of Muslims from all over the world and the electrifying atmosphere of sanctity, which reigned all around, were conducive to such a recruitment of enthusiasts, which brought them esteem in Muslim society. Eickelman[123] brings out the case of Ahmed Bin Ali al Jazuli, who in 1768 went on a pilgrimage, and on his way back he stopped in Cairo at the prestigious Al-Azhar center of Islamic learning. There, he encountered other students from Fez, Morocco, Tunisia and Egypt.

---

[121] Ibid.

[122] *New York Times*, .7 July, 1918

[123] Eickelman, Dale F. ,*Muslim travellers: pilgrimage, migration, and the religious imagination*. Vol. 9. Univ of California Press, Berkeley 1990.

He then resumed his travels, going to the Ottoman Empire. There he participated in *jihad* and was offered a high position in the capital[124].

But for Erbakan, Erdogan and Co., who did not live to experience W W I and the demise of the Empire with the momentous developments that followed, like the rise of the Muslim Brotherhood in Egypt, they have been trying in their lifetimes to make sense on the new Islamic realities. Of course, the story is long, and we don't need to narrate that entire intricate and fascinating tale. For Erdogan to become a devotee of the Muslim Brothers and to seek to champion their cause, there must be some strong link, religious and emotional, tying him to that source. Suffice it to record here that the Muslim Brotherhood was created in Egypt in 1928 by Hassan al-Banna, who had all kinds of ideas that he introduced into Islam. He did not generate or invent Islam, but he updated it, so to speak. For example, he added or rather revived to the Islamic usage two or three major terms, which injected perhaps a new life into the very operation of modern Islam. He addressed *jihad*, the holy war, which had been taken before by Muslims in the modern world as a striving, as an aspiration to be a better Muslim, an aspiration to self-strengthening, or making an effort, which can also be intellectual, not necessarily military. From now on Hassan al-Banna said that, as of old: "*jihad i*s an instrument in order to battle against the enemy." The problem was to identify who the enemy was, as the Ottoman Chief cleric had specified in his appeal to Muslims to join Jihad was against the Entente powers. And the enemy is, he said, first of all the British, who were occupying Egypt, and second the Jews, who were coming to colonize Palestine, and who are battling against the local Arabs, Muslims, and Palestinians for the same land, and therefore Muslims are duty bound to help the Palestinians against the Jews. And the second term was *shahid* or martyr. He said

---

[124] Ibid. page 76

that whenever a Muslim dies in this battle, it's not just death as one is killed in other combats. This is the death of a martyr, because then one is assured to go straight to paradise, and therefore not only were people who volunteered for the Muslim Brothers not afraid to die, they were eager to martyr themselves in battle for the cause of Islam and in the Path of Allah, and so take the shortcut from this tormenting life into eternal paradise in the entourage of Allah. The terms of *Jihad* and *Shahid* were not new ones because they had been used in the times of the Prophet himself. But due to modernization and Westernization, they fell into disuse and Banna reintroduced vigor into them and made them operative.

When Hassan al-Banna spoke on those terms, he revived a terminology which had not indeed been operational since medieval times, when Islam was great, expanding and victorious. He was impressing upon the Muslims of Egypt that: "We are under obligation to help other Muslims," that is to say those in Palestine, and not only to wage *jihad* against the Jews and the British, but also not to be afraid to die, because those who die are assured of their second life in heaven, in the afterworld. Now one can understand how the Nazi Germans picked up the usefulness of the same ideas, realizing that this was the great occasion they were looking for, quite a great opportunity to penetrate the Islamic world. They had been trying to create in Egypt an office for propaganda, for their own cause. Previously, the Egyptian population rejected that propaganda of hatred, because they had reasonably good relations with the Jews, who had lived there for many centuries. There were some eighty thousand of them in Egypt then. There was even a very famous trial, when the Germans published in French an anti-Semitic book by their Nazi office in Cairo, speaking about the threat the Jews posed to Germany. They used Nazi propaganda to warn the Arabs that: "Jews are not only a threat against Europe or against Germans, the Aryans, but are also a threat against you." And Jews in Egypt sued that Nazi office in Cairo, and they won the case. And therefore the whole idea was dismissed in public opinion, showing how Egypt was ill-prepared for a negative anti-Semitic propaganda attitude toward the Jews at that time. But here the propaganda machine of the Nazis in Egypt and later in Palestine, together with the Muslim Brothers in Egypt since the 1930s, combined with the efforts of the mufti of Jerusalem, Haj Amin al-Husseini, simply changed attitudes in the Middle East toward the Palestine and Jewish problems, whose consequences we suffer from to this very day. The Germans, who understood exactly what it was all about, jumped on the opportunity to tell the Arabs, and Muslims in general, that as a matter of fact both Germans and Muslims shared a common ideology. Both of them wanted to eliminate Jews, for both of them thought that Jews were treacherous in character, and so on, therefore, it was only natural for them to join their efforts and to collaborate in their elimination.

Against this background, we can understand that as soon as World II War broke out, the mufti of Jerusalem, Haj Amin al-Husseini, was invited to Berlin. He established together with sixty more Arabs and other Muslim broadcasters and translators, a broadcasting service, which operated from Berlin in the service of the Nazis until the very end of the war. And in the middle of the war, when more and more German divisions were needed for the eastern front, when Stalingrad went awry and the whole situation on the war front started to deteriorate, the Germans became very short on manpower, and therefore they resorted to the thirty-eight divisions of *Waffen-SS* that they recruited to fill the ranks. *Waffen* means armed, the armed SS. The SS was created initially as a police unit, some kind of elite unit, and later they were needed for battles, for selected battles. Therefore their numbers and their tasks expanded from three battalions of police at the very beginning, into thirty-eight divisions of fighting troops at the end of the war. Most of them were German, but since they ran short of recruits they started to enlist others: Lithuanians, Ukrainians, Romanians, and of course, Yugoslavs and Albanians, and so on. So, the concerned Nazis flew especially the mufti of Jerusalem—who was settled in Berlin—to Bosnia, with the task to convince the Muslim population there of his newly adopted militant Muslim Brother ideology, which he had chosen as a tool to achieve his goals in Palestine, and which prescribed that it was good to fight against the Jews, who deserved elimination, and the British because they supported the Jews, and that if one fought that war, it would be considered *jihad,* and any casualty would be regarded as a martyr, hence his automatic salvation is guaranteed to eternity when he goes to heaven to dwell in the vicinity of Allah. The mufti went from place to place in the large Muslim agglomerations of Bosnia, especially the cities, where in 1941 the Imams of the major Muslim communities of Sarajevo, Tuzla, Banja Luka, and Mostar had previously issued *fatwa* decrees, a sort of religious verdicts, forbidding the Bosnian Muslims to collaborate with the Ustasha government of NDH, which had encompassed their country under German and Italian accord, uniting Bosnia with Croatia. And here comes the mufti of Jerusalem, the great spiritual authority with the reputation and prestige of his city, and representing both the Nazis in Berlin and the Muslim Brothers in Egypt, and telling them: "No, no, no, forget about that. That verdict is not valid anymore." And in 1943, when he visited all those four cities, he convinced the local religious leadership to come out in support of the Muslim recruits, thus mobilizing some twenty-one thousand people to serve in the Waffen-SS Division Number Thirteen, notoriously known as the *Hanjar* Division, which in Turkish and Arabic means simply "dagger," as a symbol of the war itself.

Some elaboration is needed nonetheless in order to find the German-Muslim common cause against Jews and Zionists, which united them in their endeavor to provide a "final solution" for the Jews, taking advantage of the heat of the war, when they thought that it would be more difficult to attract the attention of nations to these Satanic schemes. In other words, they were especially seeking the ideological and political juncture that would allow both of them to act in concert to achieve the genocide of the Jewish people in the Middle East and in Europe, in order to aid the Axis powers against the Allies. But after the war, due to the Nazi defeat, the banner of virulent anti-Semitism definitely passed from Europe, with Nazi Germany at its centre, to the Islamic world led by the Arabs, and especially to the fundamentalist Muslims like al-Qa'ida and Iran since the end of the twentieth century. The writer who detected and researched the ideological link between Islamic fundamentalism and Nazi Judeophobia is the German Matthias Kuntzel, a political scientist and a student of anti-Semitism, in his book published in German, English, and Hebrew.[125] The only drawback in this seminal volume is that the author follows today's vogue among Western scholars, who, contrary to Erdogan's own analysis, differentiate between Islam and "Islamism," as if they were two different religions or systems of belief, attributing the built-in hatred to Jews only to the latter, while the former seems to be generally exonerated. The problem is that it is becoming more and more difficult to distinguish between the two, if there ever was a difference, since the Muslim Brothers have moved to the international Muslim consensus, and what used to be considered as fanatic "Islamism," is now the accepted norm.

It is true that those called "Islamists" are more radical and vocal about their hatred toward the Jews than the common Muslims, and this has given rise to the spurious claim that the abuses of Islam, including anti-Semitism and terrorism, are only the lot of those "radical" and "fundamentalist" Muslims, usually quantified as some 15 percent of the 1.5 billion world Muslims. In fact, we are talking about the same one creed, which upholds *Shari'a* law to various

---

[125] Kuntzel, Matthias, *Jihad and Jew-Hatred, Islamism, Nazism and the Roots of 9/11*, Telos Press, New York, 2007.

degrees, while those who do not follow it to the letter, as in any other religion, are not adepts of an alternative "moderate Islam," the one that is sometimes dubbed "religion of peace," to distinguish from the faith of aggressive "extremists." The truth of the matter is that no such Islam exists, though there are certainly many truly moderate Muslims, who have broken away from the bloody road of *jihad*, especially when they have conveniently moved to the West and can from a safe distance criticize the killing in their original countries of those dubbed "apostates" or "traitors"; or condemn the phenomenon of the *Islamikaze* bombers against Westerners and Israelis, or the culture of death, which is cultivated in many Muslim lands, or indeed the unbridled anti-Semitic calumnies that are rife in their culture. But they have yet to produce an alternative doctrine and worldview that could rival official Islam and posit a creed and a set of rules that can tempt Muslims to relinquish the aggressive aspects *Shari'a* and embrace a different path. If they did, they would no longer be Muslims in the eyes of established Islam, that is, they would be accused of apostasy, which is punishable by death. Tayyip Erdogan, being a pious man and a supporter of the Muslim Brothers, will not abandon his faith, therefore he is unlikely to alter his view against Jews and Israel.

In short, anti-Semitism has been built into Islam from its inception. Any one of the numerous Hirsi Ali's, who was brought up in Saudi Arabia,[126] and certainly Jewish individuals who lived under the yoke of Islam,[127] can attest to the phenomenon. Therefore, there is no need to attribute anti-Semitism to "Islamists," as if mainstream Islam were different, exactly as warlike *jihad*, the violent aspect of Islam, has been a common tenet of all Muslims, though

---

[126] Cited in Israeli, Raphael, *Muslim Anti-Semitism in Christian Europe*, Transaction, New Brunswick, 2009, pp. 4–5.

[127] See e.g., Bat Ye'or, the *Dhimmi*, Fairleigh Dickinson Press, Madison and London, 1985; R. Israeli, *Back to Nowhere: Moroccan Jews in Dream, Nostalgia and Reality*, Lambert Academic Publishing, Saarbrucken, 2010.

some of them practice it less than others. This is the reason why the Muslim Brothers are so popular among Arabs and Muslims in the world, and one need not be an Islamist to be a member. Similarly, hatred of the Jews has been universal among Palestinians, as it is with Erdogan, and there is no difference, in that regard, between the Palestinian Authority, which is considered "moderate," and the Hamas, who are said to be Islamist. Thus, the common enmity of Muslims toward Jews was not discovered on the eve of World War II, nor was it an innovation that was due to the Nazi propaganda, though under those circumstances of the pre-war, the Nazi machinery knew how to incite the Muslim populace, which at some times and in some places had lived harmoniously with the Jews, to rise against them when they could free themselves from the restraining shackles of Western colonial powers, like Britain in Egypt and Palestine, and France in Morocco. Erdogan, nonetheless, continues to spread relentlessly his anti-Jewish venom around, having attained the supreme power in his country where no one dares to challenge him.

In Islamic writings during the war, like those of the Brothers and of the chief mufti of Jerusalem, thoughts of violence of the Nazi type started to creep in, coupled with paranoid conspiracy theories that attributed to the Jews both an evil nature, capable of causing damage to all nations, especially Islam, and a satanic ability to carry out those schemes. It was necessary, when the moment of anti-Semitic action had come, to emphasize the evil attributes of the Jews, as the Germans did, in order to render them an easy prey to the people they dwelt within, and to facilitate their exclusion, persecution, discrimination, and ultimately their removal and physical extermination. Kuntzel's seminal innovation is that he traced the roots of the historical collaboration between Islam (that he called "Islamism") and Nazi ideology and practice, and why in the post-war era, when Nazism was wiped out, it was Islam that inherited that questionable clout and raised the banner of anti-Semitism as one of the first items on its agenda. Various champions rose successively to wave that banner : first Gamal abdul Nasser, then Saddam Hussein, and now Tayyip Erdogan. Kuntzel also claimed that it was not the Arab-Israeli dispute that caused this anti-Semitic trend to gain strength, but on the contrary, it has been the radicalization of Muslim anti-Semitism, as among the Hezbollah in Lebanon, the Hamas among the Palestinians, the Muslim Brothers and their affiliates in Pakistan, Africa, and Asia, and then al-Qa'ida and its Taliban, ISIS and other sister movements, which enabled them to dominate the Islamic discourse, aggravate the already difficult hostility to Jews and Israel, and make that conflict all the more intractable. It is not the Middle Eastern conflict that causes virulent Islamic anti-Semitism, claims Kuntzel, but like in Europe, it is the overt and covert anti-Semitism that sharpens the anti-Zionist and anti-Israeli attitudes worldwide. Today he might like to add to the causes of modern anti-Semitism the blatant factor of Erdogan and his party leading the important Muslim country of Turkey and injecting into it massive doses of anti-Jewish, anti-Zionist and anti-Israeli hatred.

This is the reason why at the time, when Nazism was universally condemned in Europe, in the Arab world it not only won currency, but it was regarded as both the savior of the Arabs from the yoke of British colonialism, and from Jewish settlement in Palestine, which the Arabs/Muslims considered exclusively theirs. Moreover, they viewed in the Nazi "final solution" an ideal platform and blueprint to reverse, not only to arrest, the Zionist great strides made in Palestine, that no other available plan, not even the British White Paper against Jewish immigration to Palestine (1936), could undo. No wonder then, that after the war, Nazi officials found shelter in the Arab world, and the remnants of Nazi ideology could find their echo in Muslim countries. *Sho'ah* denial, which has spread almost universally into the Arab and Muslim world to this day, is one manifestation of these surviving vestiges of Nazism, which at one and the same time seek to avoid worldwide criticism of the regime they had supported in Germany during the war, but also to avert any support or sympathy to the Jewish victims of the Nazis. Kuntzel's unquestioned accomplishment has been to trace the stunning persistence, even escalation, of this violent brand of anti-Semitism in the Islamic world today, not only within the growing Muslim communities in the West, but is often latently acclaimed and supported by the world media, and sometimes by the authorities of the rest of the world.

Kuntzel's focus on the Muslim Brothers in Egypt not only interpreted that movement as the beginning of modern radicalism in Islam, but he found extraordinary organizational similarities between it and Nazism and Fascism in general; for example, the subordination of the individual to the collective will, the worship of iconic leadership, hostility toward liberal and democratic principles, vitriolic rejection of Communism, extreme opposition to capitalism, and a strong ambition among Muslims to establish a universal Muslim state, ruled by the *Shari'a*, similar to the Germanic thousand-year Reich that Hitler had in mind. In that ambience of continual fighting under strict rules of conduct and their relentless enforcement, the predominance of men was paramount, the submission of women obvious, as was martyrdom for the sake of the collective, and above all, a common contempt, hatred, and obsession with the Jews, who were simultaneously feared and despised. Hence the need then to fight to the finish, both the Jews and the British, the latter being the only nation that stood up against the Nazis at the opening of the war and confronted them fearlessly under Churchill. These similarities and affinities between the two ideas and nationalities emerged during the 1930s and contributed to the forging of the alliance between the two by the time the war broke out. It was the Muslim Brothers (MB) who translated Hitler's *Mein Kampf* into Arabic and distributed it throughout the Arab world and helped channel to Haj Amin in Palestine, who was facing similar challenges, arms and funds from Germany, which sustained him in his major revolt against the British (and Zionism) in Palestine during the lead-up to the war (1936–39).

The Islamic connection, which has been becoming prevalent in Erdogan's thought, peaked when Haj Amin, who escaped British wrath during the Arab Revolt (1936-9) by moving to Iraq and aiding the short-lived Rashid Ali's Rebellion, which was also prominently anti-Semitic, as it was mainly directed against the Baghdadi Jews in what was known as the *Farhood* Pogrom, and escaped to Germany in the heat of the war (June 1941), met with Hitler in person, and harnessed his energies, his prestige as the mufti of Jerusalem, his hostility to the British and the Jews, and his skill as a propagandist to enhance the German war effort. Unlike the general ties, sympathetic exchanges and assistance in weapons and funds to face the Brits in the Middle East, which the Nazis had forged with the MB since they began their relations and collaboration, Haj Amin went a step further by proving himself to the Nazis as a practitioner. First of all, he lived in Berlin throughout the war and broadcast in Arabic over shortwave to the entire Arab world, and in other languages spoken in the Islamic world, like Turkish, Iranian, and Urdu, to try to enlist the support of much of the Muslim world to Hitler and his Nazi enterprise. From the mufti's point of view, perhaps the summit of his "achievements" was his string of meetings with the highest German hierarchy, to persuade them to scuttle any attempt of any deal to rescue Jews from the German claws in Europe, and to make sure that they were sent to their execution in the Nazi death camps. In that regard, he participated directly and heartlessly in the decimation of thousands of Jews who could otherwise have survived that fate, not least of all by fighting their entrance into Palestine.

Of course, the center of gravity of Kuntzel's interest in the MB was not only their inspiration by Nazi doctrine, but their extended influence on Haj Amin and Palestinian Arabs, which facilitated the mufti's close collaboration with Hitler. That caused him to move to Berlin during the war and after the war to invite some MB troops to participate with the Palestinians in their war against the Jews in 1948–49. Historically, the fact that the Palestinians are still struggling today to establish a state of their own, is the fruit of their and their Nazi allies' failure to wipe out the Jews of Palestine during the war, who stood after it as their main and victorious competitors. Under Nazi instigation, the Palestinians elected to claim all of Palestine undivided, instead of compromising over it with the Jews, so they ended up losing it all and entering the future with uncertainty, for it is very difficult to turn the clock back today. Kuntzel also laments the fact that the victorious allies, instead of punishing the MB and their supporters, including Haj Amin, after the war, for their collaboration with the Nazis and for concocting with them the ruin of Britain, on the contrary came to view their restored good relations with the Arab world as outweighing any doctrinal "deviation" by the mufti and his MB allies, who continue to this day to declare their abhorrence of the West, to profess virulent anti-Semitism, to vow the destruction of Israel, to advocate Holocaust denial, and to hardly hide their admiration for Hitler and the Nazis. In the current unrest in the Arab world, that has been wrongly dubbed the "Arab Spring," some of those themes are reemerging. Britain and the West, who were prepared to sacrifice their long term interests for a temporary rehabilitation of their positions in the Middle East, may be now paying dearly for that momentary lapse in their thinking. Indeed, with British and American silent consent, France had permitted the mufti, back then, to run away from her territory and so avoid his trial as a war criminal, and seek refuge in Egypt, which had become, just like Syria, Argentina, and Paraguay, a shelter for Nazi criminals after the war. This is the background that Erdogan finds congenial for his ideas, ruling style and international and inter- Muslim politics.

In spite of the many differences between Nazism and Fascism, on the one hand, and the authoritarian regimes in the Arab and Islamic worlds, on the other, there is a lasting red (now green) thread that continues to connect between the two, long after the former has waned away in Europe and the latter has begun to shake off some of the unbearable regimes that have oppressed Arab and Muslim peoples for so long. These connections persist, in spite of the doctrinal reversals that have gripped the Arab and Muslim world since the end of the world war, when Arabs and Muslims, Erdogan included, started the reversal of attributing Nazism to Israel. Devout Muslim radical practitioners, like the MB, the Hamas, and Hizbullah and similar movements, indeed often attempt to wash themselves clean of Nazism by projecting it on Israel and accusing her of having adopted it. What truly unites these movements with bygone European Fascism are indeed their common enchantment with modern technology (today it is Internet, satellites, up-to-date television and radio broadcasting, and the most modern weaponry, including weapons of mass destruction); their fascination with violence and war, and the cultivation of supreme sacrifice, to the point of encouraging self-immolation, like the *Islamikaze* (that are wrongly viewed in the West as "suicide bombers"); and the rejection of democracy and liberal values. And perhaps above all, the obsession that refuses to die, with eliminating the Jews wherever they can be found.[128] No wonder that spectacular acts of international terrorism, like 9/11, the London and Madrid mass killings in civilian subways, mass killings in the streets of Europe, hijacking airplanes and killing their passengers, or the Bali and other senseless bombings, have all an element of fanatic madness in them, reminiscent of the abuses of the Nazis. Even the Twin Towers' attack is strikingly identical to Hitler's similar fantasy to see Manhattan burning.[129]

Kuntzel's book explains what happened in Egypt in the years

---

[128] Israeli, Raphael, *Muslim Anti-Semitism in Christian Europe,* Transaction, New Brunswick, 2010, especially chapter 1.

[129] See Jeffrey Herf's splendid introduction to Kuntzel's book.

1925–45 to turn the pro-Jewish sentiment in the early years of Zionist activity in Palestine, which was thought to benefit the entire area, into a hostile ambience that kindled the violent eruptions against the Jews thereafter. He attributes the radical change to the rise of the MB in 1928 that later impacted drastically the developments in mandatory Palestine, the relations between the Arabs and the Nazi regime, and ultimately the alliance between the mufti of Jerusalem and Hitler in person. He rightly observes that in the beginning of that period, amiable relations existed between the Muslim majority and the successful and well-to-do Jewish minority. But lest anyone believe, or come to the conclusion, that the Jews had always been privileged in Egypt at all times, and in general in the Arab and Islamic world, let us remember that when the state of Israel was founded in 1948, and when the Jews found a shelter for themselves, the almost totality of the million Jews who had lived in the Arab and Islamic worlds emigrated either to the Jewish state or elsewhere in the West. American and European Jews did not leave, and there must be a reason. The reason was that Jews had lived under the discriminatory and humiliating status of *dhimmis* in the Muslim world, and there were periods that under particularly strict and harsh rulers, like the Almoravids in North Africa and the Mamluks in Egypt, or under the fanatic Shi'ites in Iran, Jews were persecuted, massacred, forced to convert to Islam, expelled, or constrained to run for their lives elsewhere.

Kuntzel speaks about contemporary Egypt, and it is there, under the pressure of the MB since 1928, on the eve of the world depression, which they could easily impute to the Jews, that the Jewish condition veered to the worse and had a direct impact on the situation in Palestine, and on the increasingly close relations between Arabs and Nazis. It was then and there that the Islamic connection to the Nazis and the Balkans began to burgeon, and it was then and there that the seeds of modern Muslim radicalism were sown, whence they would spread worldwide, including to Republican

Turkey, under different appellations, to this very day. The membership of the MB, under its charismatic leader until 1940, Hassan al-Banna, grew from eight hundred in 1936 to two hundred thousand merely two years later, and half a million in 1948, with a military arm of about forty thousand. Ostensibly, the growth and the rhetoric were directed against the colonizing power, the British, who were not forthcoming on their promise to grant full independence to Egypt. Al Banna took advantage of the post-World War I socioeconomic dislocations, and the building tensions with the British, to announce and promulgate his brand of conservative and restorative *Salafi* Islam, which professed a return to the roots, as in the times of the Prophet. He taught that Islam had lost its prestige and impact on daily life in Egypt, due to Western intrusion, which lured people to secularism and to the abandonment of religion, and he propagated the return to the divine law that is incorporated in the Qur'an and the Sunnah, which gave clear and detailed guidance to all needs of life.

The MB advocated a return to religious orthodoxy as the panacea not only for moral and social ills, but also for regaining the moral high ground that was lost to the West, by internationalizing the movement and attracting to it wide constituencies, especially of young people, and not only in the countryside where Islam had always kept its grip on the people, but also to reconquer the cities, which had fallen to the secular, westernizing, and modernizing bourgeoisie. They recruited the foreign Muslim students, who were studying in Cairo, to train them as their representatives when they returned to their countries of origin. Thus, they very early established branches of the Brothers in Lebanon, Syria, Transjordan (later Jordan), and in 1940 the Palestine Committee was set up, which encompassed the entire Middle East, and then the Far East Committee to cover the Muslim countries of Asia, and prophetically they even established the European Committee which has served its purpose only when Muslim immigration has intensified to Europe in the post-war period. Domestically, and following the European Fascist pattern of Germany and Italy, the MB demanded the dismantlement of all political parties and the abolishment of liberal democracy in Egypt. This is the main reason, though there are also others connected to Egyptian, Arab, and Muslim traditional order, why in the 1920s Egypt, and possibly also Iraq and others, were far more democratic and dedicated to women's rights than ever since, but all of them embraced varying degrees of authoritarianism following the military coups that plagued them for almost a century, until the 2010s when their "Spring" at last permitted them to talk about democracy if not to achieve it.

The Party of MB platform, which could easily be Erdogan's, proposed a new political organization modeled on the medieval universal Caliphate, based on *Shari'a* law and obeying the global Caliph, much along the lines of the thousand-year Reich, just with another content to its ideology, albeit with a similar organizational philosophy, which also prohibited any other competing all-encompassing theory like Communism. The MB soon began to pursue an organizational praxis, by penetrating Communist ranks and denouncing them to the state security apparatus. In this endeavor, too, the MB felt they were treading on the Nazi's heels, launching a spreading pattern of confrontation that pitted Islam against Communism everywhere. Since in most Communist parties in the Arab and Islamic worlds, Jews (and Christians) were more prominent than in other local political parties, due to their preferred adherence to an atheistic political entity where Islam played little or no part, Communism became also a channel to rationalize the growing hostility toward Jews, in both the MB and the Nazi political organization. Economically, the MB treaded its unique route when it forbade interest (which countered any ambition to establish a modern banking system), and created a commonality of interest between capital and labor, while at the same time recognizing, like in Nazi Germany, the significance of technology, industrialization, and work ethic, as a condition and prerequisite to gaining military preponderance and running a world Islamic regime.

The MB, again like its Nazi model, also professed a social and moral puritanism, which sought to control individual desires and ambitions by strictly adhering to conservative modes of conduct, avoiding material temptations, and aspiring to spirituality, a controlled asceticism that lent priority to satisfying the needs of the collective before turning to address personal necessities. In this light, or rather obscurity, one has to reconsider *Kristalnacht* and other abuses by Nazi thugs toward their Jewish victims that they wished to subdue by terror and violence, as well as the violent outbursts of the MB then and the Hamas today, which burned down night clubs, brothels, and movie theaters, inherited from the Palestinian Authority in Gaza. Does'nt this sound like an Erdogan prescription for a sane Muslim society ? Similarly, the Islamic Revolution of Iran, in February 1977, was triggered by the arson of a theater in a coastal city, by Muslim radicals who falsely claimed that a pornographic film was being shown, which justified the burning of the hall with its occupants inside. Since the MB, particularly their prominent leader, Sayyid Qut'b, who inherited the clout of Banna after his assassination, saw Jews as the evil of the world and the cause of its misfortunes, then, of course, all acts and institutions of immorality, such as theaters, movies, prostitution, drugs, corruption, and the deterioration of manners and values in all societies, were due to the Jewish management of world affairs. It was thought that the MB could outdo the Nazis in their obsession with anything Jewish, and in the hatred they instigated in their constituencies as a result, so much so that they naturally concocted plans together to wipe out the cause and reason of these troubles by methodically exterminating that race. Those ideas have become so rooted in general Islamic and Arab culture that one can still detect them, without much effort, more than half a century after Nazism was routed and eradicated.

However, nothing illustrates the great doctrinal breakthrough of the MB as the operationalization of the idea of *jihad*, from a dormant ideal, whose time had revolved, to an active tool to combat present day enemies, binding every individual Muslim, not only the Muslim *Umma* as a whole. The rationale was that when the house is burning, it was incumbent on each individual Muslim to carry a bucket of water and contribute to the extinction of the fire the best he can, regardless of what the state, the public or the community does or refrains from doing. The idea was that the Qur'anic tenet of *jihad*, which had been the driving force of Islam at its inception, and the engine of its expansion, and had become over the years mostly viewed as merely an endeavor for self-striving and improvement, for example by spreading and propagating Islam, ought to be revived and Muslims ought to convert the use of force from self-defense into propagatory activity. In other words, *jihad*, as a mere educational value, ought not to predominate and it should be developed into an active tool, as of old, to spread the word of Islam worldwide. Al-Banna gave this idea a very active twist, as in the times of the Prophet, essentialized in the popular slogan that is still central to MB affiliates like the Hamas: "Allah is our aim, the Prophet our model, the Qur'an our constitution, *jihad* our path, and death for Allah the sublimest of our ambitions." By promising eternal martyrdom to the casualties in battle, he turned death for the cause not only into something that does not inspire fear and abhorrence, but into a desirable ideal that every young Muslim can and should embrace, thus avoiding the torment of this worldly life and taking the shortcut to the eternal hereafter under the blissful protection of Allah. The revival of MB and *Salafi* Islam in the Arab and Islamic world following the "Spring" of 2011–2012, attests to the tenacity of this thinking.

Chapter Eight

Fethullah Gulen and the 2016 Counter-Revolution

Fethullah Gulen, an old man in his 70s, once a close ideological and political partner of Erdogan, has become his most bitter nemesis in the wake of the attempted coup of Summer 2016, which the cunning Prime Minister of Turkey has astutely used to rid himself of all his rivals in the military, the public service, intellectuals, academics and journalists . He has even been risking his links with the US in his demand that Washington agree to extradite to him "in the pursuit of justice" that man, who now finds shelter in Pennsylvania, so as to make sure that all his potential political enemies are incarcerated and constitute no longer any menace to his increasingly absolute rule. All in all, it is estimated, according to press reports, that some 40,000 people were arrested and over 100,000 officials of all sorts dismissed, most of them accused of having some link to the Gulen group. Vindictive Erdogan, who miraculously and inexplicably survived the coup, to the point that many of his detractors suspected it was a staged drama, even accused the alleged rebels of having belonged to a clandestine counter-state "terrorist" organization (FETO), that was guided from the outside, allegedly by Fethullah Gulen, with a view of dismissing the "democratically-elected government" of Erdogan and installing another in its stead. *Anadolu*, the official news agency, has launched a major publicity campaign to spread the official government narrative on the coup attempt, which was received with many suspicions and question marks both by the Turkish opposition and by the internatioal audiences. In the following days, a state of emergency was declared in the country, and requests were dispatched worldwide to close down Gulen's institutions (mainly "educational"). Taking a page from Bashar Assad's record, Erdogan has been dubbing these dissident rebels as "terrorists" to enlist public and international support to his counter-coup and to the vast reforms he wished to introduce to tighten the grip on his authoritarian rule.

At the ouset of his career, Fethullah Gulen was a fervent Muslim turned preacher, but after he retired at 40 (probably mimicking the life of the Prophet of Islam) he began focusing on social activities, many of which involved launching new enterprises, particularly media ventures and educational projects - areas which at the time were opening up to privatization in Turkey, causing his personal influence to rise throughout the country, and later abroad during the years preceding the rapprochement of his country to Israel. But towards the end of the century he decided to grow international and moved his center of activity to America, in the Chestnut Retreat at Saylorburg in the state of Pennsylvania, two years after the removal of Erbakan from power by the military, either out of disgust or of despair, and three years before Erdogan's revived Islamic party unexpectedly won the majority that brought him to power. It is hard to know whether the later rationalizations that he had moved in order to expand his Islamic educational program worldwide were created to compensate for his lack of foresight when he left Turkey on the brink of acceding to a position of power within the victorious AKP.

Gulen founded the Gulen Movement that was known as *Hizmet* (service), allegedly, based on a volunteer corps of some 5 miilion devotees, who gather around their adulated leader and adore him as Hassidic Jews venerate their Rebbe or Sufis worship their Saint in Islamic tradition. They are apt to worship him in whatever task he allocates to them, but claim to cultivate a moderate Islamic advocacy at the same time that they are said to have infiltrated, aside from their visible and legal activities, also the Turkish armed forces, police and judiciary, which explains why those were the main targets of Erdogans' repeated purges once he perceived that threat looming against his rule. Ironically, he had acted hand in hand with Erdogan in their commom combat against civil corruption and in favor of empowering religious individuals in civil life who had been practically disenfranchised in the secular Kemalist Republic's official machinery. This is the source of the bitterness, sense of betrayal and enmity that arose between them: Erdogan, who is not free from paranoia, feels wounded by the betrayal of his companion of combat who was apparently jealous of his partner's meteoric success, and is now bent on discrediting him and subverting his rule; and Gulen, who is shackled (by choice) to his exile in America and cannot repatriate for fear of being indicted for a treason he did not commit, bitter about his partner turned enemy, exasperated by the authoritarianism of Erdogan who had committed himself in the past to struggle hand in hand with his associate against corruption, for democracy and moderation in religion and politics, and determined to resist the disappointing turncoat. It is believed that the great disenchanment between two crept in during the landmark investigations against corruption in 2013, which involved also Erdogan's family members and high officials in his entourage. The Police which undertook the investiogation and gave public vent to them, which was also reputed as being loyal to Gulen, naturally give birth to the immediate accusations by Erdogan in person against his exiled erstwhile partner, thus triggering a series of broadsides, not all totally unjustified, between the two men, widely reflecting the deep hiatus that was widening between Erdogan and his ilk, supported by his massive rural power base and his hapless opposition in the large urban agglomerations which helplesslely lamented his Sultan-like style of rule.

To justify the Turkish demand for extradition from the US, and at the same time rally behind him the public opinion among which Gulen was still enormously popular, Erdogan accused Gulen of the most heinous and outrageous crimes of terrorism, subversion, treason and such, the acronym used to name his "terrorist" organization (FETO) standing for *The Gulenist Terror Organization*, which made revered Gulen sound like the basest and the most reprehensible criminal Turkey had seen, even more so than the Kurdish rebels who had been disturbing the peace in eastern Anatolia for long years. The cumulation of those alleged crimes necessitated the immediate arrest of that dangerous enemy of the people, and the docile court of law issued one, putting that popular man under the humiliating status of a fugitive from the law of the land. The issue has been of utmost concern to Erdogan who drummed it up at such a level as to place it at the top of Americano-Turkish agenda, with Turkish officials threatening, openly and indirectly, that unless and until Gulen is extradited, the relations between Ankara and Washington would not revert to normal. And to signal that Turkey needed America less than it deluded itself was the case, Erdogan did not hesitate to make advances to Moscow, to irritate Trump by embracing Ayatullah Rohani, to disinvite Israel from the Anatolian air maneuvers in spite of the American solidary withrawal from them, to sent another flotilla to Gaza which was impounded by Israel, and to bring his relations with Israel to the breaking point by his outrageous antisemitic accusations, despite the imposed "reconciliation" that Obama had compelled him and Netanyahu to embrace. It is Erdogan's simultaneous embroilment with America on the subjects of both Gulen and Israel that provide the latent link between the two events. It was sufficient for some Turkish minds that both Gulen and Israel have been extremely displeased (to use a euphemism), with Erdogan's demeanor and excesses, to make them allies.

Gulen had grown up and received religious instruction in the *madrasa*s of Ezerum in spite the ban on Islamic education under the Kemalist school system. There, he came under the influence of the dominant Islamic thinker and preacher of the time- Said Nursi, who merited the honorific *Badi' al-Zaman* (the Wonder of his Era) in recognition of his erudition and charisma. He peddled the idea that since logic and science were the way of the future, it was imperative to teach religion scientifically and he himself indulged in commenting intensively on the Qur'an in line with his convictions. He launched the Nursi movement which expressed quite early its dissatisfaction with the prevalent educational system where the secular students were deprived from religion and the religious adepts from scientific method. Due to his prodigious memory he could recite many books by heart, which aroused the admiration of his entourage, which included young Fethullah Gulen. He was active during the late Ottoman Empire as an educational reformer and advocate of the unity of the peoples of the Caliphate. He proposed educational reforms to the Ottoman Sultan Abdul Hamid's plan to put the traditional *Madrasa* (seminary) training, and the modern sciences in dialogue with each other. After his return from captivity in Russia during W W I, he was chosen to be a member of *Dar-al Hikmat al-Islamiye*, (The Islamic Wisdom Academy) which was seeking solutions for the post -Ottoman problems of the hour, especially what he considered as the negative predominance of Mustafa Kemal who relentlessly put into effect his sweeping program of secularization. Thus, he refused a post of Minister of Religious Affairs in the Republic, signaling his deep disagreement with Ataturk. He undertook, however, to update and modernize the Qur'an so as to make it "meet the requirements of modern life,", although he defied the ban to use the Arabic script and published his books using that banished alphabet, as well as calling the Believers to prayer in Arabic. His combat aroused the admiration of his entourage, for he could not countenance that secular students were deprived of religion and the religious students were banned from the scientific method. He combatted materialism and atheism as anti-scientific and urged Muslims to engage in "Jihad of the Word".

Ironically, as Erdogan strives today to erase Ataturk's heritage and replace it with his own, he at the same time accuses intellectuals and security officers of Gulenism, which is itself a sort of rebellion against Kemalism, as did the previous Kemalist governments with regard to Nursi. At any rate, alarmed by the growing popularity of Nursi's teachings, which had spread even among the intellectuals and the military officers, the Turkish Republican government arrested him for allegedly violating laws mandating secularism and sent him to exile. He was acquitted of all these charges in 1956. Isn't Gulen's biography, an almost precise replica of Nursi's? He died in 1956, but after the military coup d'état in Turkey in 1960, a group of soldiers opened his grave and buried him at an unknown place near Isparta during July 1960 in order to prevent popular veneration. His followers are reported to have found his grave after years of searching in the area, and took his remains to a secret place in an effort to protect his body from further disturbance. No wonder then that Gulen is often compared to Nursi, though the former is considered as more nationalist and state-oriented than his great predecessor. It was Gulen who tried to put into practice the ideas of his adulated mentor, first in Izmir which was totally secularized and under Western influence. He preached in various cities after his retirement and won the title of Honorary President of "Journalists and Writers Foundation " which he had helped create. However, he had surprisingly refrained from commenting on the closure of the anticedents of Erdogan's Islamic Party – the Welfare Party in 1998 and the Virtue Party in 2001. And though he did meet with civil politicians like Ecevit and Ciller, he avoided meeting or identifying too closely with the leaders of Islamic political parties.

This mixed bag in Gulen's political conduct leaves some mystery around his ultimate political orientation, but it is estimated that when he left for the US in 1999, that was a sort of self-imposed exile, maybe out of personal frustration that he did not make it to the top, or more likely due to his indictment for subverting the still army-backed civil governments of Turkey at the end of the 20th Century. In 2000, more than two years prior to the advent of Erdogan's Party (AKP, temporarily headed by Abdallah Gul), he was found guilty, in absentia, of scheming to overthrow the government by embedding civil servants in various governmental offices - an indictment that would come back to haunt him again later, and that Erdogan conveniently used after the 2016 coup against him. In 2002, after the stunning victory of AKP, Gulen was still confident that he could continue to cooperate with Erdogan, while the latter, out of an astute political consideration, probably thought that his partner could strengthen his political base by lending some ideological and popular underpinnings to the AKP which was not viewed in the public as a natural heir to the throne of national politics. However, after being re-elected in 2007 with even a stronger mandate, the AKP under Erdogan's leadership grew to regard Gulen as a potential competitor for popularity if not for power. But rather than battling him from the outside and putting the rule of Turkey under a permanent challenge, he apparently determined, like President Truman with regard to Edgar Hoover, that better to bring him into the tent and let him urinate to the outside, than combat him from the outside and compel him to urinate inside. Within a year, he would reverse the charges against Gulen, signaling a willingness to cooperate with the cleric and his global movement. In fact, Erdogan mobilized the tremendous empire Gulen had built worldwide to his benefit, especially the media and educational networks he had erected within Turkey and outside of it, for Gulen was educating in his schools pious youth who at the same time were thoroughly modernized, and that was what Erdogan was striving for, aided by Islamic banks which facilitated the transfer of funds to developing Turkey. Another common goal which facilitated the cooperation between the two leaders was the opening of Central

Asia subsequent to the collapse of the Soviet Union. The new Islamic states were in effect charmed by the educational entrepreneurship of Gulen and welcomed his aid, something that went hand in hand with Turkish policy as explained above, without heeding too much the warnings about the long-term potential subversion that an Islamic education can generate.

This collaboration was also beneficial for Gulen, though both competitors were suspicious of each other. Thus, while Erdogan viewed Gulen's input into the Islamization of Turkey as a controlled blessing, and Gulen's exile as a guarantee that he was unable to constitute any immediate threat, Gulen was elated to see his followers invading *en masse* Turkish bureacracy, educational system, the judiciary and the security forces. Viewing the collaboration between the two leaders as a sign of their joined long term program, Gulen's followers had no compunction about pursuing their course of action while the AKP called the rules of the game. Thus, even when some AKP operatives feared that the Gulenists were acting like an "underground army", the latter astutely responded that they were increasing a democratic and free dialogue within Turkish society. Until the day came, in July 2016, when the coup against Erdogan was conveniently (rightly or wrongly) attributed to the Gulenists and the all-out campaign to eradicate them was launched, while their absent leader turned into an abject criminal and terrorist, implying that his supporters too were no more than terrorist traitors.

Thus, if Erdogan's close collaborator and devoted patriot can subvert his rule and be a traitor and a terrorist, what prevents the other "terrorist" – Prime Minister Netanyahu of Israel, who has no regards for Muslim children whom he "murders in Gaza" right and left, and strives to dethrone his nemesis – the Muslim Party headed by Erdogan, out of office in Ankara, from acting together to achieve the same end under the sponsorship of that "shameless Zionist"- President Trump, who had shown his malevolence against the Muslims and in favor of the Jews? That daring thesis is not pronounced openly as yet, but some discreet analysts find it plausible. For after all, the Gulenists say that their members seek inter-religious dialogue and that they are devoted to the principle of serving others, hence their self-styled name, "*Hizmet*" - which translates as "service." This is also how they explain their abundant presence in government positions, but this is also how their opponents can claim is their innate propensity to collaborate with outsiders in their schemes to reverse the government, as Gluen himself had attempted in 1999 and had to flee into exile before he was indicted and convicted *in absentia* .

Paradoxically, the old guard generals who had maintained the intimate relations with Israel, have been dismissed and imprisonned and replaced by others more lenient towards Islam, typically from among Gulen's followers, whom they now have to ostracize in line with Erdogan's obsession with the conspiracy against his rule. At the same time, in his effort to limit Gulen's influence in Turkey and to tarnish his image, Erdogan attributed to him the corruption scandals where Erdogan's own family was involved in 2013. These revelations, one of the biggest scandals in modern Turkish history, in turn inspired the Gezi Park protests, which Erdogan quelled with an iron fist. Not only did he fight protesters with violence, resulting in 22 deaths, but he also turned onGulen, accusing him for the second time of trying to infiltrate and overthrow the government by supporting the protests. The image of Gulen as a subversive Islamist was thus cemented - an enemy of the state, whom Erdogan accused of fashioning a "state within a state" or a "parallel state." Even though Turkish authorities have tried to link the assassin of Russian Ambassador Andrei Karlov, on December 19, 2017, to moribund Gulen's global network, which he firmly denied, Erdogan's machinery's determination to accuse him of all the crimes of the world is only indicative of the President's deep paranoia and conspiracy theories which have been jolting him since the coup of

2016. Gulen's application for a visa to the US, which was rejected by the immigration authorities was finally approved only due to the intervention of high officials including the CIA. A rare citation from Gulen[130], which might "indict" him regarding potential links with Jews, was a report that he had initiated an interfaith dialogue with the Vatican and some Jewish organizations and that he had in the 1970s, "invited people to practice tolerance and forgiveness."[, something that might be inpardonable in the eyes of Erdogan whose heart is bubbling with hatred towards Jews and Israelis. On the national level, since his movement enjoyed some recognition under President Ozal, himself a religious Muslim, opposition to him was sparked by the Kemalists against his widespread educational activities which they abhorred as threatening secularism, while at the same time more radical Muslims, of the type of Erbakan and his adepts criticized him for his accommodating and conciliatory attitudes towards the West. In the 1990s he met with Pope John Paul II and other religious leaders, who included the Sephardic Chief Rabbi of Israel- Bakshi-Doron.

However, on the Gaza flotilla issue, which was staged by Erdogan to turn the corner with Israel, the Turkish Prime Miniter seems to have been directly and sorely humiliated by Gulen's conduct, and that was inexcusable. In effect, Gülen criticized the Turkish-led Gaza flotilla for trying to deliver aid to the Palestinians without Israel's consent. He spoke of watching the news coverage of the deadly confrontation between Israeli commandos and multinational aid group members as the flotilla approached Israel's sea blockade of Gaza. He said, "What I saw was not pretty, it was ugly." He has since continued his criticism, saying later that the organizers' failure to seek accord with Israel before attempting to deliver aid was "a

---

[130] Fethullah Gulen (2010), Toward a Global Civilization of Love and Tolerance. Tughra Books. *Cited in ISBN as 978-1932099683*

sign of defying authority, and will not lead to fruitful matters.[131] This was not only a direct affront to Erdogan's policies and a contradiction to his statements and incitement campaigns against Israel, but also the most challenging offense to the anti-Israeli onslaughts of the Turkish Prime Minister and public denial of all the fraudulent theses he had tried to peddle to the Turkish public and to the world in order to rationalize his braodsides against Jews, Zionism and Israel:

1. Against Erdogan's repeated accusations that Israel was killing "Palestinian children", here comes a respected leader who implied that Israel was in her rights to check the delivery of humanitarian aid to Gaza, and it was Erdogan's fault not recognize that right;

2. Against Erdogan's outcry against Israel for practicing piracy in international waters, Gülen in fact backed the verdict of the UN –commissioned report by a former Prime Minister of New Zealand that Israel's blockade was legal; and, worst of all

3. Gülen recommanded that everyone should look at the recorded evidence of the unwarranted attack by the Turks on the Israeli commandoes who peacefully descended on the *marmara* to lead it to Ashdod in Israel for inspection. He had obviously seen the film and was impressed to the point of publicly denouncing his Prime Minister's false accusations;

4. In effect, by coming to those conclusions and courageously announcing them in public, he condemned the "deal" medi-

---

[131] *Günter Seufert (January 2014).* "Is the Fethullah Gülen Movement Overstretching Itself?" *(Research Paper). Stiftung Wissenschaft und Politik. 2 August 2016.*

ated by America under Obama, which would have surely been declared by his successor as the "worst deal", that forced Israel to pay "compensation" in order to redress a wrong it did not do. At the end, after the outrageous "compensations" were disbursed, Erdogan did not repay with the promised *quid pro quo* and the relations between the countries were not really restored.

Despite this totally unexpected stand in favor of Israel on the part of Gulen, while all Turkey was bubbling with anti-Israeli propaganda and incitement, to accuse him of Zionism or pro-Jewish propensities or special links with Israel would be a wild exaggeration. His quarrel with Erdogan and the obsessive way his extradition has been pursued therefore seem as a purely personal affair of ego and oneupmanship between the two men, except that in his frantic pace of an irreversible Islamization of Turkey, Erdogan can always dismiss his opponent's accommodating ways as an obstacle worth removing in order to faciliate the ideal Islamic society he has been striving to erect and for which he gained public support, to his mind, in three or four consecutives rounds of elections and plebiscites. As evidence against his nemesis, Erdogan can always cite his repeated affirmation that secularism was not necessarily anti-religious, for as long as it allowed freedom of religion and belief, it was compatible with Islam. He was also cited as affirming that in democratic-secular countries, 95% of Islamic principles were permissible and practically feasible, and there was no problem with them while the remaining 5% "were not worth fighting for". But it is those 5% that Erdogan might insist as crucial for his Islamization program. For example, in one of his many publications[132], and against the prevailing mood among many Muslim theologians and

---

[132] *Terror and Suicide Attacks: An Islamic Perspective*, Tughra Books, 2008. ISBN 1932099743

politicians, Gulen dared to call the "suicide attacks" of Muslim terrorists by their name, distancing himself from the currently
accepted terminology of *Istishhad* (martyrdom or *Islamikaze*[133]).
Conversely, except when directed against Turkey, Erdogan has
always justified the terrorists of Hamas and Hizbullah as martyrs.

---

[133] Islamikaze, a combination of Islam and Kamikaze was coinded by this author.
See his articles and books on the topic.

CHAPTER NINE
The Looming Balkan Arena

Yet another world stage where Erdogan's Turkey and Israel have diverged in their interests and might still collide in the future, are the Balkan states which had been in the past part of the Ottoman Empire, and then partly in the Soviet Empire, but since the 1990's, after the collapse of the latter, new relationships are being woven there. One of the most remarkable phenomena in that regard has been the extraordinary warming of the links betwwen Israel and Greece, which in many respects has replaced the deteriorating relations between Ankara and Jerusalem under Erdogan. Greece, also a member of NATO like Turkey, with the added advantage of also being a member of the EU which has so far excluded Turkey, has in fact replaced its Turkish rival as a close ally of Israel, much to Ankara's displeasure. With Romania, especially under Ceaucescu, Israel has maintained a correct relationship even during the darkest hours of its mistreatment by the Soviet Bloc, and with Bulgaria it established relations recently. Communist Yogoslavia had maintained a clear distance from Israel due to Tito's relations with Nasser and the rest of the "Non-Aligned" group, but after its dismantlement and the wars of Bosnoia (1992-5) and Kosovo (1998-9) which revived Islam there, Turkish involvement was emphasized, with Western support and aid. Israel has tied good relations with independent Serbia and Croatia, Slovenia and Macedonia, who are not exactly

Ankara's friends, and also with the Muslim central government of Bosnia and its Serb component of *Republica Srpska*. The question of an independent Muslim Kosovo has been still pending in the balance due to the controvesries it occasions, both in the Balkans and worldwide.

As Bat Ye'or has copiously demonstrated in her books about dhimmitude across the Isalmic world, her most recent summary of the Balkan scene in this regard deserves notice and reference[134]. According to her, it was due to the weakness ensued by new post-Soviet Russia that President Clinton, in order to cover up for America's intrusion into Saudi and Kuwaiti territory during the 1991 Gulf War, that he rushed to dismantle Yugoslavia, prompted the former Ustasha to revive their anti-Serb rebellion in Croatia, while radical Muslims brought back to life Muslim enclaves in Bosnia, those Ottoman hotbeds of Bosniak Janissaries which had represented the insteitution of *devshirme*, that age-old agency for kidnapping, enslaving and Islamizing Christian children in the Balkans and the rest of Europe. Thus, in fact, the ancient religious hatreds are being revived which had grown under the various kinds of Imperialism which had subjugated the Balkans in the 19th and 20th centuries : the occupation by Austrian imperialists facilitated by the Croat Catholics, then the war of independence of the Orthodoc Serbs, supported by Russia, and then the Bosniak Muslim rebellions who resented the removal of their privileged position of oppressing the Christian *dhimmis* in the region. It was then that the Americans decided to play the Islamic and Turkish card, leaving to the Serbs no option that would respect their legitimate expectation, thus unleashing the war which targeted the suppression of Serbian resistance. The European and Western press then depicted the Muslim war "victims" as the duplication of the Jewish genocide

---

[134] Bat Yeor, *Bat Ye'or: Autobiographie Politique:DE la DEcouverte du Dhimmi a Eurabia*, Ls Provinciales, 2017, pp.207-210.

of W W II, while the Jewish, Serb and Roma massacre perpetrated by the Ustasha regime and the Muslim SS brigades in Bosnia and Croatia, who were reinforced by Arabs and other Asian Muslims, instigated by the Palestinian Mufti of Jerusalem, were purposely forgotten. For NATO, to quell the Serbian resistance was a children's game. Its General Secretary, Javier Solana, acting without UN approval, sent his bombers to carpet-bomb Belgrade.

Bat Ye'or finds that the violence of the press and its anti-Serb bias obstructed the way towards any objective evaluation of the situation, which was in fact replayed against the background of the alleged multi-religious and harmonious Ottoman Empire, governed by the *Shari'a's* standards of Justice. That idyllic model of European existence under the aegis of Islam, that was being erected, is aided by the encouragement of Muslim immigration into Europe, the admission of Turkey into the EU, and the fusion of Europe with Islam as envisaged by the vision of *Eurabia*[135]. The Serbs were thus rightly exasperated by Europe's and the previous Ustasha attempt to erase the history and cultures of European nations by globalization, the disappearance of national borders, and their alliance with Islam. Originally, Serbs and Muslims were members of the same people, before some Serbs (the Croats insist that they were Croats) converted into Islam in order to keep possession of their lands and weapons under Ottoman rule, while their compatriots and former coreligionists were turned *dhimmis* in their effrort to resist forced conversion. Thus, Muslims had become the oppressors of their brothers, while the Serbs became their victims. Only following decades of battles and massacres could the Serbs liberate themselves at the end of the 19th Century from the Turkish colonization. But during W W II they were afflicted by genocide on the part of the fascist Ustasha Croatians who were allied to the Nazis, and were joined in their endeavor by the Muslim Bosniaks who were incited

---

[135] This is also the title of one of Bat Ye'or's recent books.

by the Mufti of Jerusalem, Haj Amin al-Husseini who was the spiritual and religious Chief of the Muslim SS divisions recruited in the Balkans. According to Bat Ye'or, the myth of a pluralist and tolerant Islam was created in the 19th by Great Britain in Bosnia and Herzegovina in order to appease the infuriated public opinion by the massacres of Christian rebels under the Ottoman regime. At the time, the Foreign Office indeed justified its support to the Porte by the alleged inherent tolerance of Islam under which the Ottomans operated. It said that this system was best adapted to the ignorant and sub-human masses of Balkan Slavs, and this view was backed by the Turkophiles of Europe who regarded the Ottoman system as a model of multi-ethnic and multi-religious rule which guaranteed happiness and equality to all under the enlightened Islamic law, an argument that would be later picked up and hammered in by Elya Izetbegovic, the President of modern Bosnia.

However, the Consular reports of the time tell a quite different story, for they provide evidence of a cruel oppression of Christians (and Jews) under the crushing laws of the *dhimmi*, which demonstrate the utilization of the fabricated myth of Islamic tolerance only to justify the collusion of the European powers with the Ottoman authorities, much like what is done today within the strictures of *Eurabia*, which bend European governments to the Islamic will and force them to swallow the excesses of Islam and its expansion into Europe, much to the growing displeasure of the general public there. In other words this myth has survived the fall of the Ottoman Empire, but converted into the post- W W I Arab nationalism and backed by European intellectuals, politicians, clerics and writers in order to to scuttle any attempt by Christians (and Kurds) to attain their national aspirations, thus depriving Armenians, Copts, Assyrians-Chaldeans and Lebanese Maronites from attaining national sovereignty in lands that were originally theirs but where they had been occupied by conquering Islam and reduced to *dhimmis*. In the 1990s the wars in Yugoslavia and the massive bombardment of Serbia by NATO, once again took place under the widely held assumption of a Muslim Bosnia that was multi-religious and multi-ethnic and inherited the mythical Ottoman tolerance. Bat Ye'or also rebelled against dubbing the Christians under Islam who have rebelled against their discrimination in the 19th Century, generating massacres and retaliations against them, as "religious mainorities", because they in fact represented the remnants of defeated majorities which were taken over by military conquest and then rapidly eroded by conversions, voluntary and involuntary, seeking to survive or to potect their material interests, and if they retracted from their imposed conversion, were convicted for "apostasy" and sentenced to death.

This was aslo the fate of Jews under Islam for more than a millennium[136], until the rise of the state of Israel in 1948, whose robust resistance against the onslaughts of Islam, whose yoke the Jewish *dhimmis* had shaken off under the energetic jolt of the Zionist movement, in tandem with their kin in Eastern Europe and the vestiges of the European Holocaust martyrs, have become a model of revival and of defiance of their sworn Muslim enemies. This is where Serbs and Jews, Israelis and former Yugoslavs can meet and sympathize, lament their common past under Muslim oppression and plan a common future. Croats have aso joined the new bandwagon of success and optimism, but their Ustasha past is hard to forget or to forgive. Bosnia too has opened up to new Israel despite that grim past, partly due to its large Serbian component of *Republica Srpska*, which will not allow the Bosnian Federation to slide in the Islamic direction that Elya Izetbegovic had chartered for it[137].

The Ottoman state, which had reached Vienna at the pinnacle of

---

[136] See Bat Ye'ors other books on the topic (*The Dhimmi, Les Chretientes d' Orient, Juifs et Chretiens sous l'Islam, etc.*) as well as my own *Paranoia, Inferiority Complex and Religious Fanaticism*.

[137] R. Israeli, *The Islamic Challenge in Europe*, Transaction, NJ, 2008, especially Ch. 5, pp. 197-218.

its expansion in the sixteenth century, in its second quest to Islamize Europe, after the first attempt had ended in failure in the Iberian Peninsula around the same time, was deemed multi-ethnic and multi-religious, all right, but under the Muslim domination which prescribed and enforced the laws of *dhimma,* a far cry from the multi-culturalism practiced today in Europe and in Israel, of which the Muslim migrants into Europe are taking advantage to impose cultural changes to their tune in their host environments. In effct, under Muslim dominance, Christians, Jews, and others lived in a state of *dhimma* for many centuries, ostensibly as relatively free to exercise their respective faiths, but in fact they were often displaced, uprooted, lured, and at times forced to Islamize. For this coexistence was not born out of a modern concept of tolerance of the other on the basis of acceptance of differences and equality for all, and therefore on the right of free choice, but on a sense of superiority of the dominant faith and rule of Islam which when it tolerated others, that was in spite of their inherent inferiority in its eyes. Therefore, even though Muslim Turks may have temporarily constituted the minority of the population in some areas of the Empire, they reigned supreme by virtue of their Muslim master status, while the various Christian groups (and Jews for that matter) were relegated to the status of "protected people" (*dhimmis*) even when they constituted the majority of the population. Christians and others who had integrated into the Ottoman system, by embracing Islam, speaking Turkish, and going into the government service, soon became part and parcel of the Ottoman culture, even when they kept their attachment to their ethnic origin and to their mother tongue. The Bosnians were a case in point; many of them felt privileged to go into the *devsirme* system of enrolling their kidnapped boys to the prestigious Janissary Corps, and in the course of time, they were Islamized, though they maintained their ethnic and linguistic roots and often returned to their birthplace to boss around their previous compatriots and coreligionists.

The Balkans were conquered by the Ottomans from the middle of the fifteenth century on. Serbia fell to the Muslim conquerors in 1459, and four years later Bosnia and Herzegovina succumbed. Caught between the economic interest of milking the tax-paying *dhimmis* by extracting from them the *jizya*h poll tax, which necessitated maintaining the conquered population in place instead of expelling it or converting it by force; and the military and security needs that required the Muslim population to be numerous and dominant enough to ensure the loyalty to the Empire, the Ottomans tended to implement the latter choice in the Balkans. They adopted the policy of deporting part of the native populations and settling their own people, or other conquered people in their stead, thus ensuring that no local minority should envisage any insurgency among a dominant Muslim population. In Bosnia, and parts of Bulgaria, Serbia, Macedonia and Montenegro, as well as in Albania, the process of Islamization was reinforced by the local turncoats who flocked to Islam and became the worst oppressors of their former coreligionists. So much so, that the Bosnians, for example, were notorious for their role in the Ottoman administration, the military, and especially the Janissaries. Much of the anti-Christian zeal, which burst in Bosnia in the twentieth century against Serbs and Croats alike, can be traced back to those early times. As late as 1875, way after the introduction of the modernizing *tanzimat* reforms into the Ottoman system, which were supposed to redress the situation of the non-Muslims throughout the Empire, the British Ambassador in Istanbul reported that the Ottoman authorities in Bosnia recognized the impossibility to administer justice in equality between the Muslims and the Christians, inasmuch as the ruling Muslim courts accepted no written or oral evidence from Christians. One 1876 report from Bosna-Serai (Sarajevo) by the British Consul in town, tells the whole story:

About a month ago, an Austrian subject named Jean

Udilak, was attacked and robbed between Sarajevo and Visoka by nine Bashi-Bazouks. The act was witnessed by a respectable Mussulman of this time named Nouri Aga Varinika, and he was called as a witness when the affair was brought before the Sarajevo Tribunal. His testimony was in favor of the Austrian, and the next day he was sent for by the Vice-President and one of the members of the Court and threatened with imprisonment for daring to testify against his coreligionists.

As British Consul Majer tells us, Muslims, Christians (and Jews, for that matter), could keep to themselves in their own communities, with their lifestyles, rituals, and festivals running without hindrance, except in case of intermarriage. For here, the only allowed combination was Muslim men taking in Christian (or Jewish) wives, an act that consecrated their joint offspring as full-right Muslims. The result was that while non-Muslim culture merged into the predominant Islam, there was also an outside input into the Muslim civilization, with material culture (food, dress, habits, language) growing to become common to all. All this was acceptable to the Ottoman authorities who were reluctant to interfere, but as soon as the *dhimmis* became wealthy and were conspicuous in their dress and demeanor, it was considered a provocation to the Muslim population and dealt with accordingly. Christians who wanted to improve their lot in Bosnia and Albania could always do so through conversion to Islam or seek the protection of their Muslim family members.

Toward the end of the Ottoman rule, as economic problems arose and the state was no longer able to enforce law and order in the face of the nationalist awakening in the various provinces of the Empire, local rule grew more despotic in an attempt to hold on to the territories that were slipping out of the Porte's grip. The notions of equality coming from liberal Europe, which made the maintenance of legal and religious inequities untenable, were conjugated into national terms in the Balkans, and spelled out independence from the Ottoman yoke, since the idea of ruling an Empire held together by Islam was no longer operative. It was, ironically, the Ottoman attempts at modernity, opening up the system and addressing individuals instead of traditional communities, which brought to its downfall and opened the new vistas of nationalism and independence in the Balkans as elsewhere, a situation not unlike Eastern Europe after the Gorbachev Perestroika in the late 1980s and early 1990s. But in view of the Greek and Bulgarian plans for a Balkan Federation under their aegis, to take over from the Ottomans, the gradual and parallel dreams to realize a Greater Serbia, a Greater Croatia, and a Greater Albania, and the tax repression imposed on all of them by the Bosnian Muslims on behalf of the dwindling imperial authorities, the Serbs rose up in arms (1875), and many of them ran into hiding, leaving behind, to the mercy of the Muslims, children, the old and women, something reminiscent of the horrors of the Bosnian War and then the Kosovo War more than one century later. Banja Luka and Preydor were the most harmed by the insurgents when Serb churches and homes were burned.

According to reports from the time of the rebellion, the Bosnian Muslims, descendants of converted Slavs who had become the land-owners and acceded to the status of aristocracy by virtue of their conversion, now practiced their faith fanatically and ruthlessly toward their Orthodox compatriots, who would rather die in battle than submit to the tax exactions. What made things worse, again like in the recent events in Bosnia, was that the Catholics (later identified as Croats) allied to the Muslims against the Orthodox Serbs, as was to recur again during World War II when the greater combined state of Croatia and Bosnia was set up under the Ustasha. An eyewitness of the time reports:

> United under oppression, it was natural that the Serbs

should respond by rebellion. But in the entire northern part of Bosnia and Turkish Croatia, the antagonism between the two [Catholic and Orthodox] denominations is vast enough for us to have eye-witnessed Catholics marching on the heels of the Turks against Greek insurgents.... By an inexplicable aberration, the priests of the two denominations entertain hatred [toward each other] and we could say without exaggerating that, if given the choice the Catholics would rather be dominated by the Turks [Muslims] than by the Orthodox Serbs.

That reporter had concluded that the Muslims of Bosnia maintained their loyalty to the Ottomans, and that there was no chance of a fusion between the populations, in view of the fact that those Serbs (or Croats) whose ancestors had embraced Islam as a political expediency, were now too imbued with it and too captured by the teachings of their Holy Book to relent from their intense hatred, which had germinated in their bodies and taken them over completely. But this was to be only a foretaste of things to come, as henceforth the politics of Yugoslavia would be dominated by the alliance of two of its major religious groups, and later ethno-national communities, against the third. After the Berlin Congress (1878) and the occupation of Bosnia by the Austro-Hungarian Empire, the Serbs allied with the Muslims against the occupiers, who were supported by the Catholics (Croats) in the province. The Hungarian governor of the province tried valiantly to create a new Bosnian identity merging together its three principal communities, but he failed. The annexation of Bosnia by the occupiers in 1908, created a new alliance: the Serbs of Bosnia, who wished their merger with Serbia (not for the last time), were pitted against the Croat-Muslim coalition who would rather reconcile to their occupation than allow the Serbs to implement their dream. As a result, repression of the

Serbs in Bosnia, coupled with the expulsion of Serbs from Kosovo, brought to a record level the bitterness of the occupied Serbs against their oppressors. Sukrija Kurtovic, a Bosnian Muslim, sought the differentiation between ethno-nationality and religion, and pleaded for the unity of the Bosnians with the Serbs in one single national group by reason of their common Serbian roots, arguing that Islam was a common religion of the Bosnians and the Turks, but that in itself did not make them share any national common ground. The idea of Yugoslavism, a larger entity where all the ethnic and religious groups could find their common identity, came to the fore after the Balkan wars and precipitated World War I following the Sarajevo murder of the heir to the Austro-Hungarian throne in 1914. That war reinforced the Croat-Muslim alliance in Bosnia, which swore to expel the Serbs from Bosnia altogether, and acted upon its vow by perpetrating large-scale massacres of the Serbs, thus demonstrating the vanity of an all-Yugoslavian identity.

A Yugoslavian state was created in 1918 nevertheless, which once again attempted to fuse its components in the ethnic and linguistic domains and leave, as befits a modern European state, the question of religion to the realm of each individual. However, while the Serbs and the Croats of Bosnia could look up to Belgrade and Zagreb, respectively, the Muslims were left to vacillate between their Muslim, Ottoman, local and Slavic roots. At first they allied with the stronger Serbs and turned their eyes on Belgrade where they ensured for themselves some privileges; but wary of the competition between the Croats, who championed their particularistic national-ism, and the Serbs, who regarded themselves as the guardians and sponsors of Yugoslavian unity, they focused more and more on their local and religious identity in the form of a Muslim Party (JMO), while the Serbs and the Croats continued to claim that the Muslims of Bosnia were of their respective origins. The Yugoslavian kingdom, which was formed in 1918, integrated into a single state embracing the southern Slavic nations of Croatia, Slovenia, Serbia, Bosnia-

Herzegovina, Montenegro, and Macedonia. Each one of these nations dwelling in the Balkans, and being the protégé of outside conflicting interests and competing religious denominations, triggered more than once wide-ranging confrontations all over Europe, notably in Sarajevo in 1914, which launched the conflagration of the Great War in 1914 that caused the death of twenty million persons; deprived Europe of an entire generation of young lives of workers, intellectuals, artists, creative minds, and who knows who else; and instead paved the way for the larger and more cruel and destructive World War II, when frustrated madmen like Adolf Hitler and his ilk, who could not accept their country's and personal humiliation, set the world on fire. But when the first Yugoslavian state was created in consequence of that war, *inter alia* on the ruins of the Austro-Hungarian and Ottoman sick and obsolete empires, it was the result of positive Western attitudes toward its component parts, which were to shift totally later on.

The consequences of this array of alliances were the Yugoslavian wars in the wake of the dismantlement of the Yugoslavian state, once the strong man which held it together forcibly, much like Hafez al-Assad in Syria whose death occasioned the civil war and the dismembermentof the country into its ethno-religious components (Christians, Druze, Alawites, Sunnis) until great power politics interfered and are attempting to restore Bashar al Assad's authoritarian rule to make it a semblance of his father's style of rule, now instigated by Erdogan's regime after its decision to join the Putin-Rohani camp. When the Yugoslavian wars broke out, with large doses of Islam entering the fray, and foreign Jihadi Muslims converging on Bosnia (1992-5) in support of the local Bosnian Muslims and in connivance with them, the pre-Erdogan civil governments in Ankara began to realize that their joint war calculations with the Americans, which had envisaged a moderate Turkey taking the lead of the Muslim continuum from the Balkans to Central Asia was faltering. And the Americans and their NATO allies were even ready to pay the obvious price of accepting the Muslim wedge that this geo- political reality would have introduced in the heart of Europe, interrupting the Christian Greek-Orthodox continuum from Russia through Eastern and Central Europe through Greece and into the Aegean Sea. Thus the fact that they decided the wars in the Muslims' favor ended up backfiring on them. And to the extent that Turkey remained relevant in those countries, it nonetheless no longer meets the role that was designed for her by the powers. Instead, it is Saudi Arabia, with the latent support of Israel who also maintains good relations with all the Balkan countries, which ensure the ouster of Iran and its ilk from those areas (for now). As to Western interests, contrary to the American initial planning, they have been foiled by Turkey's Islamic revolution under Erdogan, and his veering towards Russia and Iran and away from democracy, moderation and NATO.

The Bosnia War, which began as a civil war between the ethnic and religious components of former Yugoslavia, and ended (at least for now) only through massive intervention of the UN, the EU and the US, continues to brew under and over the surface, due to the involvement of world Islam both in cultivating Bosnia as a Muslim entity in the heart of Europe, and in enhancing the Islamic stature in Europe in particular and the West in general. These trends did not begin with the Bosnia War *per se,* which was a direct product of the dismantling of Yugoslavia, but have deep roots in the long heritage that the Ottoman Empire has left behind when it was compelled to abandon Muslim positions in Europe, for the second time, at the end of 19th Century after a rule extending over four centuries in the Balkans. When Bosnia emerged as a separate Muslim entity, various Islamic models competed for prevalence there in order to shape it to their respective tastes, and that too has conditioned the fate of the country, in accordance with the powers who supported this or that model, rightly or wrongly. The key to understanding the implanting and growth of Islam in Bosnia, which lay at the base of its Islamization in modern times, on the one hand, and its rejection by its Christian neighbors, on the other, must be sought in the heavy heritage that the Ottomans have left behind, which turned Slavic Bosnians, who were originally either Croats or Serbs, into enemies of the latter, and into a self-conscious separate "ethnic group" which was recognized by Tito in the 1960's, as a counterpart of the other ethnic groups who made up the Yugoslavian Federation. In the Conference on the Turks and Islam at the University of Indiana, Stephen Schwartz[138] offered a brilliant analysis of that heritage. He first found it necessary to recognize the difference in the religious and cultural destinies of the peoples in the area that were brought under Ottoman rule, beginning in the 14th century C.E. Schwartz stressed that Serbian historical legend depicts all Slavs who became Muslims as "renegade Serbs" who left their past faith either under compulsion or to avoid the *Jizya* poll tax on non-Muslims that was imposed by the Muslim Empire, and to gain other advantages. There certainly were and are Serb Muslims, although many were driven out of the country during the wars, massacres, and expulsions of Slav and Albanian Muslims during the long southerly expansion of Serbian territory, beginning in 1804. *Muhajirs*[139] or refugees from persecution for their Muslim faith settled in places as distinct from one another as Kosovo, and Turkey. At least 3.5 percent of the Serbian population of 7.5 million today is Muslim, concentrated in the southwest, with Slavs, who identify themselves as Bosniaks, living in the northern part of

---

[138] Stephen Schwartz, "The Heritage of Ottoman Islam in the Balkans", Indiana University, Bloomington, Conference on The Turks and Islam, September 12, 2010. See www.islamicpluralism.org/1663/the-heritage-of-ottoman. Much of the following discussion is based on this lecture.

[139] Muslim *Muhajirs* – literally "migrants"-, have been using that same terminology to designate refugees who were either forced through "population exchanges" (Like between Turkey and Greece and later between India and Pakistan) into exile, or were constrained by circumstance to move into an alien land (Like Pakistanis in England).

the former *Sanjak* of Pazar and Novipazar, which was divided between Serbia and Montenegro after the Balkan Wars of 1912-13. The *Sanjak*, as it is known to Bosniaks today, also includes a significant Albanian Muslim presence at its eastward extremity, bordering on Kosovo.Ottoman immigration to these districts was uneven after their takeover, with some receiving considerable numbers of Turkish colonists and administrators, others fewer. Remnants of Ottoman Turkish communities, sometimes speaking archaic dialects of the language, are to be found today in Kosovo, Macedonia, Bulgaria, and Thrace. In addition, Turkish-language *ilahije* (hymns praising Allah) and spiritual songs are still sung by Sufis in the region.

Until the Communist era, Bosnia was rich with Sufi activities, including those of the main *tariqats* (Orders) aside from the Naqshbandis and Qadiris, such as the *Mevlevis,* who are said to have converted a former dignitary of the autonomous Bosnian Church (Bogamil, similar to the heretic Albigensi movement of southern France)) to Islam. On the whole, according to Schwartz, Bosnian Islam has maintained an air of pronounced Sunni "rigor" although its popular culture, as revealed in song traditions, is replete with positive references to rebels. Nevertheless, resentment of the distant authority in Istanbul is found under the surface of many Bosnian Muslim cultural products. For example, two Muslim brothers from the 18th century, the Morići, were hanged by the authorities yet are looked upon as beloved symbols of Sarajevo, and celebrated in many folk songs, as are the victims of Ottoman Turkey celebrated in Bosnian Ivo Andric's *Bridge on the Drina River.* One of the folk songs, proclaimed: "Imperial sultan, you are damned as long as your sword denies justice and the empire stands on evil; Oh, pashas and vezirs will come and go but my Bosnia will never die." These songs became patriotic anthems during the 1992-95 war in Bosnia-Herzegovina, and the reference to the evil foundation of the Ottoman Empire invariably elicits waves of applause when this ballad is included in public performances in Bosnia[140] Muslim Albanians in Kosovo and western Macedonia remained loyal to Sufism, which could not be suppressed in their regions of former Yugoslavia. By contrast, Sufism was outlawed in Bosnia-Herzegovina in the 1950s. In a certain sense, Bosnian Muslims may be said to have preferred the worldly rewards brought by the Communist system, in the form of artificial industrial development, over the spiritual bounties of the Sufis. The result of this is that Sufism has a rich tradition of local *shaykhs* and authors in Bosnia, but most of them are figures of the past, although some Sufis fought with distinction in the 1992-95 war. Today, Sufism has a more abstract, intellectual, and even folkloric quality in Bosnia-Herzegovina than in Kosovo, western Macedonia, and Albania proper. In the former it is but one among many competing cultural trends, Islamic and non-Islamic, but in the latter it maintains a strong presence in public life. Under Titoite Yugoslavia, the non-Bektashi Sufis of Yugoslavia had their headquarters among the Kosovar Albanians of Prizren, while the teaching and clerical institutions of the Yugoslav Islamic Community were centered in Sarajevo. Although Bosniaks and Kosovars speak different languages, the Islamic Faculty of Sarajevo continues to serve as the main teaching institution for Muslim religious functionaries in the western Balkans, Kosovar Albanians as well as Bosnians and others.

In April, 1998 the State Department published its annual report on global terrorism. Among other things it referred to the unidentified terrorists who acted against the international presence in Bosnia, and especially to the *Mujahideen* who had served in the Bosnian army during the civil war, but were after it engaged in warrant killings. According to that report, the Bosnian government began arresting some of those loose terrorists, and by November, 1997, it had incarcerated twenty of them, who were identified as

---

[140] Schwartz, op.cit.

Arabs or Bosnian Muslims[141]. In that same year of 1998 there were reports that Iranian Intelligence agents were mounting extensive operations and had even infiltrated the American program to train the Bosnian Army. According to those reports, more than 200 Iranian agents were identified as "having insinuated themselves into Bosnian Muslim political and social circles… to gather information and to thwart western interests in Bosnia". Those agents, it was believed, could be helpful in planning terrorist attacks against NATO forces or targets[142]. Taken together, these reports did identify the "unidentified terrorists" mentioned above. Moreover, these reports linked together into an "Islamic International" centered around Iran, most of the major terrorist activities that were carried out by Islamists then, from the Israeli Embassy in Buenos Aires (1992); the international gathering of Islamic terrorist organizations in Tehran (1997); the Hizbullah stepped-up activities against Israel in the late 1990's; the arrest in Israel of Stefan Smirak, a Muslim of Bosnian origin, a would-be "suicide-bomber" for Hizbullah (November, 1997); the attacks against American interests in the Gulf, East Africa and on American soil (throughout the 1990's)[143], to say nothing of the Muslim separatists in Northwest China (the Uyghurs of Xinjiang), and the Islamic resurgence in Bosnia and Kosovo. People spoke during the Bosnian War of the clashes between Serbs and Muslims in Bosnia, Serbs and Albanians in Kosovo, in terms of ethno-national conflicts, with the more numerous Serbs figuring as the oppressors and their rivals as the underdogs and the oppressed. *Prima facie,* the very usage of the terms Serbs (and Croats for that matter) against Muslims, equates the latter (essentially members of a faith and civilization) to the former who clearly belong to religio-ethnic groups. This points out

---

[141] *Patterns of Global Terrorism,* US Department of State, April, 1998.
[142] Policy Watch No. 296, p. 3., 1998, The Washington Institute, citing reports byThe New York Times and the Washington Times.
[143] Ilja Izetbegovic, The *Islamic Revolution,* (Serbian) Belgrade, 1970.

to the fact that not only did Yugoslavian statism and universalistic communism fail to obliterate ethnic and kinship identities (real or imagined), but that communal interest overrode the state umbrella, economic interest or even sheer common sense. But this also raises the question of whether Islam, a universal religion predominant in more than 50 countries around the world, is or can be perceived as a local nationalism that is particularistic by definition.

At any rate, the revival of Islam in the Balkans which was not sudden and did not come from nowhere, has been an acknowleged fact of life, and what use can be made of it by Turkey and other powers, to boost or restrain it, will also have a direct impact on the relations between Turkey and Israel. In 1970, well before the collapse of the Yugoslavian order that had been imposed by Tito, and the outburst of communal nationalism which instigated the process of its disintegration, a political manifesto was written by an unknown at the time Muslim in Bosnia- Alija Izetbegovic (born in 1925)- but not immediately released to the public. It was, however, duplicated and made available to individual Muslims who circulated it among their coreligionists, apparently to serve as a guide to a Muslim order to replace the Godless Communist system in Bosnia. That pamphlet is known as the *Islamska Deklaracija* (The Islamic Declaration). In 1983, after Tito's death but while the Communist state was still held together by inertia, a trial took place in Sarajevo where the author and some like-minded individuals were prosecuted for subverting the constitutional order and for acting from the standpoint of Islamic fundamentalism and Muslim nationalism. Significantly, after the fall of Communist power, the accused were publicly rehabilitated, and the *Declaration* was then officially published in Sarajevo (1990). Izetbegovic, at the head of his Democratic Action Party (SDA) won the majority of the Muslim votes in the first free elections in Bosnia-Herzegovina (November 1990), but his pamphlet was obscured and not heard of again. However, judging from the wide appeal of his later book, *Islam*

Between East and West[144], which was published in English in the USA (1984), then in Turkish in Istanbul (1987), and in Serbian in Belgrade (1988), and from the developments in the Bosnian war in the mid-1990's, one might be well advised to take a look at it. The *Declaration*, which in many respects sounds and looks like the platforms of Muslim fundamentalists elsewhere (e.g. the Hamas Charter)[145], assumed that its appeal would be heeded by Muslims around the world, not only by the immediate constituency to which it was directed, accused the West of wishing to "keep Muslim nations spiritually weak and materially and politically dependent", and called upon the Believers to cast aside inertia and passivity in order to embark on the road of action[146], a sort of open appeal to Muslims worldwide to flock to the Bosnian arena and help defend its heritage. And like Muslim radicals such as Sayyid Qutb of Egypt, who had urged his followers to reject the world of ignorance around them and transform it on the model of the Prophet of Islam, the *Declaration* of Izetbegovic also called upon the millions to join the efforts of Muslim individuals who fought against the *Jahiliyya* (the state of ignorance and godlessness which had preceded the advent of the Prophet)[147], and dedicated the text to the memory of "our brothers who have laid their lives for Islam"[148], namely the *shuhada'* (martyrs) of all times and places who had fallen in the cause of Islam.

The manifesto, again like other Muslim radicals' writings, not only addressed itself to the restoration of Islam in private life, in the family and society, but also expressly shunned local nationalism of any sort and substituted for it, as of old, the creation of a universal

---

[144] Alija Izetbegovic, *Islam Between East and West*, the US, 1984

[145] See Raphael Israeli, "The Charter of Allah: the Platform of the Hamas", in Y. Alexander (ed), *The Annual of Terrorism, 1988-9*, Nijhoff, the Netherlands, 1990, pp.99-134

[146] Introduction to the Pamphlet, pp.1-2.

[147] Ibid. p. 2.

[148] Ibid.

Islamic polity (the traditional *umma*), "from Morocco to Indonesia", much as Muslim radicals of today vow to revive the old Caliphate[149]. The author awakened his people to the reality where "a few thousand of true Islamic fighters had forced England to withdraw from the Suez Canal in the early 1950's, at a time when the nationalist armies of the Arabs were losing their battles against Israel", and where "Turkey, an Islamic country, had ruled the world" (in Ottoman times), while when it tried to emulate Europe, it dropped to the level of a third-world country. In other words, he claimed, it was not nationalism that made the force of Muslim nations, but their abidance by Islam in its universal version. Therefore, it does not befit Muslims to fight or die for any other cause but Islam, and it behooves Muslims to die with the name and glory of Allah in their hearts, or totally desert the battlefield[150]. Translated into the Bosnian scene, Muslims ought not take part in, or stand for, any form of government, which was not Islamic, and for any cause which was not connected to Islam. For the Bosnians, whom Izetbegovic addressed directly, there were only two options left: either to subscribe to Muslim revival and its political requirements, or be doomed to stagnation and oblivion[151].

The Manifesto then went into a long dissertation explaining the reasons and history of "backwardness of the Muslim nations" (pp. 5-11). Basically, it refuted modernists who regarded the notion of the Islamic *din* (faith, religion) as only religion in the European sense, and insisted on viewing it and living by it as an entire religious, cultural and political way of life, which unified "religion and science, ethics and politics, ideal and interest"[152]. In the typically fundamentalist fashion, it attacked established conservative Islam and its "*hodjas* and *sheikh*s, who organized themselves as a caste

---

[149] Ibid. p. 3.
[150] Ibid p. 4.
[151] Ibid.
[152] Ibid. p. 5.

unto itself, arrogating to itself a monopoly over the interpretation of Islam, and placed itself in the position of mediator between the Qur'an and the people"[153], a claim that mirrored the Protestant denominations in Europe and America which condemned the Catholic hierarchical system for monopolizing the link between Divinity and the Believer . It also mocked the modernists for emulating the West and worshipping its material life, ultimately producing corruption and decadence instead of spiritual uplifting. In this context, the author belittled the role of Mustafa Kemal (Attaturk) in modern Turkey, because he had wrongly thought that by ordering the *fez* out, the heads, which wore it, would also be transformed[154]. That was the reason, in the author's mind, why modern Turkey and Japan, which began from the same starting point at the turn of the century, grew in totally different directions: Japan, which knew how to integrate its own culture into modernity, but kept its traditional values and writing system, became a great power, while Turkey, which abolished her Arabic script that "ranks among the most perfect and the most widely used alphabets", in favor of introducing the Latin script, thus remaining a third-world country[155].

This total rejection of the Kemalist Turkey's model of course stood in sharp contrast and contradiction to Western, especially American, hopes to "sell" that very precedent of modernity, Europeanization and moderation to the emerging Muslim entities in Central Asia and the Balkans. As against the perceived failure of Turkey and other Muslim countries due to "the weakening of the influence of Islam in the practical life of the people, the author posited that "all successes, both political and moral, are the reflection of our acceptance of Islam and its application in life"[156]. Therefore, while all Muslim

---

[153] Ibid. p. 6.
[154] Ibid pp. 7-8.
[155] Ibid. p. 9.
[156] Ibid. p. 12.

defeats, from the Uhud Battle at the time of the Prophet (AD 625), to the Sinai War between Israel and Egypt (1956), were due to "apostasy from Islam", any "rise of the Islamic peoples, and every period of their dignity, started with the affirmation of the Qur'an" .But in today's real world the Qur'an, complained the author, was being recited instead of practiced, mosques were "monumental but empty", the form took over from substance, as the Holy Book turned "into a mere sound without intelligible sense and content"[157]. This reality was caused, lamented the author, in line with other Muslim fundamentalists, by the western-inspired or imposed school system in all Muslim countries[158]. Secularism and nationalism, the products of that foreign educational trend, took over the minds and hearts of the new generation of Muslims. The masses, who did not submit to these fleeting concepts which are foreign to Islam, chose indifference; but if they were rightly guided, they could rise to action, provided they were spurred by "an idea that corresponded to their profound feelings, and that could only be the Islamic idea", that is instilled by a new *intelligentsia*, that "thinks and feels Islam" and would ultimately "fly the flag of the Islamic order and together with the Muslim masses initiate action for its realization"[159]. This new Islamic order should unite "religion and law, upbringing and force, ideals and interests, the spiritual community and the state, free will and coercion", for an "Islamic society without Islamic rule is incomplete and impotent; Islamic rule without Islamic society is either utopia or violence"[160]. This in effect means, in the vein of other Muslim fundamentalist platforms, that the Muslim state ought to enforce ("coerce") the Islamic order, short of which violence would erupt by necessity. For, according to this scheme, and contrary to the European concept of a liberal society where the

---

[157] Ibid pp 14-15.
[158] Ibid. pp. 16-17.
[159] Ibd. p. 19.
[160] Ibid. p. 20.

individual is prized, a Muslim "does not exist as an individual entity", and he must create his Islamic milieu in order to survive, by way of changing the world around him if he does not want to be changed by others[161].

The manifesto held that there was no point to legislate laws, as has been Western wont, because they end up corrupting society. Better to educate people and teach them to obey the decree of Allah, and that would put an end to corruption and lawlessness[162]. This is the reason for the "incompatibility of Islam with non-Islamic systems"; therefore **"there can be no peace or co-existence between the Islamic faith and non-Islamic social and political institutions"**[163]. This means in effect that Muslims should not submit to a non-Islamic rule and that they should exclusively strive to create and live under an Islamic system, due to the assumption that "Islam clearly rules out any right or possibility of action of any foreign ideology [supposedly including democracy, pluralism, tolerance, freedom, equality etc] on its turf". As a result, "there is no room for the secular principle, and the state should be an expression of the moral concepts of [the Islamic] religion and supportive of them"[164]. In the light [or rather the obscurity] of these principles, which shun mysticism and stagnation and assume the right of innovation to make things adaptable to every time and place, the pamphlet defined and traced a long series of rules and regulations which ought to guide the individual Muslim (pp. 25- 40) in practically all spheres of his societal life. The core of this orientation is that "Islamic society may not be based upon social or economic interest only, or on any other external, technical factor of association. As a community of believers, it is based on a religious and emotional aspect of affiliation. This element is most clearly visible and

---

[161] Ibid.

[162] Ibid. pp. 21-22.

[163] Ibid p. 23.

[164] Ibid.

enshrined in the *jemaat* (groups, associations) as the basic unit in Islamic society"[165]. This would mean in the Bosnian context that only a religiously-based society, on the model of religious associations (*jemaat*), is viable, and no provision ought to be made for non-Muslims or for a multi-religious or multi-cultural society in its midst.

Now comes the problematic issue of the relations between the Muslim host culture, where there is one, and minority guest cultures under the Islamic order. The manifesto provided religious freedom and "protection" to the minorities, "provided they are loyal", something that smacks of the traditional Muslim attitude to the *dhimmi* (protected people) under its aegis. The interesting aspect of all this is that when the situation is reversed, namely Muslim minorities dwell in non-Muslim lands, their loyalty is made conditional on their religious freedom, not the other way around. Moreover, even under such conditions, the Muslims are committed to carry out all their obligations to the host community "with the exception of those that are detrimental to the Muslims"[166]. The question remained unanswered as to who was to determine what is detrimental to Islam, when and where. When he assumed that the status of Muslim minorities would depend on "the strength and reputation of the Islamic world community", he meant two things:

1. That there was a possibility for Izetbegovic that the Muslims of Bosnia would remain a minority; indeed, their rate is about 40% of the total population (and growing, due to higher birth-rate); and

2. if the Catholic Croats and Orthodox Serbs of Bosnia should gang up against the Muslims (as had happened in the past),

---

[165] Ibid. pp.25-6.
[166] Ibid. p. 40.

this manifesto still provided them with a chance for survival; and that was, incidentally, one of the reasons why the Muslims ended up federating with the Croats, their old-time mortal enemies, so as to create a majority coalition that could stand up to the stronger Serbs.

In any case, the Bosnian Muslims were counting on the intervention of the world Muslim community, something that was to be corroborated during the Bosnia and then the Kosovo wars. Again, like the Hamas and other branches of the Muslim Brotherhood, this manifesto proclaimed the primacy of education and preaching, in order to conquer the hearts of the people before power, which is recognized as a prerequisite for enforcing the Islamic order, is conquered. "We must be preachers first and then soldiers" [167] is the motto of the manifesto. Force to take over power will be applied, in his words, "as soon as Islam is morally and numerically strong enough, not only to overthrow the non-Islamic rule, but to develop the new Islamic rule", because "to act prematurely is as dangerous as to be late in taking the required action":[168] The author was confident that this could be done, because "history is not only a story of constant changes, but also of the continual realization of the impossible and the unexpected"[169]. The model for the new Islamic order, which the manifesto put on the pedestal, is Pakistan, the Muslim state that, in spite of its many deficiencies, remained the "great hope" of Izetbegovic[170], contrary to the preferred failed Turkish model which the West was squandering its resources for, in the killing fields of Serbia, Bosnia and later Kosovo. But his great goal was the unity of the Muslim people, and in the meantime he urged every Muslim country to be concerned about all the rest: Egypt

---

[167] Ibid. p. 45.
[168] Ibid. pp. 45-6.
[169] Ibid. p. 46.
[170] Ibid p. 48.

ought to care for the Muslims of Ethiopia and Kashmir[171], and by inference, the Muslims of Bosnia and the Balkans should be the business of all the rest of the Islamic world. He felt that the fact that sentiments of affinity for oppressed Muslim brothers everywhere were not translated into action, was the fault of the Western-educated Muslims who substituted nationalism for Pan-Islam[172]. Had he lived, Izetbegovic may have been jubilating and feeling vindicated today by the reversal that the "Arab Spring" has been producing these day. At any rate, the urge for global Muslim solidarity infers the revival of itinerant Muslim fighters who should rush from one part of the globe to another in order to preserve Islam and its prestige[173].

Under the heading "Christianity and Judaism", the manifesto determined the future relationships of the envisaged new Islamic order with those two faiths, which the author generously considered as "the two foremost religions" and the "major systems and doctrines outside the sphere of Islam"[174]. Nonetheless, the author distinguished between Jesus as a *persona* and the Church as an institution. The former said he, in line with Qur'anic teachings, was part of divine revelation, while the latter, as embodied in the Inquisition, was abhorrent to his heart. At the same time, however, as is the normative Islamic wont, he accused Christianity of "distorting certain aspects" of the divine message and accused the Church of intolerance[175]. Similarly, he differentiated between Jews and their national movement- Zionism, idealizing the times when they lived under Islam, but he totally rejected their plea for independence and nationhood[176]. So, as long as the Jews were submissive and stateless

---

[171] Ibid. pp. 49-50.

[172] Ibid. p. 51.

[173] R. Israeli, *Itinerant Jihadis*, op. cit.

[174] Ibid. pp. 55-57.

[175] Ibid 55-56.

[176] Ibid. pp. 56-7

in their *dhimmi* status within the Islamic state he envisaged, all is well, but to dare to declare independence and stand up to the Islamic world, that was unforgivable. He claimed that Jerusalem was not only a Palestinian city but first of all a Muslim one, and therefore he warned the Jews, who "have created themselves the conflict with the Arab regimes" (not the Arab or the Muslim people), that a prolonged war will be waged against them by Muslims until they release "every inch of captured land". He threatened that "any trade-offs or compromises which might call into question these "elementary rights of our brothers in Palestine will amount to treason, which can destroy even the very system of moral values underpinning our world"[177].

In sum, this passionate message of Izetbegovic, based on the Qur'an and the revival of Islam, addressed the universal congregation of all Muslims, and, like the Muslim Brothers and their many affiliates, strove to establish an Islamic world order (a Caliphate) based on Qur'anic precepts and world Islamic solidarity. The idea of nationalism, any nationalism, was totally rejected in favor of the Islamic Republic, which alone could respond to the challenges of their modern world and restore to Islam its glory and preponderance (as it has been negatively demonstrated in the separately existing republics of Iran, Pakistan, Taliban Afghanistan, Syria, Algeria and Turkey in our days, some of which he did not live to see). Like the platform of the Hamas and other fundamentalists, the text of the Qur'an, rather than the commentaries of the Muslim establishment, provides the rationale for the cultural, social and political revolution that the author proposed to undertake. ISIS or al-Qa'ida could not have expressed this platform more precisely or more forcefully. Indeed, the profuse citations from the Holy Book that we find interspersed throughout the text of the *Declaration*, bear witness to the Qur'anic hegemony in the thought and plans of the

---

[177] Ibid. p. 57.

author. Moreover, by positing the listed principles as deriving from the Holy Scripture, namely the eternal and immutable Word of Allah, the document creates, like the Charter of the Hamas (released in February 1988) the impression of a divinely guided program, which is not given to debate or consideration. The vow insinuated in this declaration, that Islam would re-conquer its people peacefully if possible, by force if necessary, might throw some light (or rather obscurity) on some of the events that took place in Bosnia in the 1990's, including Iranian and other volunteer *Mujahidun* who participated in the battles, and gained momentum later in Kosovo and elsewhere, where al-*Qa'ida* was taking root at the turn of the Millennium.

Izetbegovic is dead, after he had been compelled, against his will and expectation, to share the presidency of Bosnia with his Serb and Croat partners in his federal state under the Dayton arrangements. But it seems that Turkish Erdogan did not forgo or abandon Izetbegovic's ideology and dreams as to the Islamization of the Balkans. Consider the expression of that ambition in this latest remarkable Erdogan's measure that he takes the time to concoct and implement amidst the vast problems he is encountering with the Super-powers, Europe and Israel externally, and the refugees and the surging opposition against his rule domestically. From a report of October 19, 2018, based on a photo of a a four-minaret Ottoman-style mosque sporting a Turkish flag that was erected in the center of Pristina, the capital of Kosovo.[178] With less than 2 million people, Kosovo, which declared its independence from Serbia in 2008, is already the home of over 800 mosques and in the process of building the "Central Mosque" at an estimated cost of $35- $40 million financed by Turkey's Directorate of Religious Affairs (*Diyanet*). The Diyanet also financed the building of a similar mosque on a 10,000-square-

---

[178] Alon Ben-Meir and Arbana Xharra, "Diyanet: Erdogan's Islamic Vehicle To The Balkans", Blog, 19 October, 2018

meter parcel of land on George W. Bush Street in Tirana, Albania, the largest mosque in the Balkans, along with dozens of other mosques across neighboring countries. Turkey's president Erdogan has put in the field two state organizations, *Diyanet* and the Turkish Development Agency (TIKA), as vehicles through which Turkey could enhance its Islamic influence in the Balkans.*Diyanet* is the official state institution whose role is "to execute the works concerning the beliefs, worship, and ethics of Islam, enlighten the public about their religion, and administer the sacred worshiping places." *Diyanet* is also responsible for the religious affairs of the Turkish diaspora. In Germany alone, it administers 970 mosques with imams trained by the organization.

According to the authors of this field report, Austria as a past competitor to the Ottomans in the Balkans, was the first country to realize that the mosques built with Erdogan's money are used for political purposes to promote his Islamic agenda. In June 2018, Chancellor Sebastian Kurz ordered the closing of seven mosques built by *Diyanet*, and deported 60 imams and their families with ties to Turkey as part of the 'fight against political Islam.' Already in February 2016, German law enforcement officials revealed that clerics from the organization were involved in espionage against Gülen's followers in Germany, something that connects with the all-out struggle that Erdogan is waging against his nemesis, Fethullah Gulen. **In the same year** *Cumhuriyet*, an independent Turkish newspaper, reported that *Diyanet* was very active in collecting intelligence, specifically on the activities of Gülen sympathizers in 38 countries across Europe, including Germany and the Balkans. Accusations of espionage by the organization have existed since the 1990s, but these revelations pointed to far more extensive operations than were previously thought. Incidentally, *Diyanet* has extended its religious program also to countries whose connection to Ottoman history is tenuous by building over 100 mosques outside Turkey. The president of Diyanet, Ali Erbaş, said that they have extremely strong relations with Balkan countries and stressed that this cooperation will continue in the future, especially in relation to religious education, services, and publications. He emphasized the importance and affinity of Turkey to the Balkans and added, "The Balkans have a special place for us. Our historical ties will continue as they have done in the past."[179]

Ironically, emphasize the authors, while most of the Balkan countries suffer from unemployment, lack of foreign investments, and rampant poverty, Erdogan's investments are focused on mosques and religious educational institutions at a time when Kosovo's unemployment rate is 30%. Lulzim Peci, former Ambassador of Kosovo to Sweden and Executive Director of the Kosovo Institute for Policy Research and Development (KIPRED), is one of the most critical voices in Kosovo against Erdogan's political Islamic scheme. He agrees that the mosques built in Kosovo are political establishments to promulgate Erdogan's Islamist vision. "In the case of Kosovo and Albania, the tens of millions of dollars invested in building mosques has to do with the symbol of Turkish supremacy and influence, not only religious but also political", says Peci. Erdogan's enormous investments in Ottoman symbolism are obviously designed to influence the mindset of the population in Kosovo and the rest of the Balkans and increase the pro-Turkish-Islamist sentiments on the present and future generations. The Islamic ideology that *Diyanet* promotes and seems to be the continuation and implementation of Izetbegovic's ambitions have reportedly caused wide-spread indignation among Turkey's hardcore secularists, for *Diyanet* has outrageously stated that girls ready to get pregnant can be married at the age of 9 years old, and boys at the age of 12. Thus, the concerns over *Diyanet* activities are not limited to building mosques, but also extend to cultural and societal influence based on radical Islam of the Erdogan-Izetbegovic brand.

---

[179] Ibid.

It is said that one day following the failed coup in Turkey (July 2016) which was blamed on Gulen and his group,, crowds of Albanians and Bosniaks in Macedonia, Bosnia, Albania, and Kosovo demonstrated in support of Erdogan and his government. "It clearly visualized the potential and mechanisms that Erdogan has in the Balkans and the Turkish Diaspora, on which he capitalizes and uses whenever he wants", says Xhemal Ahmeti, an Albanian historian specializing in the Balkans."Unfortunately, Albanian mosques are confirming the thesis of Swiss Islamist Saida Keller-Messahli in her book *Islamic Centrifuge in Switzerland*, where Albanian mosques are in fact radical centers serving this kind of Islamic agenda for the radicalization of Albanian Muslims in favor of Erdogan's politics", says Ahmeti. Visar Duriqi, a Kosovo journalist specializing in religious affairs, said that the project for the construction of the great mosque with Turkish funds sends a clear political message by Erdogan to the effect that he has control over this region. "Kosovo" says Duriqi "is a country that does not need more religious buildings, certainly not ones funded by Erdogan." For mosques are increasingly being used to spread political Islamic ideologies (like *Islamska Declaracija*) to a point where only limited room is left for actual prayers. "It is no longer a question of whether those establishments are necessary, because the goal is to build as many as possible in order to strengthen the political influence from the Middle Eastern countries and Erdogan's Turkey", said Xhelal Neziri, an experienced investigative reporter from Macedonia.[180]

In the countries with Christian majority populations in the Balkans, such as Serbia, Macedonia, and Croatia, Turkey is investing in major development projects, while in Albania the investments are geared mainly toward building Islamic religious institutes. "It has been shown that the most powerful and sustainable influence in this region, especially among Albanians, is made precisely

---

[180] Ibid

through the instrumentalization of the religion", said Neziri. To be sure, anyone who even scarcely follows Erdogan's ambitions in the Balkans cannot escape the conclusion that the Turkish leader had a specific, well-articulated Islamic agenda which he is determined to entrench in the psyche of the Balkan people by building mosques and appointing imams that follow his doctrine. It is part and parcel of Erdogan's vision to restore elements of the Ottoman Empire under his leadership. Erdogan himself and many other Turkish officials have openly spoke about their dream that by 2023, the centenary of modern Turkey, the country will enjoy as much sway and influence that was once enjoyed by the Ottomans. Erdogan purposefully uses *Diyanet* as one of his main vehicles to that end though for the Balkan states, this will certainly turn out to be nightmarish unless they prevent Erdogan from exploiting them in the name of Allah as he seems to be intent to do.

Apart from Erdogan's probably donning the anti-Zionist and anti-Israeli mantle of Izetbegovic, recent reevaluations of his role in the Balkans may throw some additional light on its possible reverbations or Turkey's relations with Israel. He claims essentially that:

1. Banned from promoting his dangerous Islamic agenda across the European Union, Turkish President Erdogan is now seeking to use his growing influence in the Balkans against the Western countries. Erdogan's aggressive return to the Balkans increased concerns among critics in southeastern Europe— the region where he is pursuing more assertive policies and strategically spreading his brand of Islamist nationalism through a network of mosques and religious institutions. The EU countries have come to realize the danger emanating from his Islamic scheme. As a result, Austria, the Netherlands, and Germany banned Erdogan from organizing electoral campaigns. Furthermore, two months ago, Austria's Chancellor Sebastian Kurz ordered the closing of seven

mosques and expelled Turkish-funded Imams while placing under tight scrutiny dozens more Turkish Imams. "Parallel societies, politicized Islam or radical tendencies have no place in our country," Kurz said as was reported by the *New York Times*.

2. Austria's move to close mosques prompted a furious reaction from Erdogan, who condemned the decision, predictably labeling it "Islamophobic", and promising to retaliate against them. He used a rally in Bosnia to underline his proclivity for challenging the Western countries and declared in front of a crowd of more than 12,000 supporters that "at a time when the glorious European countries that claim to be the cradle of democracy failed, Bosnia and Herzegovina proved to be not ostensibly, but truly democratic by giving us the opportunity to gather here." Many corrupt politicians, Imams, representatives of NGOs, and members of academia in the Balkans remain united in their resolve to campaign on Erdogan's behalf, as they have been enjoying over the years the largess and comfort that Erdogan provides to his loyalists. This is how Erdogan succeeded in winning hearts and minds, especially among the region's Muslim population.

3. Albanian politician Grida Duma, representing the Democratic Party, the second-largest group in the parliament, said to us that, "For Rama, the Albanian Prime Minister,'s challenge to the EU by appeasing Erdogan is dangerous… and would create serious consequences… as the closeness between Rama and Erdogan does not serve Albania's geostrategic interests."

4. Journalists and civil society representatives from Balkan countries are concerned lest Erdogan's increasing influence in

Balkan cities might give rise to the spread of his kind of aggressive and Islamic nationalism and his anti-European rhetorics Journalists and civil society representatives from Balkan countries are deeply concerned that ERdogan might increase his anti-European rhetorics through his network of mosques and religious institutions.

5. Andi Bushati, a journalist and publisher from Albania, affirms Duma's observation and suggested that "This closeness manifests itself not only by symbolic acts, such as Rama's applause to Erdogan's statement that 'Kosovo is Turkey and Turkey is Kosovo,' but also politically, for example, by endorsing Erdogan's condemnation of Trump's recognition of Jerusalem as Israel's capital."

6. To express their admiration of this authoritarian leader, Serbian, Macedonian, Kosovar, Albanian, and Bosnian leaders hailed Erdogan's re-election and attended his inauguration in a show of solidarity.Meanwhile, Kosovo's acquiescence to Erdogan's Islamic agenda is becoming increasingly transparent. A few weeks ago, hundreds of Kosovars marched in support of "Turkish democracy" led by the Turkish Ambassador in Kosovo, Kıvılcım Kılıç. Bekim Kupina, a seasoned journalist from Kosovo, said that Kosovo's leaders must not allow Erdogan to use their country as a springboard to Europe. "Kosovo needs schools, kindergartens, and job opportunities, and not religious institutions that Turkey is building."

7. As the EU seeks to increase its influence in the Balkans, Russia and Turkey have been working hard **to strengthen their own ties to the region**. The EU's renewed interest in its southern backyard has also been prompted by fears of Moscow's mounting influence in the Balkans. Jelena Milic, direc-

tor of the Center for Euro-Atlantic Studies in Belgrade, confirmed that Erdogan and Serbian president Aleksandar Vucic are developing increasingly strong ties. "Erdogan's track record is not criticized by Serbia's government-controlled media. Erdogan and Vucic visited the Sandjak, the Bosnian Muslim populated province of Serbia, but Erdogan was <u>very</u> cautious to highlight only economic ties and investment opportunities, said Milic. According to her, Turkey's influence in the region is growing at an alarming speed.

8. Former Bosnian diplomat Zlatko Dizdarević, who served as ambassador to Jordan, Croatia, Iraq, Syria, and Lebanon, described Turkish meddling in Bosnia as a "threat" which further weakens the country by deepening internal divisions. On the night of Erdogan's re-election, Bosniak member of the Presidency of Bosnia and Herzegovina, Bakir Izetbegović, congratulated Erdogan on his victory, stating "Mr. President, you are not only the president of Turkey, you are the president of all of us." Sead Numanovic, a Bosnian journalist, said that such statement further encourages Erdogan to intensify his interference in Bosnia, which has recently opened an AKP office in Sarajevo. "Erdogan made a public promise to build a highway and speed road between Sarajevo- Novi Pazar and Belgrade. The cost of these two projects alone is over 3 billion euros", says Numanovic. He believes that the recent election's outcome in Turkey has emboldened Erdogan, who will use his power and prestige to increase his political influence in the Balkans. Erdogan is bent on doing so through financial means and investments, and there is little that can stop him because he believes he can lock horns with the EU without chancing much. Conversely, Duma said that "While the main projects were given to Turkish companies, there is no American company that has invested recently in

Albania." There is no doubt about the closeness between Albanian Prime Minister Rama and Erdogan. Beside their friendly relations, they also support each other electorally.

9. To be sure, Erdogan has made his unprincipled position clear to Western powers, stressing that Turkey will become as powerful and influential as the Ottoman Empire was during its heyday. Erdogan's ambition to reconstitute elements of the Ottoman era should have a chilling effect on any country with which Erdogan seeks active bilateral relations. There are always insidious intentions behind his overtures, especially now that most of the countries in the Balkans are in the process of negotiating entry into the European Union, especially Serbia and Macedonia, who are recognized candidates for accession. The result is that the Balkans now are Erdogan's trump card against Europe, especially after he was barred by EU countries from expanding his Islamic agenda and particularly because the door for Turkey to become an EU member has, for all intents and purposes, been shut.

10. Since the Western Balkan countries have been seeking long-lasting relations with the EU, which has facilitated the inclusion of Croatia, Bulgaria and Romania I in addition to Greece) into the Union, the EU is bound to further strengthen its relations with the Balkan states by providing financial support and investing in major projects, while continuing to encourage social, political, and economic reforms to its tune, a process also encouraged by Israel as the most efficient barrage against the expansion of Erdogan-like Islam. By commencing accession negotiations with Macedonia and Albania, which according to the European commission are ready to join, the EU will send a clear message to the rest of the Balkan states of its seriousness about their prospective

membership and will send a cautionary note to the Balkan leaders that the path to EU membership is open, but of necessity requires that they not cozy up to Erdogan, who has betrayed the EU's founding principles and is obsessed with luring the Balkans to join his Islamist nationalistic orbit.

Summary

The asymmetrical Turkish relations with Israel had been founded during their heyday on pragmatic considerations, aided by some emotional gestures characteristic to the Levant, when things went well. However, the moment Islam was introduced into the equation, aided by the irrational and uncontrollable outbursts of fury of Erdogan, things went awry. For not only verifiable, measurable and quantifiable data came into play but entirely manufactured, and at time delusive lies were thrown into the pot to make of these relations a burning hot boullion no longer palatable. It does not take much to rekindle hatred against the Jews and to revive the popular lies concocted against them, by clerical and political leaderships, who stand to gain from diffusing them among their ignorant masses, and no one can compete with Erdogan on those grounds. The lies, which provoke hatred, either in their original and traditional forms or in their new and constantly evolving novel expressions, continue to attract huge audiences in the Islamic world, even if in the civilized countries of the West they might have waned to a greater or smaller measure. While in the West it is no longer fashionable to fabricate false accusations against Jews, or to hurl against them gross antisemitic lies that are punishable by law, under various pieces of legislation geared to reduce ethnic and religious incitement, it turns out that the predisposition in many publics remains in place, especially in the radical Islamic world, ready to manufacture any kinds of calumniations against Israel, under the pretext of "anti-Zionism"in order to lash out openly at Jews. So much more so in the Arab and Islamic worlds, where that pre-disposition is always on the verge of exploding if just given the opportunity. The"poison affair" of 1982 in the West Bank[181], for example, which began as an innocent malaise among Palestinian girls but grew into a staged malicious propaganda campaign to tarnish Israel, was only avidly seized upon by the European media to castigate Israel without any justification or verification. Especially the German press was eager to show that it was not only the Nazis who had been culprits of using gas against their Jewish victims, but they found their "worthy" followers in today's Israeli Jews who allegedly pursue the same methods against Palestinians. Even when the story was proved to have been a hoax and Israel was totally exonerated from that horrible accusation, none of the respectable papers who championed the blood libel had the decency to apologize.

The Arabs and Muslims, now led by Erdogan's Turkey, are so steeped in their own propaganda and campaigns of hatred against Jews and Israel, that they have grown to believe in their own delusions, as the popular television series and books on blood libel and the *Protocols of the Elders of Zion*, which are liberally cited in the writings of radical Muslims, such as the platform of the Hamas and the public declarations that one hears from polical and religious leaders in the Islamic world attest. Those beliefs come to the fore every time Israel exercises the right of self-defense, and it is accused of "slaughters", "mass murders" and intentional "killing of children" among the Palestinians and other Arabs. Those claims are also voiced by "moderate" Palestinians and countries like Jordan and Egypt with whom Israel has maintained "peaceful" relationships for

---

[181] For the full story, see R. Israeli, *Poison: Manifestastions of a Blood Libel*, Lexington Books, 2002.

decades. That shows that making peace through concessions to those countries, and catering to doctrinaire ideologues like Erdogan and intiating gestures of goodwill towards them, do not necessarly generate changes in attitudes and behaviors among them. The hatred and lies produced, have gone so deep into the Islamic experience and are so frenquently repeated to the new generations of Muslims, that they have become part of the Muslim DNA that nothing can erase. In a way, it is tragic that Muslim culture has unwittingly embraced Goebbels' infamous mantra, that when repeated often enough a lie becomes a reality. The tragedy is that those who initiate and propagate the lies begin themselves to believe in them and therefore are victims of their own delusions. As they feed their lies into their youth, they also foreclose any possibility of letting the new generations investigate the changing situation and come to their own conclusions, as the prevailing propaganda tends to perpetuate itself, and the very few independent minds who challenge it are brutally silenced.

A case in point are the recent reports of a four year study of the Palestinian Authority (PA)'s textbooks that were used in their school system in the years 2013-2018. In September, 2017 the first report was issued, based on 201 books, and another 118 books were examined in 2017 that were published during 2018 in a separate study. This third 100 page report is based on 45 books published in 2017-8 for grades 11 and 12.[182] The main findings of this latest and most updated study can be summed up in these most disillusioning points:

- The Palestinian school children learn that that a peaceful resolution of the Middle East Dispute is not an option., for Palestine must be liberated from "Zionist Occupation", by way of an armed struggle (dubbed "revolution") and "self-sacrificing

---

[182] Arnon Groiss, *Jews, Israel and Peace in the 2017/8 Palestinian Authority Schoolbooks for Grades 11 and 12: a Complementary Study*, The Meir Amit Intelligence and Terrorism Information Center, Tel-Aviv, October, 2018.

operations", referring in one of the books[183] to the "1972 Munich Operation" where 11 members of the Israeli Olympic team were murdered during the Olympic Games, and shockingly crowing the terrorist murderers as "self-sacrificing" *Fidai's*, just like those who are struggling to "liberate the Aqsa Mosque from the Jews' sway".

- The struggle for liberation from occupation is not limited to the West Bank, where the PA pretends to aspire for the creation of a Palestinian state,, but extends over the entire territory of Israel, namely not only that occupied in 1967 but encompassing also that "occupied during the *nakbah* of 1948[184]. This means that Israel does not acquire legitimacy within any borders, and is invariably referred to as the "Zionist entity" or the "Zionist occupation".

- The Palestinian refugee descendants, amounting now to 5 million, should return to return Palestine, only then putting an end to the Palestinian catastrophe (and also, incidentally, to the State of Israel);

- The 6-7 million Jewish citizens of the Jewish-majority state, are presented as "colonizing settlers" motivated by racist sentiments [185], who massacred and expelled many of the original inhabitants and have been holding the rest under occupation to this very day. Thus, even the modern day Jewish cities o like Tel-Aviv and Eilat, appear on Palestinian maps in their Arabic translation, to deny any Jewish legitimacy to them.

---

[183] History Studies, Grade 11, Part II, 2017, p. 54
[184] Management and Economics, Grade 11, Part II, 2017, p. 55.
[185] History Studies, Grade 12, Humanities, 2018, p. 5.

- The historical link of the Jews to their ancient land is denied, while the Jewish holy places like the Wailing Wall and the Tomb of the Patriarchs are presented as exclusively Islamic ones.[186].

- In plain anti-Semitic bias, Jews are demonized in Islamic terms, based om Qur'anic verses, so as to lend a religious, scared and immutable character to their abject nature. Hence all actions of the Jewish state must necessarily be tinged by Jewish evil, even its defensive acts against aggression and terror, while Palestinian violence is overlooked.

- The upshot of this sorry tale is that not only are Palestinian youth "educated", indeed indoctrinated, like other Arabs and Muslims around the world, to disregard facts, science and history, in favor of propaganda and manufactured lies, but are being prepared, for a fourth generation now, to pursue warfare and violence instead to being predisposed to negotiation and peace. This will certainly ensure that no peaceful settlement will be possible for the intractable dispute that has been plaguing the Middle East in the last century.

It was symbolic that on the eve of Passover 2002, when 29 Israelis who sat for the *Pessach seder* in Park Hotel in Netanyah, they were murdered by a Palestinian terrorist, in a horror that wiped out entire families of innocent civilians which included children. This time it was Jewish children who were sacrificed on Pesach eve, contrary to the blood libel millennial accusation against Jews that they used Christian and then Muslim children blood to make their *matza* bread. Hardly any reaction or expression of sympathy was

---

[186] Arabic Language 1: Reading, Grammar, Prosody and Expression- Academic Path, Grade 12, 2018, pp. 38-9

triggered in the Arab and Islamic world, which regarded that Passover murder with indifference, sometimes even with elation. But when Israelis launched a few weeks later a counter-attack against terrorists who had dug themselves among the civilian population of inner Jenin, and at the price of 23 Israeli soldiers killed, carefully dislodging and eliminating that nest of terror, Palestinian, Arab, Muslim, European, and UN outrage was heard from one end of the world to the other decrying the "massacre" that the Israelis were again accused of having committed. Moreover, in the course of time, Palestinian "moderate" Abu Mazen, recognized the culprit of the horrendous Park Hotel massacre as a national hero and posited him as a model to be emulated by Palestinian youth. That is exactly the stuff that perpetuates propaganda and lies to justify that hatred. Like in the poison affair of 1983, the Jews were conveniently charged of a massive "massacre" of innocent Palestinian civilians who never did any wrong to anyone. "Moderate" Sa'ib Arekat, the spokesman of the Palestinians at that time, cited a fantastic number of "3000 innocent Palestinian civilians who were wantonly attacked and annihilated by the murderous Israelis". Names of 9-children families were eulogized for their falling victims to the "bloodthirsty" Israelis. It was difficult to fight back this blood libel, even against the background of the true slaughter that had happened a few weeks earlier against Jews in Netanyah's Park Hotel. At the end, it turned out that most of the 50 (not 3,000) Arab dead in Jenin were armed combatants who were killed during the fighting, which had levied such a heavy price on the Israelis, who could otherwise have leveled that part of the city with artillery or from the air without incurring one casualty of their own, had they chosen to use the Park Hotel method of mass killing that Palestinian terrorists had resorted to. The lie was uncovered, but the popular belief among the Palestinians that the Jenin massacre had been perpetrated by Israel persisted. And Arekat, the master lier, was promoted to "chief negotiator" for the Palestinian Authority.

The false accusations against Israel have persisted nonetheless. Films were done on the "Jenin massacre" which do not relate to any reality, and charges are still hurled daily by Muslim countries, notably Erdogan's Turkey, at Israel whenever it dares to retaliate against the targeted Palestinian culprits every time they launch missiles or trigger arsons indiscriminately against Israeli civilian population and nature reserves. Somehow, massive and indiscriminate murder of Israelis by Palestinian terrorists is more tolerated, by Muslims and Europeans alike, than the targeted surgical retaliatory attacks against the perpetrators in their nests, which admittedly sometimes cause unfortunate collateral damage to their neighborhoods. "Moderate" Abu Mazen and Erdogan, Ahmedinejad and other Muslim leaders, let alone the murderers themselves, immediately ritually decry the new "Israeli crime", and the "massacre of innocent Palestinian children", while the Hamas or Islamic Jihad- initiated murders are forgotten if not justified. This is reminiscent of the traditional blood libel when the Jews were always the accused victims while the perpetrators were invariably exonerated, because, as Erdogan said, "Muslims simply cannot perpetrate genocide".Nevermind that the greatest numbers of murders occur in and by the Muslim world, if one considers the Darfur massacre (that Erdogan could not see), the Syrian killings fields with 500,000 victims or more, the daily terrorist attacks by Muslims against Muslims in Afghanistan, Iraq, Pakistan, not to speak of the scattered killing events which occur constantly in Libya, Tunisia, Yemen, Somalia, Egypt, Iran and all the rest, where death is not reported as anything extraordinary. Only when it refers to Jews and Israelis, the headlines advertise the "new massacres" that they committed against the innocent Muslims.

In an interview by Egyptian salafist Muhammed al-Zawahiri, brother of al-Qa'ida leader, Ayman al-Zawahiri, he said that even though he was not a member of any organization, he supported the vision of a *Shari'a* state in Egypt and declared that fighting Israel and the Jews is a religious duty incumbent upon all. The Egyptian government [of Mursi at the time] should have been fighting the Jewish enemy. Perhaps due to circumstances, its weakness or its interests, the Egyptian government ignored a religious duty incumbent upon it. Not just the Egyptian government - the Jordanian one as well. This is a religious duty incumbent upon all Muslims"[187].

As other "moderate" muslims, whose countries had made peace with Israel, continue to delegitimize it and deny the Holocaust which they regard as the basis of Jewish nationhood in the first place, in spite of the paradox involved, hatred continues to spread towards the Jews in general, for forging their Jewish identity while they hail from the Khazars of the Caspian area, and owe their state to Hitler, while at the same time Muslims and Arabs claim that the Sho'a is a hoax.[188] Some Jordanian writers attacked President Obama for celebrating the Jewish Passover in the White House, ignoring the "blood of gentile children that Jews used for their Matza bread". This kind of garbage, which is backed by many other articles of the same writers, which attribute September 11 to Jews, or to an Israeli-American conspiracy, or deny the Holocaust altogether, is not likely to endear Jews to the Islamic world even in the relatively "moderate " countries which have made "peace" with Israel, some of them have visited it, and they should know better. Nevertheless, there is demand in those countries and beyond to the most libelous nonsense written about Jews, because no sane voice is raised against thee lies and no government sanction is taken to deny and refute them, they not being considered illegitimate incite-

---

[187] MEMRI, clip No 3611, 4 October, 2012.
[188] MEMRI, Special Dispatch No 5022, 23 October, 2012

ment as in Western Europe. Quite the contrary, calumniators of this caliber are often considered a sort of popular heroes, and they see no reason why to discontinue their work of libel, hatred and lies, and to lose thereby their fame and readership in the Muslim world.[189]

Worse than that it is, when advanced students in Arab-Muslim universities undertake new "pathbreaking research" and win new academic titles, based on hoaxes and lies, for that means that the hatred and culture of lies that was transmitted to them will be faithfully passed on to the next generation and perpetuated *ad infinitum*. In January, 2012, a doctoral student at the Yarmouk University in Jordan published an article analyzing the present malaise in the Arab world, heaping the entire responsibility, once again, on a Jewish conspiracy. This untenable analysis, which it is worth to explore, not only draws a desperately negative verdict about the primitive level of research at this university, as in others of its kind, but signals to the Muslims and to the world that the next generation has been valiantly taking over the banners of hatred, bigotry and lies from their predecessors. Let us read for ourselves from this pathbreaking doctoral dissertation:

> Reading the Introduction to the *Protociols of the Elders of Zion*... I was surprised to discover the scope of the global Zionist conspiracy. But I was even more surprised that I could not find any other explanation for the current reality [in the Arab world], except that it is the realization of this conspiracy...
>
> Out of respect for your intelligence, my readers, I will not belabor the idea, I will only quote from the introduction to the book and leave it to you to analyze the con-

---

[189] MEMRI, 7 April, 2013, www. Memri.org.il/cgi-webaxy/sal/sal.pl?lang=he&ID=107345memri&act=show&dbid=articles&dataid=3359

spiracy in light of the reality, or to analyze the reality in light of the conspiracy…

The Jews have had a secret plan to dominate the entire world to promote their exclusive interests… The *Protocols* state:" the Jews aim to eliminate all the regimes in the world and replace them with a tyrannical Jewish monarchy…One of the steps they have taken is to entice the monarchs to oppress their people, and entice people to rebel against their monarchs by spreading the principles of liberty, equality and the like interpreted in their specila way so as to harm both sides… They corrupt the rulers and leaders, while quashing any display of awareness among the non-Jewish peoples… They use women, money, positions and trickery, among other means…

They sow dissent and schism in all countries by means of secret political and religious societies, labor unions, sports foundations, Masonic temples and various clubts and societies, they want to bring the countries from a state of tolerance to a state of political and religious radicalism, socialism licentiousness, anarch and inability to implement the principle of equality…

How long will our Arab nation continue to ignore these facts and wander aimlessly? My brother, the reader, after citing these statements there is no need for me to analyze or explain any further. Suffice it to quote the word of Allah :"Those of the Children of Israel who went astray were cursed by the tongue of David and of Jesus. That was because they rebelled and used to transgress (Qur'an 5:78)….[190]

For this trash to be considered "academic research", his approving

---

[190] *al-Asawsana.com electronic journal, 24 January, 2012*

university must be at the level of a backward primary school at most. He takes for granted that the *Protocols*, which were confirmed by courts of law in civilized countries, as a forgery by the Czar secret police at the turn of the 20th Century, are a reliable source to cite. And then he pathetically tries to tell his readers, without "insulting their intelligence", that neither he nor they have to seek any evidencefor showing, that Israel's [democratic, sane and stable regime] was conspirational, while the [dictatorship, unstable and unrepresentative] monarchies of the Arab world were the victims of Jewish conspiracies. How primitive and insane is his thinking, (if he cares to think at all), and how destructive and uneducative are his teachers who direct him to write these idiotic words, and lead their student -prodigy to believe that he deserves a superior academic title. That is the true insult to intelligence, and a disastrous omen for any improvement in the Arab-Muslim mentality of hatred and lies in the foreseeable future. This mentality and upbringing seem to be so deeply steeped in religion, that is taken as the Word of Allah, namely as true, eternal and immutable, and that there is no chance, even no attempt to alter it or ignore it. When school children learn Ibn Ishaq's authoritative *Sirah (biography)* of the Prophet, for example, and they are instructed by it how how to hate the Jews and mistreate them, why would they be expected to behave differently? The Sirah, in effect, said :

> The Apostle said: "Kill any Jew that falls into your power". Thereupon, Muhayyisa b.Mas'ud lept upon Ibn Sunayma, a Jewish merchant with whom he had social and commercial relations, and killed him. Huwayyisa was not a Muslim at the time, though he was the elder brother of Muhayyisa.. When Muhayyisa killed the Jews, his brother began to beat him, saying: " You enemy of Allah, did you kill him when much of the fat on your belly comes from his wealth?". His brother answered: "

Had the one who ordered me to kill him ordered me to
kill you, I would have cut your head off". He said that
this was the beginning of Huwayyisa's acceptance of
Islam. The other replied: "by Allah, if Muhammed had
ordered you to kill me, would you have killed me?" Yes,
responded the other: "if he had ordered me to cut off you
head, I would have done so".. His brother exclaimed: " a
religion that can bring you to do this is marvelous", and
he became a Muslim.[191]

Reverend Mark Durie discusses the issue of whether this story
reflects the strength of the weakness of Islam, as the words of the
Prophet have become absolute commands for his followers, and the
intolerance of Islam towards any apostate or any insult of the faith
is treated wih violent reactions, as we have witnessed for example in
the Rushdie Affair (1989), or the Cartoon Affair (2006. He thinks
that this story reflects the intimidating, even traumatic effect of
encountering a religion which inspires dealy violence in someone
you thought you knew as a reasonable person. The fact is that such
trauma can jolt someone to the side of Islam, which has the spiritual muscle to dictate violent acts in violation of the most stringent
civilized social norms. Apparently Ibn Ishaq thought that this was
a splendid and exemplary story which reflected well on Islam and
which later generations would be proud to follow. He was not far
from the cruel reality, which unfortunately is still being followed by
a massive killing in and by Islam both of Muslims and of others
who are hated for not sumitting to Islam, and all manner of lies are
heaped on them to justify their elimination[192].Much of the web of
lies woven by the Nazis about the Jews and Western democracies,

---

[191] Alfred Guillaume, *The Life of Muhammed, p. 369. Cited and interpreted by
Mark Durie, mark@markdurie.com, 7 February, 2013.*
[192] Durie, Mark, "Hatred Sounds Sweeter in Arabic?", markdurie.blogspot.com,
December, 15, 2012

and by the Communist world against capitalism (and also against the Jews), could not be undone and refuted before those regimes crumbled, because their very subsistence sustained those systems of lies and prevented their refutation, and only their collapse could permit their end. Thus, maybe only the end of Islamic regimes of this sort, to which Erdogan has been adamant to belong, can begin to portend the end of hatred and lies in the Islamic world.

In addition to the building of walls of suspicion between Erdogan and Europe and his blunt opening up to Iran and Russia, mainly on the problems of adjacent Syria, he has made the unwise measures that have complicated his relations with his erstwhile more reliable ally – the US. According to an estimate of the Israeli Institute of Strategic Studies[193], the deterioration in the relations were caused by several factors, mainly centered around the Middle East, therefore of direct concern to Israel, especially the arrest of an American priest who was accused with terrorism, the most likely calumniation o pass among the Turkish public. American sanctions have had the immediate effect of the free fall of the Turkish Lira rate of exchange, but has had reverberations also on Turkish standing in NATO and in Europe, its relations with Israel, and possibly also a serious erosion in the personal relations between Erdogan and Trump.

---

[193] "The Turkish-American Crisis: an Israeli Military Reevaluation", INSI Podcast 35, July, 2018.

Bibliography

Documents

The Holy Qur'an

Communique of the 1990 Cairo Islamic Cooperation Conference (later Cooperation)

The Hamas Charter

Written and Electronic Media

Ariel Center for Policy Research

Associated Press (AP)

China Brief

CNN World News

Cumhuriyet (Turkey)

(The)Economist

Encounters with Islam in German Literature and Culture

FBIS

(The) Guardian

Flash TV

Foreign Affairs

*Haaretz (*TeL Aviv)

Hamizrah He-Hadash (The New East, Tel Aviv)

Hurriet (Turkey)

(The) Israel Journal of Foreign Affairs

Israeli TV- Channel 10
Jerusalem Post
(The) Jerusalem Review
(The)Jewish Exponent
Journal of Modern Hellenism
Journal of Palestine Studies
Journal of the British Academy
MEMRI-(Jerusalem and Washington)
Middle East Quarterly
Middle East Review
Milli Gazette (Germany)
National Post
(Al) –Monitor
Newsweek
New York Times
New Yorker
Orbis
Patterns of Global Terrorism, (US Department of State),
PJ Media
Policy Watch, (The Washington Institute)
*Policy Studies (*Singapore*)*
Standpoint
Stiftung Wissenschaft und Politik
(The) Times
Turkeyscope (T A U)
US Institute for Peace Journal
Valeurs Actuelles
Yeni Safak, (Turkey)
Http://www.thememriblog.org/turkey/blog_personal/en/2595.
   htm.
Htpp://www.milligorusarsiv.com/videolar/file.php?f=
http://www.haaretz.com/news/diplomacy-defense/hamas-admits-
   600-700-of-its-men-were-killed-in-cast-lead-1.323776 9

Books

Alexander, Yonah (ed) *The 1988-9 Annual of Terrorism, NIjhoff, Boston, 1990*

Andric, Ivo, *The Bridge on the Drina*, Dereta, Beograd, 2011, R. Israeli and A. Banabou, *The Bosnia War (1992-5)*, Strategic Books, Tx, 2013

Bat Ye'or, the *Dhimmi*, Fairleigh Dickinson Press, Madison and London, 1985

Bat Yeor, *Bat Ye'or: Autobiographie Politique:DE la DEcouverte du Dhimmi a Eurabia*, Ls Provinciales, 2017, pp.207-210.

Ben-Arieh, Yehoshua, *The Changing Landscape of the Central Jordan Valley*, Scripta Hierosolymitana, Jerusalem, 1968.

Bostom, Andrew, *The Legacy of Islamic anti-Semitism*, Prometheus Books, 2010

Brockelmann, Carl, *History of the Islamic Peoples*, Capricorn NY, 1960. Pp 259 ff

Cahen, Claude, *Islam* (Hebrew Translation), Dvir, Tel-Aviv, 1995

Davutoglu, Ahmet, *Strategic Depth: Turkey's International Position* (Turkish), Istanbul, 2001.

1974

Eickelman, Dale F. ,*Muslim travellers: pilgrimage, migration, and the religious imagination.* Vol. 9. Univ of California Press, Berkeley 1990

Erlich, Haggai, *Introduction to the Modern History of the Middle East, Vol I (Hebrew), Open University, Tel-Aviv, 1987*

Haggai

Fernandez-Morera, Dario, *The myth of the Andalusian Paradise*, ISIS Press Wylmington, 2016

Fenton, Paul and David Littman, *Exile in the Maghreb*, 2012, Paris

Gilley, Bruce, and Andrew O'Neil (Eds.), *Middle Powers and the Rise of China*,Georgetown University Press, 2014), pp. 192-212.

Groiss, Arnon, *Jews, Israel and Peace in the 2017/8 Palestinian Authority Schoolbooks for Grades 11 and 12: a Complementary*

Study, The Meir Amit Intelligence and Terrorism Information Center, Tel-Aviv, October, 2018.

Gulen Fethullah, Toward a Global Civilization of Love and Tolerance. Tughra Books. Cited in ISBN as 978-1932099683, (2010)

Guvendiren, Ekrem, *A Concise Report on Turkish-Israeli Relations*, Foreign-Economic Relations Board, Istanbul, 1990

Hedin, Sven, *Till Jerusalem* (Swedish), Albert Bonniers Forlag, Stockholm 1917

Hodgson, Marshall, *The Venture of Islam*, Vol III, Univ of Chicago Press, *1972*

Israeli, Raphael *The Internationalization of ISIS: The Muslim State in Iraq and Syria*, Transaction, NJ, 2016, Chap. One, pp. 1-48

Israeli, *Raphael, Hatred, Lies and Violence in Islam*, Transaction, NJ 2012

Israeli, Raphael, *Who is Right and Who is Left: the Fate of Weak Nations Among Great Empires*, Strategic Books, TX, 2018.

Israeli, Raphael, *From Arab Spring to Islamic Winter*, Transaction, NJ, 2013.

Israeli, Raphael, *The Blood Libel and its Derivatives*, Transaction, NJ, 2012.

Israeli, Raphael, *Absence of Evidence and its Consequences in Travesties of Justice*, Cambridge Scholars, Cambridge, 2018

Israeli, Raphael, *The Islamic Challenge in Europe*, Transaction, NJ, 2008, especially Ch. 5, pp. 197-218.

Israeli, Raphael, *Muslim Anti-Semitism in Christian Europe*, Transaction, New Brunswick, 2009

Israeli, Raphael, *Back to Nowhere: Moroccan Jews in Dream, Nostalgia and Reality*, Lambert Academic Publishing, Saarbrucken, 2010.

Israeli, Raphael, *Ethnic Cleansing, Migrations and Population Transfers* (forthcoming).

Israeli, Raphael, *Islamikaze: Manifestation of Islamic Martyrology*, Frank Cass, London, 2003.

Israeli, Raphael, *Paranoia, Inferiority Complex and Fanaticism: Muslim Attitudes to Jews*, Strategic Books, TX, 2018

Israeli, R and Albert ben-Abou,_*The Bosnia War (1992-5)*, Strategic Books, Tx, 2013

Israeli, Raphael, *Retreating from the Mirage of Multi-culturalism: the Cases of Holland, Britain and Israel*, Strategic Books, TX, 2018

Kuntzel, Matthias, *Jihad and Jew-Hatred, Islamism, Nazism and the Roots of 9/11*, Telos Press, New York, 2007.

Lecker, Michael, Muhammad and the Jews (Hebrew), Jerusalem, 2012.

Maoz, Moshe (ed), *Palestine Duringthe Ottoman Period:Documents from Archives and Collections in Israel*, The Institute of Asian and African Studies, Hebrew University, Jerusalem, 1970.

Murray, Douglas, *The Strange Death of Europe: Immigration, Identity, Islam*, Bloomsbury, London, 2017.

Nachmani, Amikam, *Israel, Turkey and Greece: Uneasy Relations in the Eastern Mediterranean*, Frank Cass, London, 1987

Nachmani, Amikam, *Turkey and the Middle East*, BESA, Bar Ilan University, 1999

Rafaelovich, *Y., The Land of Israel and its Moshavot* (Hebrew and German), Ariel Press, Jerusalem,1979, a Reproduction of the First Album of the settlement in the Land of Israel, dated 1899.

Rubenstein, Richard L. *Jihad and genocide*. Vol. 1. Rowman & Littlefield, Lanham 2010

Sebag-Montefiore, Simon, *Jerusalem, the Biography*, WEidenfeld and Nicolson, London, 2011

Shmuelevitz, *A. (ed.), Turkey and Israel in a Changing Environment*, BESA Center for Strategic Studies, Bar Ilan University, 1996

Spencer, Robert (ed), *The Myth of Islamic Tolerance : How Islamic Law Treats non-Muslims*, Prometheus, NY, 2005

Stave, Erik, *Genom Palestina- Memories from a trip, Spring 1891*, (Swedish)P.A. Norstedt & Soners Forlag, Stockholm,

Stillman, Norman, *The Jews of Arab Lands*, The Jewish Publication

Society of America, 1979

Tshelebi, Evliya, *Travels in Palestine (1648-50)*, Translated from Turkish by St H. Stephan, Arield Publishing House, Jrerusalem, 1980

Yang, C. K. *Religion in Chinese Society*, U.C. Berkeley, 1967, Chap. XII.

Articles

Barkho, Leon, "Iraq Betting on Oil Wealth to End Isolation", *Associated Press (AP)*, March 1, 2000.

Bengio, Ofra, "Turkey's Quiet Revolution and its Impact on Israel", in *The Israel Journal of Foreign Affairs*, Vol Four, No. One, 2010, pp. 15-21

Bone, James, "Turkey Denies anti-Semitic stance in wake of leaked documents", *The Times, 30 November, 2010*

Bostom, Andrew, "Islam or Islamism? Islamist or Islamic?", .http://www.thememriblog.org/turkey/blog_personal/en/2595.htm. posted on 12 November 2009.

"Central Asia: The Silk Road Catches Fire", *The Economist*, 26 December 1992- 8 January 1993' p. 80.

"Centeral Asia", *Newsweek*, 3 February, 1992, p.20

Daliglu, Tlin, "Turkish Intelligence Service Targets Jewish Population", *Al-Monitor* 19 December, 2012.

Dombey, Daniel and Funja Guler, "Turkish book on Darwin Sparks Outrage", 19 October, 2012 www.ft.com/cms/s/0/f27adba8-1a01-11e2-a179-00144feabdc0.html#axzz2A3AovbTy

Mark, Durie"Hatred Sounds Sweeter in Arabic?", markdurie. blogspot.com, December, 15, 2012

Erbakan, PM Necmettin, TV Interview given by previous to Flash TV on 1 July, 2007 as part of a pre-election program

Htpp://www.milligorusarsiv.com/videolar/file.php?f=

"Erdogan's anti-American and Antisemitic rant in 1993", lifted from Israeli Channel 10 broadcast on 18 March, 2010.

Feiler, F., "Economic Relations Between Turkey and Israel" (Hebrew) in A. Shmuelevitz *(ed.), Turkey and Israel in a Changing Environment,* BESA Center for Strategic Studies, Bar Ilan University, 1996

Gruen, George, "Turkeys' relations with Israel and its Arab Neighbors:The Impact of Basic Interests and Changing Circumstances", *Middle East Review,* Spring, 1985,, pp. 33-43

Hamad, Fathi, "on the Hamas casualties during the Gaza War", in http://www.haaretz.com/news/diplomacy-defense/hamas-admits-600-700-of-its-men-were-killed-in-cast-lead-1.323776 9 November 2010.

Ibrahim, Raymond, *"*The Hagia Sophia Church to turn again into a Mosque*", PJ Media,* June 18, 2013

Inbar, Efraim, "Israeli-Turkish Tensions and Beyond", *The Israel Journal of Foreign Affairs,* Vol Four, No. One, 2010, pp. 27-35

Israeli, Raphael, "Arab and Muslim Anti-Semitism", *Ariel Center for Policy Research*, April 2000.

Israeli, Rphael, "The Charter of Allah: The Platform of the Hamas", in Y. *Alexander (ed.)*

Israeli, Raphael, "The Turkish-Israeli Odd Couple", *Orbis,* January 2001, pp 165-179.

Khamenei, Ali, public speech on Iranian media, February 20, 2006.

Koch, Ariel, "Al-Qaeda's Propaganda in the Virtual Turkey " in *Turkescope,* Tel Aviv University, October 15, 2018

Kushner, David, "Before and Beyond the 'Freedom Flotilla': Understanding Turkish-Israeli Relations", *The Israeli Journal of Foreign Affairs,* Vol. 4, No. 3, 2010, pp. 21-30.

"La Grande Turquie", *Valeurs Actuelles,* 27 January, 1992

Lappin, Yaakov, " Changes in Turkey" http://web.archive.org/web/20100428140334/http://eng.akpati.org.tr/english/lifestory.html.

"Lessons from Central Asia", *US Institute for Peace Journal,* June 1992

Liel, Alon, " Israeli-Turkish Retaltions under Strain", *The Israel Journal of Foreign Affairs*, Vol Four, No. One, 2010, pp. 23-26

MagShamhráin, Rachel . "Displacing Orientalism: Ottoman jihad, German imperialism, and the Armenian genocide," *Encounters with Islam in German Literature and Culture* (2009).

Miskin, Maayana, "Erdogan: Israel worse than Sudan, Muslims do not cause Genocide", 8 November, 2009 www.israelnationalnews.com/news/news.aspx/134297#. ULQrSGdryCk

Nachmani, Amikam,"The Remarkable Turkish-Israeli Ties", *Middle East Quarterly*, June, 1998, p. 22

Nachmani, Amikam, "Turkey and the Middle East", in *Journal of Modern Hellenism, Vol. 15 (1999)*, p. 15; and *Turkey and Middle East* BESA, Bar Ilan University, 1999

Norwitz, Trevor, Conference delivered to the Lawfare Project Conference, Jerusalem, October 5, 2010.

Olcott, Martha, "Central Asia's Catapult to Independence",*Foreign Affairs*, November, 1992; "Lessons from Central Asia", *US Institute for Peace Journal*, June 1992

Parkinson, Joe, "Erdogan Tightens Grip on Turkey, Putting Nation at Crossroads", 27 June 2013. http://online.wsj.com/article/SB1000142412788732330000457 8557693146971554.html?KEYWORDS=germany+turkey

"Rachel's Tomb was never Jewish", *Jerusalem Post, 7 March, 2010.*

Ravid, Barak " Israel accuses Erdogan of inciting anti-Semitism, *Ha'aretz,* 26 January, 2010. That was before the Marmara incident of May, 2010, so it could not be the reason, just a pretext.

"Report from Turkestan", *New Yorker*", 6 April, 1992;

Rogan. E, "Rival jihads: Islam and the Great War in the Middle East, 1914–1918". *Journal of the British Academy, 4*, pp.1-20.

Rose,. Charlie, "Turkish PM Erdogan: Hamas Rockets is a hoax", 28 June, 2010 www.youtube.com/watch?v=Ptwir8pCnBU

Schwartz, Stephen, "The Heritage of Ottoman Islam in the Balkans", Indiana University, Bloomington, Conference on The Turks and Islam, September 12, 2010. See www.islamicpluralism.org/1663/the-heritage-of-ottoman.

Seufert, Günter). "Is the Fethullah Gülen Movement Overstretching Itself?" *(Research Paper). Stiftung Wissenschaft und Politik. 2 August 2016.*

Shihor, Yitzhak, "Turkey and China in the Post Cold War World :Great Expectations," in: Bruce Gilley and Andrew O'Neil (Eds.), *Middle Powers and the Rise of China,*Georgetown University Press, 2014), pp. 192-212.

Shichor, Yizthak, "Ethno-Diplomacy: The Uyghur Hitch in Sino-Turkish Relations", *Policy Studies 53,* The East-West Center, 2009, Singapore

Shichor, Y., "Turkey Trot: Military Cooperation Between Beijing and Ankara", *China Brief,* Vol IX, Issue 8, April 16, 2009, pp. 4-7

Shmuelevitz, A., "The Attitude of the Islamic Press in Turkey Toward Israel" (Hebrew). in *Hamizrah He-Hadash (*The New East), 1997-8, pp. 114-24

Tart, Robert,"Iran is our Friend, Says Turkish PM Erdogan", *The Guardian,* October 26, 2009, cited by Inbar, p. 30.

Totten, *Michael J.,* " Blood Libel: The Sequel*", Commentary blog, 11 November 2010.*

"Turkish Jews", *Yeni Safak*, 13 December, 2012

Weiker, Walter "Turkey, the Middle East and Islam", *Middle East Review* Spring 1985, pp. 27-32

Werner, David Amram, "The Jews of Fez and Politics in Morocco",*The Jewish Exponent, No 1308, 3 May, 1912, pp.1-2.*

Yanarocak, Hay, "TURKEY'S ONE-MAN SHOW", *Turkeyskope,* The Moshe Dayan Center, Tel-Aviv University, Summer, 2018.

Lappin,Yaakov, " IHH and MIlli Gorus", http://web.archive.org/web/20100428140334/http://eng.akpati.org.tr/english/lifestory.html

Yavuz, Hakan, "Turkish-Israeli Relations Through the Lens of the Turkish Identity Debate", *Journal of Palestine Studies,* vol. 27, no 1, 1997, pp. 22-37

Analytical Index

Names, Places, Terms and Events

"Government is not a solution to our problem;
government is the problem."
—President Ronald Reagan

Looking all around us, it is evident that the United States of Americ
heading down a course of economic, financial, and social ruin that
in most part, to an irresponsible and careless government. Author
Williamson, through his passionate writing, shows us why he believes that
out-of-control government no longer cares about our Constitution, econo
businesses, or families. It is a government ruled not by the people but
progressive reformers who seek to place restrictions on our individual freedo

Through his powerful words, G. Williamson suggests that the key
turning around this unrestrained government is to understand the reasons
its malfunction. From bailouts, to the economy and jobs, to foreign policy
our tax system, he effectively informs us of the self-destructive and risky p
our government is leading us down. He also describes what we as Ameri
citizens can do to reverse this dangerous and precarious direction in which
country is heading.

Don't be left in the dark about the issues in our country any longer. Pick
this motivational and encouraging book today and delve into the *Thoughts*
American Taxpayer.

G. WILLIAMSON graduated from Southeast Misso
State in Cape Girardeau, Missouri, with a Bachelor
Science in Business Administration. Although he grew
in the Midwest, he currently resides outside of Houston

www.sbprabooks.com/GWilliamson   Author's website: www.thepatriotsview

Strategic Book Publishing and Rights
$17.50 / ISBN: 978-1-952269-27-1

Review Requested:
If you loved this book, would you please provide a review at
Amazon.com?